D0342625

ADVANCE PRAISE FOR
THEY'RE NOT LISTENING

"No welfare for illegal aliens, no gay marriage, Brexit, Trump—we vote and we vote and we vote and yet, somehow, we can never *win*. Feudal subjects had more say in their governance than citizens in today's showpiece 'democracies.' Our bureaucratic-media-judicial rulers treat voters as an irritation to be ignored at their convenience. As disgust with this dysfunctional system reaches a boiling point, Ryan Girdusky and Harlan Hill show how the sneaky and the pushy have managed to defeat democratic institutions and tell us what can be done about it."

— Ann Coulter, Author of Thirteen Bestsellers Including
*Resistance Is Futile!: How the Trump-Hating Left Lost Its
Collective Mind*

"Listen up! Ryan James Girdusky and Harlan Hill have written a critically important guide to nationalism-populism here in America and around the world. Devoid of the hysterics, condescension, and bias that permeate elitist media coverage, Girdusky and Hill's book delves into the roots of the anti-establishment revolution and its universal principles: preservation of family, law and order, borders, common identity, and national sovereignty. *They're Not Listening* eschews empty fear-mongering for astute analysis of the disruptive political movement that paved the way for Trump—and, God willing, the salvation of the corrupt and crumbling West."

— Michelle Malkin, Journalist and Bestselling Writer of
Open Borders Inc.: Who's Funding America's Destruction?

"In this insightful new book, Ryan Gidursky and Harlan Hill chronicle various populist movements all over the world and the issues that underlie their political strength. Interesting and readable, *They're Not Listening* contains important lessons for an international political class that seems uninterested or unwilling to come to grips with the political instability that roils their respective countries. Whether you, like me, see the rise of populism as a useful corrective to forty years of bad policies, or wish it would just go away, I suspect you'll learn something from this intelligent, readable overview."

— JD Vance, Bestselling Author of *Hillbilly Elegy*

THEY'RE
NOT
LISTENING

THEY'RE NOT LISTENING

How The Elites Created the Nationalist Populist Revolution

RYAN JAMES GIRDUSKY & HARLAN HILL

BOMBARDIER
BOOKS

A BOMBARDIER BOOKS BOOK
An Imprint of Post Hill Press
ISBN: 978-1-64293-499-1
ISBN (eBook): 978-1-64293-500-4

They're Not Listening:
How The Elites Created the National Populist Revolution
© 2020 by Ryan James Girdusky and Harlan Hill
All Rights Reserved

Images and charts designed by and used with permission from Zach Goldberg.

No part of this book may be reproduced, stored in a retrieval system, or transmitted by any means without the written permission of the author and publisher.

Post Hill Press
New York • Nashville
posthillpress.com

Published in the United States of America

TABLE OF CONTENTS

PREFACE

IN THE WAKE of Donald Trump's victory and the UK's referendum on the European Union, national populism became a political force that has gained traction worldwide. Cosmopolitan elites around the globe never saw this populist uprising coming and few today have bothered to understand why voters have begun to question and reject liberalism, globalism, and the post-Cold War political consensus. Most pundits dismiss it as an illegitimate movement and boil it down to old white reactionaries living in dying towns and elevating strongmen and wannabe fascists.

Outside of the simplistic world of cable news, media pundits, and opinion writers, the reason for the growing tide of national populism is nuanced and complex. One thing is clear: national populism poses an immense threat to the liberal democratic order.

Our current national populist revolt started long before Donald Trump came down his golden escalator or British Prime Minister David Cameron agreed to hold a referendum vote on the EU. Trump's victory and Brexit may have awoken the general public to the rise of national populism, but it has been going on for decades. There are many common misconceptions about national populism, including that its groundswell is isolated to rundown towns in Northern England or the American Midwest. Critics believe that it's rise is an overall rejection of the political class spurred solely by demographic changes and that the national populist voting bloc is relegated to just older generations who will soon fade away. None of this is true.

Over the last twenty years, nearly every region of the world, in nations as varied as India, Colombia, Hungary, Poland, Brazil, Japan, Pakistan, and the United States, has seen a rise of national populist ideals, politicians, and political parties.

Modern-day national populism is hard to define in the global sense. Israeli philosopher Yoram Hazony has said that populism and nationalism are two movements that are very different but currently coexist in a single movement in defiance of the elites that are pushing for globalization and the demise of local culture, tribalism, and the nation-state. Nationalism is a movement toward national freedom, while populism is a class conflict.

Nationalism and populism date back to the Roman Republic. The current incarnation has formed as a reaction to various political and social global changes, including mass immigration, identity politics, victimhood culture, crony capitalism, and corruption. British academic Matthew Goodwin states that the rise of populism comes down to the four D's: distrust of politicians and institutions, destruction of national groups' historical identity and established ways of life, deprivation as a result of rising inequalities…and a loss of faith in a better future, and de-alignment caused by weakening bonds between mainstream parties and institutions.[1]

National populist parties and politicians who have been successful at winning elections have channeled voters' frustrations regarding the failures of neoliberalism and addressed the political, economic, and cultural concerns of their nation and people.

---

1   Matthew Goodwin, *National Populism, The Revolt Against Liberal Democracy,* 2018, p. xxiii.

Each party and its politicians are as different as the nations they govern or hope to govern. Some are focused on over-throwing corrupt establishment figures and want more of a direct democracy, while others campaign on preserving long-standing ethnic and cultural norms. There's no exact mold that fits all national populist parties.

While all national populist movements differ on policy, there are some universal principles that overlap globally. Here are nine points that best define what national populists believe:

- The nation contains unique and valuable people, culture, and history that are worthy of preservation.

- The government exists to protect its citizens. All government policies—especially on trade, sovereignty, immigration, austerity, and wars—should serve the interests of the people.

- Those in the government should live by the same laws of the people they govern.

- Economic interests should never benefit the few while displacing the many.

- Nation build at home, not abroad.

- Law and order are the cornerstones of prosperity.

- The media more often than not distort the truth and divide countrymen.

- No industry, including technology, should have more power than the state.

- The preservation and prosperity of the family should be the main priority of the government.

The national populist agenda is neither traditionally right-wing nor left-wing; it could be considered radically centrist, illiberal, and reactionary. National populism opposes the ideological trappings of other political movements. Libertarians and their ilk insist that the most efficient form of government is the creative destruction of the free market and it will inevitably lead to maximum prosperity sometimes at the expense of societal stability. Likewise, socialists seek an egalitarian society through the means of government force even if it limits prosperity.

Both extremes of those political ideologies are more concerned with the process than the outcome; that's where national populists differ. National populists are more capitalist than they are socialist, but, understand that the chaos of life creates the need for a social safety net. They support businessmen and innovators who can amass a vast sum of wealth but don't believe taxation is theft. Every citizen has a duty to help create a more sustainable society. Citizens' duty is not just to the government in the form of paying taxes, but to their fellow patriots and the institutions that keep society from collapsing.

This rationale extends through most national populists' political beliefs. That's why when the media dubs national populism far-right, it does so as a tool to box national populists within the left-right paradigm that voters are used to hearing, but this is not an honest assessment of national populists' beliefs.

Remedies national populists prescribe can vary greatly from country to country. Almost all have an end goal of spurring economic prosperity for their nation's working class but have stark contrasts in their methods. For example, politicians like Donald Trump have reduced taxes and deregulated the economy, while Marine Le Pen has campaigned on increased government control.

Most crucially, critics of the national populist movement should realize that their political uprising didn't need to happen. It occurred because of the actions of the governing class, not despite their efforts. The elite had countless opportunities over the last three decades to signal to voters that they were listening to their concerns, that the current system could work toward their best interests, and that the global liberal agenda was worth protecting.

Of course, the governing class didn't make reforms because the ruling elites across the globe aren't listening. They have become adherents to the liberal democratic orthodoxy, a political religion that silences and punishes heretics.

Through the latter half of the 20th century, governments around the globe have become divorced from those they govern and have pushed forward their ideology that people, cultures, and countries are interchangeable and replaceable.

Voters have repeatedly voiced their outrage at the elites, from conversations at kitchen tables all the way up to the ballot box. They never consented to the abdication of their sovereignty, mass immigration, globalism, or a growing gap of income inequality. None of these early concerns persuaded the governing class to alter their plans. Those in positions of privilege absorbed most of the benefits of this liberal democratic order while those left behind were told to bury their discontent in cheap goods manufactured in developing nations.

In the US, mass immigration and foreign intervention were always perceived as reasonable and necessary. This logic was reinforced by the mainstream media as well as both Democrat and Republican politicians. Americans were told repeatedly that diversity is a strength, America is a nation of immigrants, peace through strength, we live in a global economy, and military interventionism is part of what made America exceptional. When anyone questioned the drawbacks of such policies, they were called racist, bigoted, backward, simple, incapable of understanding world affairs, or they were just ignored.

More than 30 million people came to the United States over two decades, a number so high it eclipsed all other periods in American history.[2] Polls showed Americans consistently stated that they felt uncomfortable with the high levels of both legal and illegal immigration. They questioned what benefits had come from decades of war and what exactly happened to all the middle-class jobs that politicians promised would come out of free trade agreements. Yet the establishment persisted in refusing to meet their concerns with even a legitimate debate.

So, when a bombastic billionaire entered the presidential race in 2015 and questioned US' involvement with NATO, called the Iraq War a mistake, and said it was imperative to reduce legal immigration, pundits and experts were as horrified as Pope Urban VII when Galileo said the sun, not the earth, was the center of the universe. They had to compete with a celebrity they couldn't ignore who was expanding the Overton window and challenging their orthodoxy.

As Trump defied expectations and won the Republican primary, it became apparent that those in the establishment hadn't spent enough time speaking to Americans outside the Acela corridor who were tired of Washington D.C.'s, fight the world, invite the world policies. Almost no elected officials—both Democrat and Republican—altered or acknowledged the holes in their orthodoxy, so much so that even three years after Trump's election, some still believe they can make America normal again if they can just get rid of Trump.

In Europe, an increasingly authoritarian European Union overruled democratic elections, spurred mass immigration from both within Europe as well as Muslim-majority nations

---

2　　Stephen A. Camarota, "A Record-Setting Decade of Immigration: 2000-2010," Center for Immigration Studies, October 5, 2011.

and led to the demise of national sovereignty. Millions of new immigrants from vastly different belief systems transformed towns and cities, committed acts of terrorism, and stripped many parts of the European continent of its Christian and classical liberal roots. All the while, austerity measures, stagnant economic growth, and lack of job opportunity devastated working-class Europeans.

And national populism isn't contained to white-majority countries in the West. After decades of failed leadership by their elite, nations in South America and Asia like India, Brazil, Pakistan, Japan, and Colombia voted for national populists to combat the rampant levels of crime, unspeakable corruption, and lack of opportunity.

Aside from internal politics, international forces also moved people toward national populist parties and candidates. For instance, NATO's intervention in Kosovo during the '90s helped lead to the populist uprising in Switzerland. The terrorist attack on 9/11 was partially responsible for right-wing nationalist victories in Denmark. The ousting of Muammar Gaddafi in Libya helped give rise to Salvini in Italy. Hugo Chávez's pressure to recognize the Revolutionary Armed Forces of Colombia moved the needle in favor of the national populist Democratic Center in the 2014 election.

Establishment political parties and leaders who have favored military intervention across the world have inadvertently fed the national populist movements back at home. Politics doesn't exist in a bubble, the action and reaction of military intervention in one country affects others.

This book explains what this movement wants and how the establishment political parties could have stopped it over the last few decades. Furthermore, this book shows the internal forces being used to undermine democratic elections. We will describe how the media and corporate class have distorted the message of the national populist movement, creating a fear-based campaign to turn countrymen against each other.

Once we describe what the national populist movement wants and how it is being stopped, this book shows how the movement must move forward in remaking the world's political future.

CHAPTER 1

SWAMPS AROUND THE WORLD

THE NATIONAL POPULISM revolt wasn't supposed to happen. The governing elite had come to the consensus that Francis Fukuyama was correct when he wrote in 1992 that history had come to an end. That the fall of the Soviet Union was not just the passing of a communist state but the end of history as such: that is, the endpoint of mankind's ideological evolution and the universalization of Western liberal democracy as the final form of human government.

In the minds of the governing class, humanity would forever and always surrender all previous forms of the government to Western liberal democracy. This orthodoxy that consumed the ruling elite became so pervasive, it filtered into nearly every layer of the national psyche including politics, the media, and the economy.

Pulitzer Prize-winning writer Thomas Friedman summarized Western elites' hopes and dreams in his book *The Lexus and the*

Olive Tree: "The spread of free markets and democracy around the world is permitting more people everywhere to turn their aspirations into achievements…[erasing] not just geographical borders but also human ones…Globalization tends to turn friends and enemies into competitors."[3]

Friedman and those who subscribed to this worldview saw globalization and the spread of liberal democracy as a political orthodoxy. Culture, tribalism, nationalism, and traditional religion could all be erased by the prospect of buying a flat-screen TV at a lower price. Neoliberalism, like Jesus Christ rising from the dead, could provide salvation against the human race's original sin of God, country, and flag.

Human nature is not as flexible as 20th and 21st-century political leaders in the West would like to believe. Despite the growing rebellion throughout the West against globalization, mass immigration, and growing income inequality, most neoliberals like Friedman were unwilling to concede that their prophecies were incorrect.

At least Fukuyama had some level of humility when he wrote an opinion article for *The Wall Street Journal* in 2014, admitting that he had been overly idealistic when he wrote the end of history twenty-five years prior. He acknowledged that democratically elected governments were failing to provide substance of what people want from their government.[4]

By 2014, trends were clear that there was a growing global backlash against liberalism and in favor of national populism. Nigel Farage and Marine Le Pen were already winning national elections in the UK and France, respectively, nationalist right-wing governments were part of a ruling coalition in many

---

3   Thomas Friedman, *The Lexus and the Olive Tree,* (New York: Random House, 2010) p.12.

4   Francis Fukuyama, "'End of History' Still Stands Democracy" *The Wall Street Journal,* June 6, 2014.

Eastern European nations, the Tea Party movement took hold in the United States, and Narendra Modi was already the prime minister of the world's largest democracy.

Despite the growing evidence that times were changing, most of the political class still had their heads firmly in the sand. They believe that the political instability brought by the economic recession, mass immigration, terrorism, the loss of national sovereignty, and depleted faith in civic institutions were just passing fads. Within twenty-nine months of Fukuyama's op-ed, neoliberals around the world were shell-shocked by the advancement of national populism with the election of Donald Trump and Brexit.

Neoliberals couldn't understand the intensity of the backlash against their political religion, nor were they willing to surrender on any portion of their orthodoxy to make concessions to the rising tide of national populists. To do so would be heresy.

In the decades leading up to the election of Donald Trump, not only did the ruling elite do nothing to stop the rise of national populism, but their policies drove people into the arms of Trump, Le Pen, Farage, Modi, Bolsonaro, and Salvini. Neoliberalism traded national identity for individualism and decadence, which left millions with serious grievances.

Governments that subscribed to neoliberalism fed the social decay creeping into communities across the West and forged a wedge between segments of society. National capitols became swamps filled with bureaucrats, entrenched interest groups, and politicians that had little to no connection to the people they governed.

In the United States, it began before the fall of the Soviet Union, but the reality of a nuclear holocaust kept a lid on the ongoing social, economic, and moral decay. After the fall of the USSR, many Americans, including some Cold Warriors who had been supportive of President Reagan's efforts to dismantle the Evil Empire, hoped the US would return to pre-World War II normalcy and give up ambitions of being a global police force that combated bad actors around the world.

Any chance of that happening evaporated quickly with the Gulf War and George H. W. Bush's subsequent State of the Union address in 1991, where he stated that America had a mission in a post-Cold War world to forge a new world order.[5]

H. W. Bush's words served as foreshadowing for his son's second inaugural address, where George W. Bush declared it was the policy of the United States to end tyranny in our world.[6] This is a commitment to permanent war to create permanent peace. It is a religious declaration that had vast consequences for the world and the advancement of the national populist movement.

Likewise, the immigration reform bill signed by President Johnson and the amnesties signed by Presidents Reagan and Bush moved America toward the most radical demographic transformation in the modern world. They reasoned that Americans were not an actual people with a distinct culture, but just a collective group of individuals holding to similar ideas. American politicians told citizens that there was no difference between eighth-generation dairy farmers who had ancestral ties to Northern Wisconsin and immigrants who did not speak the same language, hold the same history, or believe in the same role of government. In the eyes of American politicians, these people were totally interchangeable.

In the time between and after the two Bush presidencies, Democratic presidents also pursued an agenda that most

---

5   President George H.W. Bush, Address Before a Joint Session of Congress on the State of the Union, Washington D.C., January 29, 1991.

6   President George W. Bush, Inaugural Address, Washington D.C., January 20, 2005.

Americans did not vote for and did not agree with, causing a disintegration of trust between the country and Washington, D.C.

According to Gallup, 72 percent of Americans had a great deal or quite a lot of confidence in the president in March of 1991, the period right after the Gulf War, and at the end of the Cold War. The percentage steadily declined throughout the following two decades, only briefly reaching over 50 percent in 1998 following the economic boom, in 2002 during the early days in the war on terror, and in 2009 right after the election of Barack Obama. Those moments, however, were fleeting, and by the end of Obama's presidency, just 36 percent of Americans held confidence in their commander in chief, a 50 percent drop in twenty-five years.[7]

By June of 2013, Americans said they were dissatisfied in the way the federal government handled criminal justice, education, energy, environmental issues, foreign affairs, healthcare, public housing, job creation, labor and employment issues, national parks, transportation, responses to natural disasters, immigration, and veterans' affairs. The belief among voters that the government wasted a majority of their tax dollars ballooned from 11 percent in 1986 to 35 percent by 2014.

A Pew Research poll found in 2015 that just 19 percent of Americans trusted the government always or most of the time, down from 77 percent in 1964.[8]

Given that millions of Americans felt betrayed and alienated by their government, is it any wonder that they supported such an unlikely candidate as Donald Trump, who promised to burn the system to the ground? A significant portion of Trump's base

---

7   "In Depth: Government," *Gallup*, Accessed September 15, 2019, https://news.gallup.com/poll/27286/government.aspx.

8   Pew Research Center, "Public Trust in the Government 1958-2019," April 11, 2019, https://www.people-press.org/2019/04/11/public-trust-in-government-1958-2019/.

in the Republican primary believed that people like me don't have a say in what the government does.[9]

America wasn't alone; Europeans in Central Europe already began gravitating toward national populists in the late '90s as a method to gain control of their borders, reduce immigration, and fight back against the growing demands of the EU. This surge of support among national populist parties in these countries occurred before the economic recession.[10]

By the early 2010s, trust in the European Union was in freefall. According to a Eurobarometer poll in 2013, just 31 percent of people living in the European Union had trust in the EU, down from 57 percent in late 2006.[11]

The economic recession led by the downturn of the American housing crisis was the final nail in the coffin for many Europeans. They were living with near-record-high youth unemployment while being forced to bail out Greece and deal with German-imposed austerity measures. And these falling poll numbers were two years before Europeans became accustomed to more than a dozen Islamic terrorist attacks annually.

Voters throughout Europe would go on to believe that the promise of the European project, which was to offer peace and prosperity, had failed them on both counts.

National populist candidates and political parties became viable because the ruling elites in West Europe were divorced

---

9   Michael Pollard and Joshua Mendelsohn, "RAND Kicks Off 2016 Presidential Election Panel Survey." *The Rand Blog*, January 27, 2016, https://www.rand. org/blog/2016/01/rand-kicks-off-2016-presidential-election-panel-survey. html.

10   Daniel Stockemer, "Structural Data on Immigration or Immigration Perceptions? What Accounts for the Electoral Success of the Radical Right in Europe?" *Journal of Common Market Studies*, 2016, p. 999-1016.

11   Nassos Stylianou, "Trust in EU at an all time low latest figures show," *The Telegraph*, January 22, 2014, https://www.telegraph.co.uk/news/worldnews/ europe/eu/10586961/Trust-in-EU-at-an-all-time-low-latest-figures-show.html.

from reality and governments in post-Cold War Eastern Europe and the developing world were engulfed in mass corruption.

People fed up with the establishment sought democratic means as a way to resolve their growing issues with globalization. However, even when national populists started winning elections throughout the world, they saw a series of roadblocks preventing them from enacting their agenda. The deep state and plutocracy were hellbent on stopping national populists even if they won at the ballot box.

DIVORCED FROM REALITY: THE PLUTOCRATS

Two years after losing the 2016 presidential election, Hillary Clinton gave a speech in Mumbai painting the picture that there were two Americas: the country that voted for her and the one that voted for her opponent.

"If you look at the map of the United States, there's all that red in the middle where Trump won," Clinton said, "I win the coast...I won the places that represent two-thirds of America's gross domestic product. So, I won the places that are optimistic, diverse, dynamic, moving forward. And his whole campaign, 'Make America Great Again,' was looking backwards."[12]

Clinton wasn't wrong: there are two Americas. One where childless coastal elites with college degrees have benefited enormously from the policies of globalization, and the other of the non-college-educated struggling from the effects of mass immigration, deindustrialization, and automation. The two very different places want almost nothing to do with each other aside from the fact that they are forced to live in the same country.

---

12 "Bitter Hillary Clinton Trashes America's Heartland, Calls States That Didn't Vote For Her 'Backwards,'" YouTube video, March 12, 2018, https://www. youtube.com/watch?v=3KKPpjN5PTc&feature=youtu.be.

This tale of two countries is not exceptional to the United States. Look at France in 2017, during the first round of the French presidential election, Marine Le Pen won nearly 7.7 million votes and won the heavily immigrant populated southern areas of the country as well as former industrial towns in the northeast. Brexit wasn't much different; while London wanted to stay in the EU, the rest of England wanted to leave.

The upper class, whether they live in London, Paris, New York, or Los Angeles, grew increasingly segregated from their working-class counterparts. Over the last half century, that segregation caused the upper class and the working class to have vastly different life experiences as well as political and cultural opinions. They grew isolated from each other and throughout the late 20th and early 21st centuries, it became less likely that the two groups would live in the same neighborhoods, attend the same church or schools, or even associate with someone with vastly different education or income. Those differences slowly but surely affected national and international politics as those living in cosmopolitan bubbles made decisions for the working class stuck in the middle.

As British journalist David Goodhart put it, populism is rising because of the friction between citizens who proudly live somewhere and those able to live anywhere. The people living somewhere have their identities tied to a place, while those living anywhere will go to any global city with Western values and features.[13]

Mobility is one of the main driving factors behind the growing isolation between the upper class and the working class. Children from well-to-do and upper-middle-class families

---

13   David Goodhart, "On the Road to Somewhere, the Divide between Elites and Populists," *National Review*, August 21, 2017, https://www.nationalreview. com/2017/08/road-to-somewhere-populist-revolt-david-goodhart-somewhere-people-anywhere-people-brexit-trump-election/.

attended expensive universities where they paired off with spouses or created business connections that took them far from their hometowns and pulled them into cosmopolitan bubbles. They self-segregated into elite zip codes in gated suburbs and pricy city dwellings, closing themselves off from the rest of society.[14]

As a consequence, some areas experienced a brain and wealth drain where those with youth, money, and high IQs left their hometowns for major cities. Places like Michigan, Nord-Pas-de-Calais, and Northern England lost their future to places like New York City, Paris, and London. In exchange, those destination cities' working class lost their past as they were economically displaced by gentrification.

New York City is a perfect example of this evolution. In 1960, a majority of adults who lived in Manhattan south of the black-majority neighborhood of Harlem did not have a high school education and had a median income of just $46,164 (in 2019 dollars), which was close to the national average. Even on the Upper East Side, which was always considered an elite part of the city, only 23 percent of adults had college degrees, and the median income was equivalent to $65,076 (in 2019 dollars.)

That all changed over the course of a few decades as the working-class population was economically displaced. The number of people working industrial blue-collar jobs shrank from 40 percent in 1960 to 5 percent in 2000. The median income for residents living south of Harlem increased from $46,164 to $180,579 and the Upper East Side's average increased from $65,076 to $290,503.[15] Those with a college

---

14   Douglas S. Massey, Jonathan Rothwell, and Thurston Domina, "The Changing Base of Segregation in the United States," *Annals of the American Academy of Political and Social Science 626*, 2009, p. 74–90.

15   Charles Murray, *Coming Apart*. (New York City, Crowne Forum, 2015) p. 77.

education rose from 23 percent to 75 percent, which is more than twice the national average.[16]

In just forty years, Manhattan went from a county that, in many ways, reflected the national average on income, education, and blue-collar employment to a city for only the wealthy. Immigrants and working-class natives were forced either into government projects or into the city's outer boroughs or suburban counties.

"By the middle of the 2010s, the great sort had been nearly completed across the US. Fewer affluent kids live in poor neighborhoods and fewer poor kids live in rich neighborhoods," wrote Robert Putnam, a professor at Harvard, in 2015.[17] For the most part, the wealthy and educated lived among each other at that time. In the United States, the top twelve wealthiest zip codes also had ten of the top twelve best zip codes.[18]

Cities like Paris, Milan, London, and New York became isolate from their working-class counterparts like Calais, Palermo, Blackpool, and Scranton.

This rift between the working class and the college-educated wealthy has real-world consequences in terms of politics and policy. Those willing to live anywhere dominate Western culture, college campuses, and politics while those from somewhere have little representation in governments in America, the UK, or Europe but make up a majority of the population.

Identity and representation are two subjects the American media loves to dwell on, especially when it comes to Congress. In the 116th Congress, 22 percent of the House was nonwhite,

---

16   Reid Wilson, "Census: More Americans have college degrees than ever before," *The Hill*, April 03, 2017, https://thehill.com/homenews/state-watch/326995-census-more-americans-have-college-degrees-than-ever-before.

17   Robert Putnam, *Our Kids*. (New York: Simon & Schuster 2015) p. 217.

18   Charles Murray, *Coming Apart: The State of White America, 1960-2010* (Crown Forum, 2015) p. 71.

23 percent were women, and 33 percent were non-Christian.[19] The American press and bloggers published countless articles, news segments, and blog posts celebrating the increasing racial, religious, and gender diversity in Congress. One group that has shrinking representation and wasn't mentioned much by the media is the working class.

As of 2018, slightly more than half of Americans were considered working class. They make up roughly the same percentage of the population as women. Yet when it comes to politics, the working class is even more underrepresented than all religious, race, or gender groups who get national media attention.

Working-class people are 52 percent of American citizens, but only 10 percent of city council members, 3 percent of state legislators, 2 percent of members of Congress, and 0 percent of governors spent their adulthood as members of the working class.[20]

The average member of Congress spent less than two percent of his or her entire pre-congressional career doing the kinds of jobs most Americans go to every day. No one from the working class has gotten into politics and gone on to become a governor, or a Supreme Court justice, or the president, wrote Dr. Nicholas Carnes, a political scientist at Duke University and author of *White-Collar Government.*

The underrepresentation of the working class has been consistent in American politics for decades. The number of people from working-class backgrounds in the state legislatures

19   Claire Hansen, "116th Congress by Party, Race, Gender, and Religion," *US News and World Report,* January 3, 2019, https://www.usnews.com/news/politics/slideshows/116th-congress-by-party-race-gender-and-religion.

20   Dr. Nicholas Carnes, "Working-class people are underrepresented in politics. The problem isn't voters," *Vox,* October 24, 2018, https://www.vox.com/policy-and-politics/2018/10/24/18009856/working-class-income-inequality-randy-bryce-alexandria-ocasio-cortez.

has actually declined from about 5 percent in the early '90s to about 3 percent in 2018.

Carnes said part of the problem is that elites recruit other elites for political office and there is no foundation or institutions spending the money necessary to recruit people from working-class backgrounds.

The situation in the UK is not much different. As of 2015, women are vastly underrepresented in the British Parliament (only 32 percent is female); other marginalized groups include gays and lesbians (7 percent) and nonwhites (8 percent).[21] None of those groups were as poorly represented as Brits who did not have a university education. As of 2014, only 42 percent of UK citizens between the ages of twenty-five and sixty-four had a university degree—less than half of the average of Conservative, Labour, and Liberal Democratic Members of Parliament (MPs). More than one in three Tory MPs went to elite schools like Oxford and Cambridge.

In 2015, only 3 percent of British MPs previously worked manual labor jobs and an additional 1 percent were farmers. This is down significantly from 1979 when over 19 percent of MPs had some form of a blue-collar background. At that time, MPs from a working-class and business background had similar representation.

In 1979, 147 MPs had a business or white-collar background, whereas 121 had experience working a manual labor or farm job. By 2015, the divide had grown to 263 MPs with a white-collar or business background and just twenty-six who previously worked in manual labor or farming.

The fastest-growing group of MPs by profession are those who only worked as professional politicians or for political organizations. While just twenty-one MPs came from that

21   Lukas Audickas and Richard Cocknell, "Social background of MP's 1979-2017," *House of Commons Library*, November 12, 2018.

background in 1979, that number catapulted to 107 MPs. By 2015, professional politician was the second most common profession in the House of Commons—aside from business.

Think about that for a moment: in 1979, it was more common for an MP to have previously been a farmer and miner than it was for them to have been a professional politician. By 2015, farmers and miners combined barely made up one-eighth of the number of professional politicians in Parliament.

Americans and Brits aren't alone, a 2019 study published by Cambridge University found that it was basically reflective of world leaders as a whole.[22] About 2 percent of political elites come from blue-collar backgrounds, and outside of Europe and America, it's even far less than 2 percent. Europe had the largest sample of political elites who come from a blue-collar background; at 4 percent, they doubled the world average.

An astonishing 22 percent of the governing class around the globe had either no work experience or only ever worked in politics. That included 16 percent in North America, 21 percent in Europe, and 26 percent in Asia. This trend is only slightly smaller in countries with democratic governments (21 percent) than it was in autocratic governments (25 percent).

Only 4 percent of European, 10 percent of North American, and 8 percent of Asian politicians came into politics with no prior experience. About 38 percent worldwide come in through partisan political machines and 16 percent come from local government. This is especially true in Europe.

As elected officials became less likely to have experienced blue-collar living, so did their staff.

Eisenhower's and Kennedy's respective cabinets were much more economically diverse than Obama's and Trump's. In

---

22   John Gerring, Erzen Oncel, Kevin Morrison, and Daniel Pernstein, "Who Rules The World? A Portrait of the Global Leadership Class," *Perspective on Politics*, December 2019, p. 1079–1097.

Ike's administration, only two of his initial cabinet members were born to affluent families, while the others were the sons of farmers, a bank cashier, a teacher, a small-town lawyer, and one was even a high school dropout. Likewise, Kennedy had three cabinet members whose parents were farmers. He also had cabinet members who were the sons of a small business owner, an immigrant factory worker, and another first-generation American whose father peddled produce.[23] That was when there were just ten federal departments, the children of working-class Americans made up a majority of the cabinet.

Despite the fact that the number of federal departments has more than doubled since Eisenhower and Kennedy, the number of members from working-class backgrounds hasn't. In the Obama administration, only Bob Gates, Eric Holder, Tom Vilsack, Gary Locke, Hilda Solis, Ray LaHood, Eric Shinseki, and Ron Kirk came from what could be considered working-class or homes of moderate income. Just eight out of twenty-two.

The Trump administration was only slightly better, with ten out of twenty-two coming from less than privileged backgrounds: Rex Tillerson, Jim Mattis, Jeff Sessions, Ryan Zinke, Alex Acosta, Ben Carson, Rick Perry, John Kelly, Mike Pompeo, and Linda McMahon.

Although these men and women spent some time in their childhood as blue-collar folks, most were millionaires by the time they landed in Washington. They had some relation to the working class, but it was distant.

This gap in income, access, geography, and education has had broad political ramifications. Those who live anywhere, do not share the same burden that those living somewhere do when it comes to mass immigration, free trade, terrorism, globalization, and war.

---

23   Murray. *Coming Apart.*

As cities in Northern England, the Midwest, and Northeast France became hollowed-out shells of their former selves and mass immigration fundamentally altered the character and composition of communities across the West, elites living in their cosmopolitan bubble felt very little change. These are the conditions that not only allowed national populism to thrive, but to take the elite by complete surprise.

In their bubbles, nothing was wrong.

CORRUPTION: THE RISE OF NATIONAL POPULISM IN THE DEVELOPING WORLD

While Western governments and societies grew increasingly distant from the working class, political leaders in the global south and the newly liberated former Soviet states in Eastern Europe were rife with corruption, crime, and terrorism. The failure of these governments to perform the most basic protections for civil society thrust voters into the arms of national populist parties.

One of the earliest victories for modern national populist candidates was in Hungary's 1998 election, where Viktor Orbán's Fidesz party captured 28 percent of the votes and ousted the Hungarian Socialist Party (MSZP). This radical change in government did not come without an immense amount of suffering.

Hungary transitioned to a democracy in 1998 and suffered from post-communist identity crisis after forty years under the control of the Soviet Union. The MSZP party won 33 percent of the vote in 1994, but their poll numbers sank as their government became mired in controversy, economic depression, and domestic terrorism.

The early part of the decade was rocked with a massive recession that took a significant toll on the Hungarian economy. In 1995, the socialist government introduced a politically unpopular economic austerity program to curb welfare spending.[24] In October of the following year, the establishment was rocked again with a money scandal when the directors of the Hungarian Privatization and State Holding Company, which is responsible for selling Hungarian state assets, were dismissed for improper financial dealings.[25] A 1997 investigation by the Parliament found that government officials were responsible.

A crime wave seized Hungary; more than a hundred bombings struck the tiny Eastern European country over a two-year period as both foreign and domestic gangs battled for territorial control.[26] Hungary's voters felt their government had lost dominance to mob justice and was no longer interested in protecting the lives and prosperity of their citizens.

Orbán campaigned on cracking down on corruption and crime as well as bringing back economic prosperity for the Hungarian people who in less than a decade saw the end of communism, economic recessions, and waves of crime and domestic terrorism.

The Fidesz party campaigned on both a law-and-order platform as well as economic populism. Orbán highlighted the growing income inequalities, especially between those living in the cities and those in rural areas. He also talked about reinvesting in education and prioritizing tax cuts for Hungarian owned businesses.

---

24   Marina Popescu and Gabor Toka, "Campaign Effects in the 1994 and 1998 Parliamentary Elections in Hungary," (ECPR Joint Sessions of Workshops, Copenhagen, 2000) p. 5.

25   Europa Publications, *A Political Chronology of Europe*, (London, Taylor & Francis e-Library, 2001) p. 113.

26   Edward Wright, "Bombings Increase in Hungary," *The Los Angeles Times*, July 26, 1998, https://www.latimes.com/archives/la-xpm-1998-jul-26-tr-7210-story.html.

Hungary's embrace of national populism only came after nearly a decade of chaos, crime, and pain for their citizens. Life became so intolerable that they had no choice but to support a radical change.

Brazil, pre-Bolsonaro, had a similar story. The Workers' Party (PT) controlled the Brazilian presidency from 2002 through 2018. Their tenure was marked by a series of scandals and crises that were both economic and cultural.

President Dilma Rousseff, the second consecutive president elected by PT, became involved with a money-laundering scheme in early 2014. The probe known as Operation Car Wash led to the indictment of 429 people, mostly comprising of elite businessmen and politicians, and resulted in the conviction of 159. Rousseff was impeached, her predecessor Luiz Inácio Lula da Silva was indicted, and many other politicians ended up in jail.

Operation Car Wash led to a complete breakdown in the faith of the political class. Brazilians hoped Rousseff's replacement would clean up the system, but her successor, President Michel Temer, was business as usual. He was ultimately charged with racketeering and obstruction of justice, and he had an approval rating of 5 percent (yes, just the single-digit).[27] A top Temer aide was also jailed after police found suitcases filled with US $16 million in his apartment.

During the time, that Brazil's political and financial elite were abusing their power and breaking the law, the South American nation became the murder capital of the world. Brazil became completely ravaged with crime with more than 63,000 homicides occurred in 2016 alone. From 1980 to 2014, the homicide rate increased by 485 percent and the number of

---

27   Brian Winter, "System Failure: Behind the Rise of Jair Bolsonaro," *Americas Quarterly*, January 22, 2018, https://www.americasquarterly.org/content/system-failure-behind-rise-jair-bolsonaro.

child homicides increased by more than 475 percent.[28] Rapes increased by 8 percent, to an insanely high total of 60,018 Brazilians reporting being raped in 2017.[29] No one was spared from the carnage.

Part of the reason for the rise in violent crime was a war between the country's two main drug trafficking organizations, the First Capital Command and the Red Command. The two groups had a longstanding truce that fell apart in 2016 and their violent drug war spilled into the cities and countryside of Brazil.

The Brazilian economy was also in a terrible position under the Worker's Party. In 2015 and 2016, the country's GDP contracted by 3.5 percent each year,[30] and the economy shrunk by 10 percent on a per-capita basis during the course of the recession. Investments were already declining before the recession, but after it hit, they all but collapsed and inflation grew to 10.6 percent. By March 2017, nineteen months before Bolsonaro was elected, unemployment hit 13.7 percent. An estimated 14 million people were without work.

Public trust was decimated, no one had faith in the political class and their promises to grow the economy, reduce crime, and end their culture of corruption. This breakdown of civil society allowed Bolsonaro to seem like the nation's only option.

It took half a decade of pain and a perfect political storm to push Brazil toward Bolsonaro. The failure of the meritocracy in nations like Brazil, Hungary, Colombia, and Pakistan is how

---

28   Julio Jacobo Waiselfisz, "Homicides of Children and Adolescents in Brazil," (Igarape Institute, December 2017).

29   Tom Embury-Dennis, "Brazil breaks own record for number of murders in single year as deaths hit 63,880," *The Independent*, August 10, 2018, https://www.independent.co.uk/news/world/americas/brazil-murder-rate-record-homicides-killings-rio-de-janeiro-police-a8485656.html.

30   Mario Braga, "Brazil's recession is over, but the crisis is not," *The Brazilian Report*, May 07, 2018, https://brazilian.report/money/2018/05/07/brazils-recession-crisis/.

the global south and former Soviet states altered their political alignments and embraced these nationalist-populist political parties and leaders.

Just like in the West, national populism grew as a reactionary force against a governing class that was divorced from their countrymen. The only difference was in the cases of the global south and the former Soviet states, it led to a breakdown of civil society.

THE DEEP STATE: HOW THE ESTABLISHMENT IS THWARTING DEMOCRACY

When national populists have been successful in winning elections and taking control of governments through proper democratic means, it's often the case that institutional forces from both in and outside the government are at work to stop them from enacting their agenda. Those forces include international associations like the EU, internal nonelected entities like the bureaucracy, and the political and judicial class.

The EU is one of the most anti-democratic institutions in the West. They have been holding voters in contempt whenever their views differ from the European project's goal of creating a multicultural superstate. During his tenure as Prime Minister of Luxembourg, Jean-Claude Juncker said of the EU politicians, "We decide something...and wait a while, what happens. If there is no big shouting and no uprisings, because most of them [the voters] do not understand what was decided, then we continue – step by step, until there is no going back."[31]

In some ways, the EU is what political scientist Colin Crouch defined as post-democratic, which is a society that has all the institutions of democracy, but it's just a formality. A small

---

31   Dirk Koch, "2000: foreign countries: the Brussels Republic," *Der Spiegel*, December 27, 1999, https://www.spiegel.de/spiegel/print/d-15317086.html.

circle of the political and economic elite makes a majority of the decisions.

Since the late '90s, the EU has fought against efforts by the peoples of Europe to regain any semblance of national sovereignty and opposed democratic elections when the outcomes did not favor the EU.

An early example of this was in 1999 when Austrians voted to put Jörg Haider's Freedom Party (FPÖ) into power. Haider was a controversial figure for his criticisms of democracy, mass immigration, and his praise for the Third Reich's sound employment policies.[32] He also received pushback for referring to Nazi concentration camps as punishment camps.

Despite Haider's bombastic personality and the FPÖ's history of associating with Nazis, Haider campaigned as a traditional national populist. His 1999 Contract with Austria pledged to support increasing social benefits, introducing a 23 percent flat tax, decreasing immigration, reducing the size of government, fighting corruption, and reviving the economy. On election day, his party captured nearly 27 percent of the vote, ahead of the center-right Austrian People's Party (ÖVP).

Under normal circumstances, Haider should have become Austria's chancellor; however, foreign critics from the EU and Israel wouldn't stand for it. The EU said Haider was in violation of Articles 6 and 7 of the Treaty on the EU that binds member states to the principles of liberty, democracy, respect for human rights, and fundamental rights as well as a common distaste for all forms of discrimination.[33] Haider's slogan to stop the over-foreignization of Austria and promise of zero immigration caused concern among the ruling elite in the EU, but given

---

32   Heather B. Freeman, *Austria: The 1999 Parliament Elections and the European Union Members' Sanctions*, 25B.C. Int'l & Comp. L. Rev.109 (2002), http://lawdigitalcommons.bc.edu/iclr/vol25/iss1/5.

33   European Union, *The Treaty of the European Union,* The Official Journal of the European Union, October 26, 2010.

that the Austrian government had not violated any terms of the Treaty it did not warrant action under Article 7.

Nonetheless, the fourteen member states of the European Union coordinated diplomatic sanctions and froze bilateral relations with the tiny Central European country at a huge economic cost to Austria,[34] Israel announced that Haider would not be allowed to visit the Jewish state and was withdrawing its ambassador from Vienna[35], and Belgian Foreign Minister Louis Michel threatened to kick Austria out of the EU. Even the largest Dutch bank, ABN Amro NV, announced it was freezing its offer to help finance a child support program in Haider's home province.

European politicians reasoned that trying to stop the effects of a democratic election was fine and completely in line with their thinking. Glyn Ford, a British Labour Member of the European Parliament (MEP) said, "Some say that it is not right for us to interfere in Austrian politics. They are wrong. Some say we have to accept the outcome of democratic elections, but elections do not always make democrats."

Haider and ÖVP leader Wolfgang Schüssel issued a commitment to EU values on February 3, 2000, but it wasn't enough to satisfy the EU and on February 28, Haider resigned as leader of the FPÖ. Schüssel became the Chancellor of Austria and the EU lifted its sanctions.

After leaving the FPÖ, Haider founded a new party called the Alliance for the Future of Austria, which received nearly 11 percent of the vote in the 2008 national legislative election. Haider set his eyes on a political comeback, but it was not to be.

---

34   "No Way Out," *The Guardian*, February 29, 2000, https://www.theguardian.com/world/2000/feb/29/austria.comment.

35   Ian Black, "Europe rallies against Haider coalition," *The Guardian*, February 4, 2000, https://www.theguardian.com/world/2000/feb/04/austria.ianblack.

Just weeks after the election, he died in a car accident and the new party crumbled without his leadership.

Nothing has changed with the EU since Haider's victory in 1999. The EU continues to act at best as a bully against democratic nations within its boundaries that voice opposition to their European mission, and at worst as a post-democratic institution.

In 2005, both France and the Netherlands held referendums on the European Constitution just three days apart from each other. Both countries rejected the Treaty by double-digit margins, with 55 percent of French[36] and nearly 62 percent of Dutch voters[37] casting ballots against the EU Constitution.

The EU leadership in the aftermath of both stunning defeats halted the Constitution process fearing that more countries would defect. Instead, they narrowed the scope to just seven articles that incorporated all the main reforms sought by the EU Constitution. On December 13, 2007, the Lisbon Treaty was signed by the twenty-seven European prime ministers and presidents.

A ratification process occurred throughout 2008: the Lisbon Treaty was voted on by members of their respective nations' legislatures. Leaders would not allow for national referendums on the matter because they feared more nations would vote down the Treaty.

"This is nothing less than a massive exercise in deceit," Nigel Farage, then the leader of the United Kingdom Independence Party (UKIP) said during the debate in the EU Parliament as

---

36   Elaine Sciolino, "French No Vote on European Constitution Rattles Continent," *The New York Times*, May 31, 2005, https://www.nytimes. com/2005/05/31/world/europe/french-no-vote-on-european-constitution-rattles-continent.html.

37   Staff and agencies, "Dutch say 'devastating no' to EU constitution," *The Guardian*, June 2, 2005, https://www.theguardian.com/world/2005/jun/02/eu.politics.

he recalled that former Prime Minister Tony Blair promised voters a national referendum.[38]

Yet that is the modus operandi of the EU, only allowing for democratic reforms when they suit their interests.

It didn't matter if the country or countries in defiance of the EU weren't member states as was the case when the Swiss voted to reform their legal immigration system.

In 2014, the Swiss People's Party (SVP) held a national initiative against mass immigration aimed at reducing immigration through quotas[39] and returning the country's immigration policy to the way it had been previous to their 2002 agreement with the EU. It posed a direct challenge to the EU's Schengen Agreement, of which Switzerland is a member although it was not a part of the EU.

When the vote was held on February 9, 2014, the international markets were stunned when 50.3 percent of the Swiss population voted in favor of the initiative. This sent shock waves through the EU and the Swiss financial institutions that heavily opposed the measure.

Eamon Gilmore, the Irish foreign minister, said the vote posed a major threat to the freedom of movement "which is the cornerstone of what the E.U. is all about."[40] Viviane Reding, the justice commissioner of the EU at the time, said of the results that leaders of the country had to reject the national referendum or reject being in a single market with the EU. As was the case of Austria during Haider's election, the EU punished

---

38   "EP approves Lisbon Treaty," *The Irish Times*, February 20, 2008, https://www.irishtimes.com/news/ep-approves-lisbon-treaty-1.818912.

39   Switzerland, Political Rights: Popular Initiatives, *Federal popular initiative 'Against mass immigration,'* last modified October 12, 2019, https://www.bk.admin.ch/ch/f/pore/vi/vis413t.html.

40   Steven Erlanger, "Swiss Vote Seen as Challenge to European Integration," *The New York Times*, February 10, 2014, https://www.nytimes.com/2014/02/11/world/europe/swiss-immigration-vote-raises-alarm-across-europe.html.

Switzerland for participating in a free and fair election that posed a threat to their agenda, they suspended their participation in research and student programs with Switzerland.

The Swiss government was given three years to find a way to implement the results of the election and like Brexit, they presented a watered-down version of what voters wanted.

In December of 2016, the EU approved a new Swiss law that would allow EU citizens to work in Switzerland in direct violation of the initiatives call for quotas. Instead, all the new law did was give priority to Swiss-based job seekers in locations that had above-average unemployment rates.[41]

The SVP called the move unconstitutional, and even members of the media criticized its implementation. "Never has a law of application been so far removed from the requirements of the Basic Charter," said Bernard Wuthrich in *Le Temps*.[42] The National Council surrendered and opted for a national priority light—a solution that does not correspond to the approach of autonomous management of immigration. "Those who claim otherwise deliberately mislead the public," wrote Daniel Foppa in *Tages Anzeiger*.[43]

Nonetheless, the SVP refused to hold another vote and by 2019 Switzerland's foreign population swelled to 2 million or 25 percent of the nation's residents.[44]

---

41 "No quotas in 'compromise' Swiss immigration bill," BBC, December 16, 2016, https://www.bbc.com/news/world-europe-38340407.

42 Bernard Wuthrich, "Immigration: la cacophonie inachevée," *Le Temps*, September 21, 2016, https://www.letemps.ch/opinions/immigration-cacophonie-inachevee.

43 Daniel Foppa, "Kapitulation mit Ansage," *Tages Anzeiger*, September 22, 2016, https://www.tagesanzeiger.ch/schweiz/standard/kapitulation-mit-ansage/story/21087006.

44 Duc-Quang Nguyen, "Defining the 25 % foreign population in Switzerland," *Swissinfo.ch*, November 19, 2017, https://www.swissinfo.ch/eng/society/migration-series-part-1-_who-are-the-25-foreign-population-in-switzerland/42412156.

After decades of suppressing national elections and national initiatives, the EU finally skirted its own parliamentary rules in 2019 in order to suppress the vote of tens of millions of their own citizens.

The 2019 EU parliamentary elections were a watershed victory for national populist parties, who came in first or second place in Belgium, France, Hungary, Italy, Poland, and the UK. Altogether the right-wing Eurosceptic parties had 179 MEPs.[45]

According to the EU's D'Hondt method of distributing leadership positions among the parliamentary groups, Eurosceptic politicians were expected to control several committees, including the Employment and Social Affairs Committee, the Agriculture Committee, and the Committee of Legal Affairs.[46]

The 519 Pro-EU MEPs blocked all but one Eurosceptic from every chair and vice-chair positions by suspending democratic norms—even though Eurosceptic parties received the greatest percentage of the vote in any given country and had the largest political party in the EU Parliament.

Aside from the heavy hand of the EU, national governments and institutions in Europe have pushed back against national populist parties, politicians, and electoral mandates that are democratically decided by the people.

In 2018, Italian voters had enough of the status quo and a slim majority voted for two radically anti-EU parties: Matteo Salvini's Lega Party and Beppe Grillo's Five Star Movement. The pair entered a coalition government soon after the election and became the first Western European nation to be run entirely by populists.

---

45   "The coming Eurosceptic surge in the European Parliament," *The Economist*, May 21, 2019, https://www.economist.com/graphic-detail/2019/05/21/the-coming-eurosceptic-surge-in-the-european-parliament.

46   David M. Herszenhorn and Maia De Le Baume, "Mainstream parties block Euroskeptics from top Parliament posts," *Politico*, July 10, 2019, https://www.politico.eu/article/mainstream-parties-block-euroskeptics-from-top-parliament-posts/.

Within a few months after their election, the coalition government nominated Paolo Savona as minister of economy and finances. Savona was a well-respected economist and professor who spoke publicly about Italy needing a Plan B in case the Euro collapsed and discussed the prospect of reintroducing a national currency.[47]

Italy's outgoing president, Sergio Mattarella, exercised his right under the nation's constitution to block Savona's nomination over his support for reintroducing a national currency. While the move to block a nomination wasn't unprecedented, it was the first time a president denied a cabinet-level position on the grounds that it was bad for the EU and the Italian economy. Many Italian leaders in the past sank the country's economic fortune and ran up trillions in debt, but that wasn't enough to block them from senior governmental positions because they supported the European project.

Mattarella designated Carlo Cottarelli, a former economist and former director of the International Monetary Fund, to lead a technocratic government. Nothing says more about the inability of establishment politicians to understand the mood of a country than stopping a democratically elected government from nominating a minister and instead appointing someone who represents the global elite.

Salvini and Luigi Di Maio, the thirty-one-year-old leader of the Five Star Movement, refused to concede. Di Maio called the appointment of Cottarelli Italian democracy's darkest night and Salvini said, "This isn't democracy, this isn't respect for the popular vote. It's the latest slap in the face."[48]

---

47   Matthew C. Klein, "Why Italy Needs a Euro Exit Plan,"
      Barron's, May 30, 2018, https://www.barrons.com/articles/
      why-italy-needs-a-euro-exit-plan-1527684618.

48   Lucy Adler, "Italy's caretaker PM assembles a cabinet almost certain to be
      rejected," *The Local*, May 29, 2018, https://www.thelocal.it/20180529/
      italy-carlo-cottarelli-cabinet-elections-impeachment.

The pair called for the impeachment of Mattarella, nationwide protests, and new elections. Within days of Cottarelli's appointment, it became clear that the pro-EU establishment was backed into a corner. Polling companies showed that the Lega Party was surging in popularity[49] and both Lega and the Five Star Movement would win an even larger majority if another election were held.

After five days, Mattarella, Di Maio, and Salvini came to an agreement that Savono could serve in the government but under a different capacity. He was appointed minister of European affairs[50] and the coalition government was allowed to continue without another flash election.

Former prime minister of the UK Theresa May can also be accused of attempting to thwart Brexit from 2017 through 2019.

May was never a Brexiteer; she campaigned for the UK to remain in the EU and warned that Brexit could damage the economy and security of Britain and said that it would be fatal for the union with Scotland.[51]

That's why it seemed a bit odd that she would be chosen as the UK's prime minister after David Cameron stepped down. She didn't share the same belief with Brexiteers, many of whom made up the base of the Conservative Party.

In July 2018, May's government published a white paper called the Chequers agreement that would be the basis of the Brexit negotiations. The agreement would keep the UK close to the EU and give it continued access to the European

---

49   "Sondaggi elettorali TP: Censtrodestra oltre il 40%, M5S in calo," *Termometro Politico*, May 31, 2018, https://www.termometropolitico.it/1305423_ sondaggi-elettorali-centrodestra-4.html.

50   "Paolo Savona, the Eurosceptic to oversee Italy's relations with Europe," *The Local Italy*, May 26, 2018, https://www.thelocal.it/20180526/ paolo-savona-the-eurosceptic-at-the-heart-of-italys-standoff.

51   Alan Robertson, "Theresa May: Brexit could prove 'fatal to Union with Scotland,'" *Holyrood*, April 25, 2016, https://www.holyrood.com/articles/ news/theresa-may-brexit-could-prove-fatal-union-scotland.

Single Market, and in exchange, the UK would continue to abide by the EU's standards on the environment, social rules, employment, and consumer protection. The UK would also apply the EU's tariffs and trade policy on goods and not apply a hard, physical border between the Republic of Ireland and Northern Ireland.[52]

Essentially, the UK would be tied to the EU's rules but would not have representation in the EU Parliament—a watered-down version of what the people mandated when they voted for Brexit.

When the details of the Chequers agreement were unveiled, May's own Tory government rebelled. Within days of the agreement's release, Brexit Secretary David Davis, Brexit Minister Steve Baker, Foreign Secretary Boris Johnson, Parliamentary Private Secretary (PPS) Chris Green, and PPS to the Foreign Secretary Conor Burns all resigned.

"We are now in the ludicrous position of asserting that we must accept huge amounts of precisely such EU law, without changing an iota, because it is essential for our economic health - and when we no longer have any ability to influence these laws as they are made," Johnson said in his resignation letter, echoing the concerns of other members of May's government who also resigned. "In that respect we are truly headed for the status of colony and many will struggle to see the economic or political advantages of that particular arrangement."[53]

By the end of 2018, nineteen high-level members of May's government resigned over her handling of Brexit, insisting that she was not respecting the wishes of the voters.

Although the EU criticized the plan, they ultimately agreed to the centerpiece of the Chequers agreement. Jean-Claude

---

52   Chris Morris, "Brexit: What does the government White Paper reveal?" BBC, July 12, 2018, https://www.bbc.com/news/uk-44807561.

53   "Boris Johnson's resignation letter and May's reply in full," BBC, July 9, 2018, https://www.bbc.com/news/uk-politics-44772804.

Juncker said, "It was the best deal possible…this is the only deal possible."[54]

Throughout the following year, May brought up several watered-down versions of Brexit for a vote and one by one, they were all voted down by Parliament.[55, 56, 57] During the process, May faced two votes of no confidence and was ultimately forced to resign.

May stated in an interview with the BBC that she failed at Brexit because she underestimated entrenched positions by some Brexiteers and opponents of Brexit.[58] By the end of May's time as prime minister, Brexit became the most important issue to Tory voters.

A YouGov poll taken in June 2019 found that Tory voters would support Brexit even if it meant Scotland left the UK, it damaged the economy, Northern Ireland left the UK, and even if it destroyed the Conservative Party.[59]

---

54   "EU leaders agree UK's Brexit deal at Brussels summit," BBC, November 25, 2018, https://www.bbc.com/news/uk-46334649.

55   United Kingdom, Parliament, House of Commons, *European Union (Withdrawal Act)*, January 15, 2019, https://hansard.parliament.uk/ Commons/2019-01-15/division/B975E889-89F5-42D3-9C18-7562AFD1977C/ EuropeanUnion(Withdrawal)Act?outputType=Party.

56   United Kingdom, Parliament, House of Commons, *United Kingdom's Withdrawal from the European Union*, March 29, 2019, https://hansard.parliament.uk/ Commons/2019-03-29/division/B6052BBD-43BE-4A30-8365-E3A8B108009E/ UnitedKingdom%E2%80%99SWithdrawalFromTheEuropeanUnion?output Type=Party.

57   "British parliament rejects plan to hold more Brexit indicative votes on Monday," Reuters, April 3, 2019, https://uk.reuters.com/article/ uk-britain-eu-votes/british-parliament-rejects-plan-to-hold-more-brexit-indicative-votes-on-monday-idUKKCN1RF26X\.

58   Jacob Jarvis, "Theresa May: I underestimated MPs' entrenched positions on Brexit," *Evening Standard*, July 12, 2019, https://www.standard.co.uk/ news/politics/theresa-may-i-underestimated-mps-entrenched-positions-on-brexit-a4189011.html.

59   Matthew Smith, "Most Conservative members would see party destroyed to achieve Brexit," *YouGov*, June 18, 2019, https:// yougov.co.uk/topics/politics/articles-reports/2019/06/18/ most-conservative-members-would-see-party-destroye.

May's refusal to deliver a Brexit that the people voted for had the ultimate cost of her premiership.

Europe isn't the only continent plagued with political institutions fighting tooth and nail against national populist reforms.

Donald Trump had his dealings with the institutional opposition to national populism both before and after he was elected president.

During the 2016 campaign, there was an attempt by people within the intelligence community to stop Trump from ever becoming president. Federal officials used a dossier created by Christopher Steele and paid for by Hillary Clinton's campaign and the Democratic National Committee to obtain a FISA warrant to surveil Trump aides.[60] The dossier was unverified opposition research: by law, when someone submits a FISA application, they must sign an affidavit that the information is correct to the best of their knowledge, but the dossier had more holes in it than a cheese grater.

Yet even after he defied the experts, the intelligence community, two political dynasties, and both the establishment Republican and Democratic parties, Trump still had a sea of people working to stop him from accomplishing his agenda using anti-democratic means.

During the 2016 campaign, Trump promised voters that if elected, he would drain the Washington swamp, but legally, it was easier said than done. The executive branch of the US federal government has more than one million employees, and nearly a third belong to a union that makes it very difficult to

60   Catherine Herridge and Gregg Re, "DOJ's Bruce Ohr wrote Christopher Steele was 'very concerned about Comey's firing – afraid they will exposed,'" *Fox News*, August 17, 2018, https://www.foxnews.com/politics/dojs-bruce-ohr-wrote-christopher-steele-was-very-concerned-about-comeys-firing-afraid-they-will-be-exposed.

fire them.[61] Trump signed three executive orders on May 25, 2018, to make it easier for agencies to fire federal workers and place limits on government union activities. By August 25, an Obama-appointed district court judge ruled that the executive order was unconstitutional.[62] That decision was overturned by the appeals court on July 16, 2019,[63] but during that fourteen–month legal process, career bureaucrats slow-walked President Trump's agenda.

Citizen journalist James O'Keefe's organization Project Veritas caught a staffer from the Government Accountability Office admitting that he is a socialist who was trying to stop the Trump administration's agenda whenever he could.[64] He's not alone in this mission.

In mid-2019, when Trump demanded that the State Department cut off financial aid to Central American countries whose citizens flooded the US's southern border, unelected bureaucrats slow-walked the president's orders.[65, 66] It became a regular

---

61   Alexander Fernandez Campbell, "Trump wants to fire federal employees at will. A federal judge said he can't," *Vox*, August 27, 2018, https://www.vox.com/2018/8/27/17786324/trump-fires-government-employees-union.

62   United States, US District Court for the District of Columbia, "National Federation of Federal Employees, AFL-CIO v. Donald Trump," August 25, 2018, https://ecf.dcd.uscourts.gov/cgi-bin/show_public_doc?2018cv1261-58.

63   Tal Axelrod, "Appeals court rules for Trump in fight over federal worker restrictions," *The Hill*, July 16, 2019, https://thehill.com/regulation/court-battles/453352-appeals-court-rules-for-trump-in-fight-over-federal-worker.

64   Brett Samuels, "GAO investigating after employee featured in Project Veritas video," *The Hill*, September 20, 2018, https://thehill.com/homenews/administration/407578-gao-investigating-after-employee-featured-in-project-veritas-video.

65   Elaina Plott, "Ignoring Trump's Orders, Hoping He'll Forget," *The Atlantic*, May 15, 2019, https://www.theatlantic.com/politics/archive/2019/05/trump-aides-ignore-president/589489/.

66   Christopher Flavelle and Benjamin Bain, "Washington Bureaucrats Are Quietly Working to Undermine Trump's Agenda," *Bloomberg News*, December 18, 2017, https://www.bloomberg.com/news/features/2017-12-18/washington-bureaucrats-are-chipping-away-at-trump-s-agenda.

practice for the administration's staff to agree with Trump to his face and then defy his orders once they left the room.

The State Department, Department of Homeland Security, and the Justice Department became infamous for regularly carrying out this practice.

On September 5, 2018, *The New York Times* published an anonymous op-ed titled, "I Am Part of the Resistance Inside the Trump Administration"[67] that detailed how senior-level members of Trump's White House were conspiring to stop the national populist agenda Trump campaigned on.

"That is why many Trump appointees have vowed to do what we can to preserve our democratic institutions while thwarting Mr. Trump's more misguided impulses until he is out of office," the anonymous author wrote. "Although he was elected as a Republican, the president shows little affinity for ideals long espoused by conservatives: free minds, free markets and free people. At best, he has invoked these ideals in scripted settings. At worst, he has attacked them outright."

In the minds of the political elite, they were going to save the Republic by stopping the democratically elected president from fulfilling the promises made to the voters. America showed signs of moving toward Crouch's post-democracy.

While the author of the piece was never identified, rumors floated that it could be anyone from then Director of the Office of Management and Budget Mick Mulvaney to Department of Homeland Security Secretary Kirstjen Nielsen to White House Deputy Press Secretary Raj Shah—all of whom denied writing the op-ed.[68]

---

67 Anonymous, "I Am Part of the Resistance Inside the Trump Administration," *The New York Times,* September 5, 2018, https://www.nytimes.com/2018/09/05/opinion/trump-white-house-anonymous-resistance.html.

68 Katie Mettler and Nick Kirkpatrick, "These officials have denied writing the Trump's 'resistance' op-ed," *The Washington Post,* September 6, 2018, https://www.washingtonpost.com/graphics/2018/politics/amp-stories/the-fix-these-trump-officials-have-denied-writing-nyt-resistance-op-ed/.

The fact that so many of Trump's cabinet members were suspect showed both the failure of the president and his team in staffing the administration with people willing to carry out his agenda and how difficult it is for unconventional candidates to reform the way Washington works.

A large part of that is Trump's fault, given the fact that he relied too heavily on members of the Republican National Committee who both vocally and quietly opposed his candidacy to fill his administration. He also lacked a formal transition team structure once he won the election.[69]

Yet despite Trump's inadequacies in his staffing decisions, the failure of national populists to carry out their agenda is almost universal. International organizations, private businesses, elected officials, and unelected bureaucrats are all committed to the neoliberal order that has been moving governments away from the people for the last half century. Some are doing it for personal profit, but most are doing it because it's fundamentally what they believe in. By 2019, a YouGov/Economist poll found that a plurality of Americans believed the deep state was trying to overthrow President Trump.[70]

This refusal by the political class to allow democracy to function will have grave consequences for the future, which we will discuss in the last chapter.

---

69   Ryan Hutchins, "Christie: Warning about Flynn among reasons I was fired from Trump transition," *Politico*, December 6, 2017, https://www.politico.com/states/new-jersey/story/2017/12/06/christie-warning-about-flynn-among-reasons-i-was-fired-from-trump-transition-136432.

70   The Economist/YouGov poll, "Do you think the 'deep state' is working to overthrow President Trump?" *The Economist*, October 13–15, 2019, distributed by *The Economist*, https://d25d2506sfb94s.cloudfront.net/cumulus_uploads/document/kvoamfqbbo/econTabReport.pdf.

CHAPTER 2

THE ENEMY OF
THE PEOPLE

AS DIVIDED AS the political elite are from the rest of their countrymen, no group is more insular and inwardly focused than the news industry. The media is one of the facets of society where the social isolation between the citizens and the elite is the most profound. Those in the media are cosmopolitan, college-educated, liberal, white, and have values that are in contrast from the somewheres.

Progressives, liberals, and globalists dominated most of the media for decades until alternative avenues became available for those offering differing narratives and opinions. Cable news, talk radio, the internet, and social media allowed for more intellectual diversity, but that came at the cost of news becoming more balkanized. People went to news outlets that confirmed the preconceived biases of their political, religious, or socioeconomic community. In the 21st century, there are so many news options that people look for outlets that confirm their worldviews. When faced with the facts that challenge their worldview, it is more common for a person to ignore facts that challenge their opinions and search instead for opinions that confirm their biases.[71]

This system became very bad for those trying to deliver unbiased reporting. Journalists and media figures became pseudo-celebrities and brands with hundreds of thousands, if not millions, of followers on social media.

The larger the brand, the better the access, opportunity, and pay. A city journalist who writes about local issues may be lucky to just get by, but a cable news host or social media celebrity could earn millions with an opportunity for book deals, speaking tours, and merchandise or endorsement deals.

Surviving as a journalist meant falling into this practice and over time, it created distrust in the media long before the rise of Trump, Bolsonaro, or Brexit.

According to a Gallup poll, trust in the American media sank from 72 percent in 1976 to 32 percent in 2016.[72] Americans cited bias as the reason they lost faith in the media as a whole, but interestingly enough, they still trusted the media outlet that confirmed their preconceived positions.

From 1985 to 2018, Pew Research found that a growing percentage of Americans regardless of political party believed that the media favored one side over another when presenting the news.[73] This included 52 percent of Democrats and an

---

71 Elizabeth Kolbert, "Why Facts Don't Change Our Minds," *The New Yorker*, February 19, 2017, https://www.newyorker.com/magazine/2017/02/27/why-facts-dont-change-our-minds.

72 Jeffrey M. Jones, "U.S. Media Trust Continues to Recover From 2016 Low," *Gallup*, October 12, 2018, https://news.gallup.com/poll/243665/media-trust-continues-recover-2016-low.aspx.

73 Jeffrey Gottfried, Galen Stocking, and Elizabeth Grieco, "Partisans Remain Sharply Divided in their Attitudes About the New Media," *Pew Research Center*, September 25, 2018, https://www.journalism.org/2018/09/25/democrats-and-republicans-remain-split-on-support-for-news-medias-watchdog-role/.

astonishing 86 percent of Republicans. A 2018 study by the Knight Foundation and Gallup[74] found that 69 percent of Americans say they have lost faith in the media over the last decade. When asked why, 45 percent said that the news industry offered misleading reporting, alternative facts, or fake news, and another 42 percent said they thought the media offered biased reporting. Nearly a third of Americans said that their distrust of the media could not be repaired, including 39 percent of Republicans and 29 percent of Independents.

Despite this growing distrust for the media as a whole, 67 percent of Americans said they trusted some news sources, while 16 percent said they trusted none. By political party, 35 percent of Democrats said they trusted all or most news sources, which is far more than the 13 percent of Independents and 3 percent of Republicans who said the same thing. Between a fourth and a fifth of Independents and Republicans said they do not trust any news organizations.

It's arguable that Democrats were more likely to trust media outlets because more outlets and well-known media figures presented the news with a narrative agreeable to them.

Very little of that distrust had to do with Donald Trump; only 5 percent of respondents said that attacks on Trump made them distrust the media and on the other side of the political aisle, just 3 percent said their negative opinions of the media had to do with outlets protecting the 45th president.

Americans aren't alone in this lack of faith in the fourth estate. A poll conducted by Cambridge University and YouGov in August 2018 found that trust in the media had also fallen across the UK and Europe. Just 32 percent of Italians, 27 percent of Poles, 40 percent of French, 44 percent of Swedes,

---

74   Gallup/Knight Foundation, "Indicators of News Media Trust," *The Knight Foundation*, 2018, distributed by the Knight's Foundation, https://www. knightfoundation.org/reports/indicators-of-news-media-trust.

44 percent of Germans, 14 percent of Hungarians, and 18 percent of Brits had either a great deal or fair amount of trust in journalists.[75] On the flip side, 67 percent of Italians, 71 percent of Poles, 54 percent of French, 52 percent of Swedes, 48 percent of Germans, 84 percent of Hungarians, and 77 percent of Brits had not much trust or no trust in journalists.

That level of distrust only increased after Brexit and Trump's election, when many media outlets saw themselves as part of the resistance against national populism. A 2019 study by the Reuters Institute for the Study of Journalism that was conducted in twelve countries including the US, the UK, Germany, Finland, France, Denmark, Spain, Japan, Brazil, Australia, and Ireland found that on average, there was a 4 percent drop in the number of people who trust the news most of the time after national populist victories in 2016 and 2017.[76] The countries that suffered from the most significant drop in trust include Finland (9 percent), the UK (11 percent), Germany (13 percent), and France (14 percent).

This ongoing disintegration of trust between the news industry and the general public is why it was easy for national populist candidates like Trump to gain support for attacking the media's fake news, or for people to believe Bolsonaro when he said journalists were printing negative stories of him to overthrow the government.[77] They're both saying exactly what millions of people, some of whom aren't their voters, already believe.

---

75   YouGov/Cambridge Centre, "Conspiracy Theories," distributed by *YouGov*, August 13–23, 2018.

76   Jacob Granger, "2019 Reuters Digital News Report finds that trust in the media continues to fall," *Journalism.co.uk*, June 13, 2019, https://www.journalism.co.uk/news/reuters-digital-news-report-finds-that-trust-in-the-media-continues-to-fall/s2/a740147/.

77   Jon Allsop, "Brazil's Bolsonaro smears reporters investigating his son," *Columbia Journalism Review*, March 12, 2019, https://www.cjr.org/the_media_today/bolsonaro_twitter_press_threats.php.

The media's bias and alienation from the masses can be attributed to two main factors: 1), like the political class, the media has become an elitist, homogenous, and cosmopolitan, and 2) the media was not held accountable for pushing fake news.

THE ELITIST MEDIA

The media is obsessed with democratic representation. It's not just in Congress, as was mentioned in the last chapter; it's in all walks of life. Google the phrase "there aren't enough women in" or "there aren't enough people of color in" and immediately you find over 479 million and 200 million articles and videos on each subject, respectively.

There are countless academic studies, articles in respected publications, and tweets by journalists with blue checkmarks about how various institutions are not proportionally representative of society as a whole. One of the worst offenders of not having proportional representation is the American media, but it's not just because there aren't enough women or people of color.

Salena Zito, a Pennsylvania-based writer who was one of the few journalists to correctly predict Trump would win the 2016 election, said a huge problem with the news industry was the lack of intellectual diversity and journalists of working-class backgrounds.

"Another problem with newsrooms is a lack of diversity," Zito said at the City Club of Cleveland, "I'm not just talking about not enough minorities, because there's not enough minorities in newsrooms. There's also not enough people that come from a state school, there's not enough people that come from the zip codes in the center of the country, there's not enough people that grew up in a blue-collar background, there's not enough people that go to church on Sunday, there's not enough people who own a gun, that go hunting, or concealed carry for protection."[78]

Zito is right: journalists in America are a pretty homogeneous crowd that aren't representative of the nation. They're overly educated (92 percent have a college degree),[79] overwhelmingly registered Democrat (just 7 percent are Republican),[80] and are mostly confined to major cities like New York and Washington, D.C.[81]

Journalists and Americans that voted for Trump in 2016 are not just segregated by economics, culture, and education. Journalists also don't physically live in places that voted for Trump or any Republican for that matter. According to one study, 61 percent of people employed in the publishing industry worked in counties that President Obama won in 2008; 32 percent of them lived in landslide counties where he won them by thirty points or more. By 2016, that number grew to 72 percent of people in the publishing industry lived in Clinton counties and 51 percent lived in counties that Clinton won in a thirty-or-more-point landslide. Only 11 percent lived in counties Trump won in a landslide.[82]

---

78   "Salena Zito 6.1.18." YouTube video, June 1, 2018, https://www.youtube. com/watch?v=i4YJOSdVOuw.

79   David H. Weaver and Lars Willnat, "The American Journalist in the Digital Age," *School of Journalism, Indiana University*, Bloomington, IN, 2014.

80   Reid Wilson, "Census: More Americans have college degrees ever before," *The Hill*, April 3, 2017, https://thehill.com/homenews/state-watch/326995-census-more-americans-have-college-degrees-than-ever-before.

81   Paul Farhi, "Charting the years-long decline of local news reporting," *The Washington Post*, March 26, 2014, https://www.washingtonpost. com/lifestyle/style/charting-the-years-long-decline-of-local-news-reporting/2014/03/26/977bf088-b457-11e3-b899-20667de76985_story. html?utm_term=.95522dad4019.

82   Jack Shafer and Tucker Doherty, "The Media Bubble Is Worse Than You Think," *Politico Magazine*, May/June 2017, https://www.politico.com/magazine/story/2017/04/25/media-bubble-real-journalism-jobs-east-coast-215048.

Not much is different overseas, according to a survey conducted by City University London: 98 percent of recent and 86 percent of all British journalists are university-educated. An astounding 36 percent hold master's degrees; that's nearly the same amount of the adult population with any university degree.[83] As is the case in America, they disproportionately live in areas that voted to remain in the EU. A whopping 36 percent of all journalists live in London, a city that houses just 13 percent of the British population.[84]

People in the media had the cultural, educational, and political characteristics of cosmopolitan voters. That was the world most of them understood and the viewpoint they represented in their work. Many journalists became ideologically driven to defend globalism and denigrate national populists.

In the vote for Brexit, thirty major British newspapers and magazines endorsed the Remain campaign, double the amount of major publications that supported Leave. During the 2016 US presidential election, the weight of the media was even more one-sided. More than five hundred daily, weekly, college, and international newspapers and magazines endorsed Clinton for president. Trump received just twenty-eight endorsements.

It's not just in endorsements, but also in coverage. The day after Marine Le Pen and Emmanuel Macron came in the top two positions in the first round of the French presidential election, the French media portrayed Macron's second-round victory as inevitable.[85] The NBC Nightly News announced after

---

83   "Higher Education Student Statistic: UK 2016/2017-Qualifications achieved," *Higher Education Statistics Agency,* January 11, 2018, https://www.hesa.ac.uk/news/11-01-2018/sfr247-higher-education-student-statistics/qualifications.

84   Oscar Williams, "British journalism is 94% white and 55% male, survey reveals," *The Guardian,* March 24, 2016, https://www.theguardian.com/media-network/2016/mar/24/british-journalism-diversity-white-female-male-survey.

85   "Marine Le Pen and the French media - The Listening Post (Lead)," YouTube video, May 1, 2017, https://www.youtube.com/watch?v=46sxxBPk7eo.

Trump's victory, "deeper concerns tonight that the world's shining light of democracy has gone dark."[86] *New York Times* journalist Maggie Haberman laughed out loud during a cable news show when a prominent Democrat predicted Trump could win the Republican nomination.[87] When the national populist Coalition Avenir Québec won in 2018, *USA Today* summed up the political party with the headline, "Anti-Immigrant Party in Canada Thrives with Big Victory in Québec."[88]

Not populist, not nationalist, not conservative, but anti-immigrant, national populists are often defined by what they're against. It's a favorite tactic of journalists, along with declaring they're far-right and extreme-right.

All of the examples above are by journalists, not even opinion writers who use more colorful language to describe national populist candidates and political parties.

Given that opinion writers and journalists were too urban, too educated, too liberal, and wrong about both Brexit and the election of Donald Trump, you could imagine that the media wanted to expand their intellectual diversity after 2016. You'd be wrong.

Although the major media outlets in the United States who endorsed Clinton in 2016 all added a token Republican or center-right opinion writer to their payroll, none of them understood the national populist movement or correctly

---

86   "WATCH: The Biggest Media Meltdowns to Trump's Win," YouTube video, November 11, 2016, https://www.youtube.com/watch?v=UtJvYdX4GKM.

87   Maggie Haberman, "That was a really bad moment of mine that I would undo. But repackaging it consistently as laughing at Ellison as opposed to, as Steve says, the idea that Trump, who had threatened to run repeatedly and whose own advisers predicted he would drop out by the fall, is untrue." November 4, 2018, https://twitter.com/maggienyt/status/1059141850517397506.

88   Adam Kovac, "Canadian anti-immigrant party thrives with landslide victory in Quebec," *USA Today*, October 3, 2018, https://www.usatoday.com/story/news/world/2018/10/03/anti-immigrant-party-canada-thrives-big-victory-quebec/1510886002/.

predicted the rise of Trump. For example, *The New York Times* hired columnist Bret Stephens, a Never Trumper; *The Washington Post* hired Max Boot, a Never Trumper; *The Atlantic* hired and then quickly fired Kevin Williamson, a Never Trumper; and *The Dallas Morning News* hired Jay Caruso, a Never Trumper.

The most surefire way to succeed as a conservative opinion columnist in Trump's America was for all of your insight, predictions, and opinions to have been absolutely wrong about the most significant political trend in the world. Of course, there were a few exceptions to this rule, but they were notably few. For the foreseeable future many parts of the media, both opinion-based and non-opinion-based, are working around the clock against national populism.

FAKE NEWS

As long as there has been journalism, there has been fake news, yellow journalism, political bias, and the like. This is not a recent phenomenon, and although some media outlets still produce interesting and compelling work, the changes in the media's business model because of the internet have had an overall negative effect on the industry. Newspapers are going out of business and those that still exist don't have the budgets to do as many groundbreaking investigative stories.[89] Those that survived resorted to clickbait and sound bites. It just became more economically feasible to cover what a celebrity said on social media than it did to do investigative reporting.

The changes in the market also affected journalists themselves. The industry doesn't pay much outside of lucrative television and book deals. Beat reporters or city desk journalists

---

89   Jack Shafer, "Where Did All the Investigative Journalism Go?" *Reason Magazine*, April 2017, https://reason.com/2017/02/22/where-did-all-the-investigativ/.

will never get rich for their efforts. That's why with the changes to the industry, it became more beneficial for reporters to become an opinion brand rather than a straight journalist.

Outright opinion journalists compromise a large chunk of the media, especially in America and now with social media platforms like Twitter, most journalists give out their opinion on a minute by minute basis. Anyone can see that most journalists are willing to share their personal bias openly and without consequence.

It used to be that journalists had to at least fake that they were straight down the line, but now it's all fair game.

In 2010, *The Washington Post*'s Dave Weigel tweeted a false accusation that there was a video of conservative Matt Drudge molesting a child.[90] Weigel claimed it was just a joke and he suffered no major repercussions. Then a few months later, emails where he discussed how he wished Matt Drudge would set himself on fire and said other disparaging things about Republicans like Ron Paul, Newt Gingrich, Pat Buchanan, and Rush Limbaugh were leaked.[91] He resigned from the paper in disgrace but quickly moved to MSNBC and ultimately back to *The Washington Post* just five years later. Since then, he's tweeted fake reports about President Trump's rallies being mostly empty.[92]

Former *Guardian* reporter Ben Jacobs did something similar but was met with no repercussions at all. In 2014, he tweeted about how he had the urge to punch a sixteen-year-old

---

90   Jennifer Harper, "Inside the Beltway," *The Washington Times*, May 3, 2010, https://www.washingtontimes.com/news/2010/may/3/drudge-smudge/.

91   Tom Scocca, "Ratfuckers, Crybabies, and Schoolmarms: The Dave Weigel Affair," *Slate*, June 27, 2010, https://slate.com/news-and-politics/2010/06/ratfuckers-crybabies-and-schoolmarms-the-dave-weigel-affair.html.

92   Emily Yahr, "President Trump calls for Washington Post reporter who apologized for inaccurate tweet to be fired," *The Washington Post*, December 9, 2017, https://www.washingtonpost.com/lifestyle/style/president-trump-calls-for-washington-post-reporter-who-apologized-for-inaccurate-tweet-to-be-fired/2017/12/09/2fb467de-dd4b-11e7-b1a8-62589434a581_story.html.

conservative in the face while he was at the Conservative Political Action Committee.[93] This outward expression of wanting to physically assault a minor didn't harm his career in the slightest. Just days before the 2016 election, he tweeted a quote from Trump out of context. Jacobs tweeted, "We are going to deliver justice the way it used to be in this country." Trump's full quote was, "We are going to deliver justice the way justice used to be in this country, at the ballot box on November Eight."[94] His followers had no idea about the full quote and replied that they thought Trump was advocating for lynching black Americans. It's one of many incidents where the media created racial tensions.

On May 16, 2018, Trump held a White House meeting on immigration where the conversation turned to the violent gang MS-13. The president described the violent gang members as animals. *The New York Times* tweeted, "Trump lashed out at undocumented immigrants during a White House meeting, calling those trying to breach the country's borders animals."[95]

They dropped the fact that Trump was talking about gang members, leaving the readers to believe that Trump was talking about all illegal aliens.

Increasing racial tensions is something the American media does especially well, including CNN's hosts Sally Kohn, Mel Robbins, and Margaret Hoover using the hands up, don't shoot

---

93   Ben Jacobs, "Left, right and center, straight news and opinion, journalists at CPAC have one thing in common, the overwhelming urge to punch Benji Backer," March 8, 2014, https://twitter.com/bencjacobs/status/442428951752097792.

94   Ezra Dulis, "The Guardian's Ben Jacobs Caught Sliming Trump With Out-Of-Context Quote," *Breitbart News*, November 7, 2016, https://www.breitbart.com/the-media/2016/11/07/guardian-ben-jacobs-caught-sliming-trump-with-out-of-context-quote/.

95   Oliver Darcy, "Media outlets take Trump out of context to suggest he called undocumented immigrants 'animals,'" CNN, May 17, 2018, https://money.cnn.com/2018/05/17/media/media-trump-animals-immigrants/index.html.

symbol on a live broadcast[96] while discussing the shooting death of Michael Brown at the hands of police. Protestors believed Brown said this phrase to the police right before they shot and killed him; according to President Obama's Attorney General Eric Holder, it turned out to be a lie.[97] Nonetheless, all three women held their hands up and perpetuated that falsehood.

Once Trump became a candidate the number of media outlets and public figures who promoted fake hate crimes and race hoaxes became endemic. This includes Jim Acosta tweeting that a church in Indiana had been vandalized with the words Heil Trump right after election day.[98] It turned out that it was committed by the church's organist as a hoax.[99] *The New Yorker* wrote an article about a Muslim woman who was attacked by three men on the New York City subway, she said the attackers were yelling "Donald Trump" while trying to remove her hijab.[100] It turned out she made the whole thing up.[101] And

96   Jackson Connor, "CNN Hosts Under Fire For Putting 'Hands Up' On Air, Critics Claim Bias," *The Huffington Post*, December 14, 2015. https://www.huffpost.com/entry/cnn-hands-up-host-under-fire-critics-claim-bias_n_6327546.

97   United States, Department of Justice, "DEPARTMENT OF JUSTICE REPORT REGARDING THE CRIMINAL INVESTIGATION INTO THE SHOOTING DEATH OF MICHAEL BROWN BY FERGUSON, MISSOURI POLICE OFFICER DARREN WILSON," Washington D.C., March 4, 2015, https://www.justice.gov/sites/default/files/opa/press-releases/attachments/2015/03/04/doj_report_on_shooting_of_michael_brown_1.pdf.

98   Jim Acosta, "Church in VP-elect Pence's home state of Indiana vandalized with words 'Heil Trump,'" November 14, 2016, https://twitter.com/Acosta/status/798184912465575936.

99   "Organist who vandalized Indiana church with slurs fired," *IndyStar*, May 16, 2017, https://www.indystar.com/story/news/fox59/2017/05/17/organist-accused-vandalizing-indiana-church-slurs-fired/326614001/.

100   Gabriella Paiella, "New York Woman Who Claimed 3 Trump Supporters Tried to Remove Her Hijab Reportedly Recants Story [Update]," *The Cut*, December 14, 2016, https://www.thecut.com/2016/12/muslim-woman-reportedly-harassed-by-trump-fans-on-nyc-subway.html?mid=twitter_nymag.

101   Christopher Mele, "Muslim Woman Made Up Hate Crime on Subway, Police Say," *The New York Times*, December 12, 2016, https://www.nytimes.com/2016/12/14/nyregion/manhattan-yasmin-seweid-false-hate-crime.html.

then there was a reporter from *The Intercept* who faked a series of hoax bomb threats against Jewish centers.[102]

The apex of these fake hate crimes under Trump's presidency came on January 18, 2019, when a video emerged of teenage boys from Covington Catholic High School wearing Trump's Make America Great Again (MAGA) hat had a standoff with a Native American activist who was playing the drums and singing. It's hard to overstate how much the media overacted after this video went viral on Twitter.

The Covington Catholic video had everything the media could dream of: a white boy with a MAGA hat using his privilege to shame a Native American elder. They were able to attack the main boy featured in the video, sixteen-year-old Nick Sandmann, on the basis of race, privilege, toxic masculinity, and being a Trump supporter. It was perfect fodder for an opinion-based news industry that lives for clickbait. So, without getting any facts, respectable media figures and outlets destroyed the teenager's reputation, made wild accusations, and ignited a mob against him.

This reaction came from both conservative media figures like S. E. Cupp, Meghan McCain, and Charlie Kirk[103] as well as liberals like Patton Oswalt, Ana Navarro, and Jeet Heer. CNN contributor Bakari Sellers even went so far as calling for violence when he tweeted about Sandmann some people can be punched in the face. Many more verified Twitter accounts called for violence and even some demanded the boys be

---

102   United States, Department of Justice, "Juan Thompson Sentenced in Manhattan Federal Court to 60 Months in Prison for Cyberstalking and Making Hoax Bomb Threats to JCCs And Other Victim Organizations," Southern District of New York, December 20, 2017, https://www.justice.gov/usao-sdny/pr/juan-thompson-sentenced-manhattan-federal-court-60-months-prison-cyberstalking-and.

103   Katelyn Caralle, "Conservative press apologizes for saying students harassed a Native American protestor," *The Washington Examiner,* January 21, 2019, https://www.washingtonexaminer.com/news/conservative-press-apologizes-for-saying-students-harassed-a-native-american-protester.

murdered. *GQ* writer Nathaniel Friedman tweeted that he wanted all the teenagers doxed and their private information to be made public[104] and *New York Daily News* columnist Brandon Friedman said the fact that the children are minors shouldn't matter when it comes to releasing their private information.[105]

The New York Times, The Washington Post, and *National Review* all immediately released biased articles condemning the boys without getting the most basic facts.[106]

When the smoke cleared, it turned out that the media portrayed the entire incident incorrectly and the Native American activist lied about his side of the story. Only one journalist, Erik Abriss from *Vulture,* lost their job from the incident after he tweeted that he wanted the boys to f**king die.[107] For some unexplainable reason, *USA Today* columnist Kirsten Powers tweeted that the real victims in the whole situation were journalists.[108]

The real victims, of course, were the teenage boys, who received death threats and the threat of expulsion from their

---

104 Jon Levine, "GQ Writer Regrets Tweet Calling for Covington Students to be Doxxed," *The Wrap,* January 21, last updated January 22, https://www.thewrap.com/gq-writer-regrets-call-for-doxxing-covington-catholic-high-school-students/.

105 Allum Bokhari, "Twitter Allows 'Verified' Calls For Violence Against Conservative High School Kids," *Breitbart,* January 21, 2019, https://www.breitbart.com/tech/2019/01/21/twitter-allows-verified-calls-for-violence-against-conservative-high-school-kids/.

106 Joe Concha, "In Covington students' controversy, media forgets to 'get it first – but first get it right,'" *The Hill,* January 23, 2019, https://thehill.com/opinion/civil-rights/426597-in-covington-students-controversy-media-forgets-to-get-it-first-but.

107 Jessica Chasmar, "Journalist loses job for tweets wishing Covington students would 'f-ing die,'" *The Washington Times,* January 22, 2019, https://www.washingtontimes.com/news/2019/jan/22/erik-abriss-journalist-loses-job-tweet-wishing-cov/.

108 Sarah D, "'Own your failure!' Kirsten Powers gets torched for the 'hottest take yet' on media's Covington eff-up," *Twitchy* (blog), January 23, 2019, https://twitchy.com/sarahd-313035/2019/01/23/own-your-failure-kirsten-powers-gets-torched-for-the-hottest-take-yet-on-medias-covington-eff-up/.

high school.[109] Some of the boys sued certain media figures for defamation, and the case is still ongoing as of the writing of this book.

Regardless of whether they win the lawsuits or not, it should not be forgotten that members of the media were absolutely fine with destroying the reputation and possibly threatening the life of teenagers. Using their Twitter accounts as weapons for the sole purpose of gaining notoriety and reflexively showing that they had enough moral integrity to call out the bigotry of a stranger from the safety of their home.

Journalists and pundits who partake in this puritan activity of publicly shaming people they disagree with are almost never held accountable for their actions. As was mentioned before, it's becoming increasingly rare that they'll be fired for ginning up racial tensions or attacking private citizens they disagree with on politics. It'll likely keep happening with increasing frequency until news outlets start firing them en masse.

The media loves consensus, especially if the consensuses has a globalist bend. The media will work overtime to defend these mutually agreed-upon opinions about foreign policy, race, immigration, globalism, and populism. Even when it turns out that a consensus isn't shared with the rest of the country or is just a disaster for the nation as a whole, the media will defend it.

American media outlets obsessed over the Mueller investigation on Trump and Russian collusion, churning out dozens of fake stories. Some of their biggest hoaxes include *New York Magazine*'s story that Trump lawyer Michael Cohen went to Prague,[110] CNN's report that James Comey was going to

109 "Videos Show a Collision of 3 Groups That Spawned a Fiery Political Moment," *The New York Times*, January 22, 2019, https://www.nytimes.com/2019/01/22/us/covington-catholic-washington-videos.html.

110 Joshua Caplan, "Mueller: Buzzfeed Report Claiming Trump Directed Michael Cohen Testimony 'Not Accurate,'" *Breitbart News*, January 18, 2019, https://www.breitbart.com/politics/2019/01/18/mueller-disputes-buzzfeed-news-report-claiming-trump-directed-michael-cohen-testimony/.

refute Donald Trump's claim that he was told he wasn't under investigation,[111] ABC's Brian Ross reporting that Michael Flynn was going to make a plea deal that Trump had directed him to contact the Russians,[112] *NBC* reporting that the government wiretapped Trump's personal attorney,[113] and the *Buzzfeed* story that Trump directed Cohen to lie to Congress about a proposed Moscow project.[114]

The list goes on and on. The American media was drunk on the belief that Trump colluded with Russia and that he was guilty. Media outlets oversold stories about Russian collusion. It got so bad that even liberal writer Glenn Greenwald said, "I genuinely feel sorry for MSNBC viewers who have had their brains filled with (stories of Russian collusion)... for two straight years and uncritically believed what they were hearing."[115]

After the Mueller probe ended with the conclusion that Trump did not collude with Russia to change the 2016 election, *The New York Times* staff had a meeting that leaked to *Salon*. In

---

111   Joe Concha, "CNN issues correction after Comey statement contradicts reporting," *The Hill,* June 7, 2017, https://thehill.com/blogs/blog-briefing-room/336871-cnn-issues-correction-after-comey-statement-contradicts-reporting.

112   "ABC's Brian Ross suspended for erroneous report on Flynn plea deal," *BBC News,* December 3, 2017, https://www.bbc.com/news/world-us-canada-42214214.

113   Oliver Darcy, "NBC News corrects explosive story on Michael Cohen," *CNN Business,* May 3, 2018, https://money.cnn.com/2018/05/03/media/nbc-news-michael-cohen-correction/index.html.

114   Kate Sullivan, "Buzzfeed: Sources say Trump directed Michael Cohen to lie to Congress about proposed Moscow project," *CNN Politics,* January 18, 2019, https://www.cnn.com/2019/01/17/politics/buzzfeed-trump-cohen-lie-congress-moscow/index.html.

115   Glenn Greenwald, "I'm not saying this to be mean. I genuinely feel sorry for MSNBC viewers who have had their brains filled with stuff like this for 2 straight years and uncritically believed what they were hearing. The damage to the discourse will never be undone," February 28, 2019, https://twitter.com/ggreenwald/status/1101152656905641985?lang=en.

the closed-door meeting, Executive Editor Dean Baquet told his staff that they had been too flat-footed, meaning that they were creating a narrative that wasn't true.

In a meeting on August 11, 2019, Baquet said Trump became emboldened politically because their reporting rooted for a Russian collusion narrative that never materialized. He told his staff that they need change, but from here on out, they would cover Trump's remarks as being racist and dividing America.[116]

That was their big come to Jesus moment. The paper of record was moving from one narrative to another to guide the public to their consensus.

The media took a consensus-based approach to news long before Trump. Take the Iraq War, for example, the news industry had a pro-war consensus. Nearly every major American publication and cable news network had war hawks peddling stories that favored a military invasion of Iraq: Judith Miller from *The New York Times*, Larry Kudlow of CNBC, Richard Cohen and Fred Hiatt of *The Washington Post*, everyone at *The Weekly Standard*, Paul Gigot of *The Wall Street Journal*, Joe Scarborough of MSNBC, Bret Stephens of *The Jerusalem Post*, David Remnick of *The New Yorker*, Jeffrey Goldberg of *The Atlantic*, as well as myriad other liberal and conservative talking heads and political analysts.[117][118]

---

116   Ashley Feinberg, "The New York Times Unites vs. Twitter," *Slate*, August
       15, 2019, https://slate.com/news-and-politics/2019/08/new-york-times-
       meeting-transcript.html.
117   Matt Taibbi, "16 Years Later, How the Press That Sold the Iraq War Got
       Away With It," *Rolling Stone*, March 22, 2019, https://www.rollingstone.com/
       politics/politics-features/iraq-war-media-fail-matt-taibbi-812230/.
118   Nick Fernandez and Bobby Lewis, "The Iraq War cheerleaders
       who are still around 15 years later," *Media Matters for America*,
       March 20, 2018, https://www.mediamatters.org/sean-hannity/
       iraq-war-cheerleaders-who-are-still-around-15-years-later.

The media helped the Bush administration sell a war that would cost over 100,000 lives and $2 trillion in lost treasure.[119] When everything they predicted—stockpiles of weapons of mass destruction, alleged plans that Saddam Hussein was attempting to get a nuclear weapon, or a connection that Iraq was working with al-Qaeda—all turned out to be false, no one in the media was held accountable for selling the greatest foreign policy mistake in American history to the public. Almost all of those names listed above still have prominent jobs either in the media or the government. They still make money spouting off their opinions and few have ever apologized to the families of the 4,572 Americans[120] who died in Iraq fighting a war America didn't need to fight.

It's not because the media loved Bush (they didn't), but American media favors military conflict in general. When President Obama considered taking military action in Syria and Iraq against ISIS, the media presented a pro-intervention narrative. Of the eighty-nine guests that appeared on Sunday news programs leading up to Obama's military intervention, just one was an outspoken critic of furthering US intervention in the Middle East.[121]

Even President Trump, who rarely gets love from the mainstream media, earned praise from the editorial pages of *The Wall Street Journal, The New York Times, USA Today, New York Daily News, The Washington Post,* and *Chicago Sun-Times* when he bombed Syria in April 2017. Out of the forty-seven major

119   Daniel Trotta, "Iraq War costs U.S. more than $2 trillion: study," Reuters, March 14, 2013, https://www.reuters.com/article/us-iraq-war-anniversary-idUSBRE92D0PG20130314.
120   "U.S. Fatalities by State," *icasualties.org* (blog), 2019, http://icasualties.org/USMap.
121   Peter Hart, "Debating How-Not Whether-to Launch a New War," *Fair* (blog), November 1, 2014, https://fair.org/extra/debating-how-not-whether-to-launch-a-new-war/.

editorial papers in the US, only one, *The Houston Chronicle,* opposed the airstrikes.[122]

When Trump tried to pull troops out of Syria, however, he was met with nearly universal resistance from the media. MSNBC's Rachel Maddow ran a segment where she hashed out a conspiracy that the pullout had to do with former Trump official Michael Flynn and the nation of Turkey,[123] Fox & Friends host Brian Kilmeade called it stunning and irresponsible,[124] *The New York Times* editorial board said they wished Trump listened to his hawkish advisor John Bolton more,[125] and *The Washington Post* writer Max Boot said it was a gift to our enemies.[126] In the end, Trump buckled under the mounting media attacks and pushback from the military-industrial complex and kept troops in Syria.

The American media is always on the side of war and when the war turns out to be a mistake, they are never held accountable, no one is fired, and the anywheres that make up the elite members of that industry just go on while the somewheres pay the price.

---

122   Adam Johnson, "Out of 47 Major Editorials on Trump's Syria Strikes, Only One Opposed," *Fair* (blog), April 11, 2017, https://fair.org/home/out-of-46-major-editorials-on-trumps-syria-strikes-only-one-opposed/.

123   Ian Schwartz, "Maddow: Trump Pulls Out of Syria A Day After Flynn Admitted He Sold Out Country," *Real Clear Politics,* December 20, 2018, https://www.realclearpolitics.com/video/2018/12/20/maddow_trump_pulls_out_of_syria_a_day_after_flynn_admitted_he_sold_out_country.html.

124   Howard Kurtz, "Conservative media challenge Trump on border wall, Syria pullout," *Fox News,* December 21, 2018, https://www.foxnews.com/politics/conservative-media-challenge-trump-on-border-wall-syria-pullout.

125   The Editorial Board, "Trump's Decision to Withdraw From Syria Is Alarming. Just Ask His Advisers," *The New York Times,* December 19, 2018, https://www.nytimes.com/2018/12/19/opinion/editorials/trump-syria-withdrawal.html.

126   Max Boot, "Trump's surprise pullout is a giant Christmas gift to our enemies," *The Washington Post,* December 19, 2018, https://www.washingtonpost.com/opinions/global-opinions/trumps-surprise-syria-pullout-is-a-giant-christmas-gift-to-our-enemies/2018/12/19/c032c7e4-03ae-11e9-b6a9-0aa5c2fcc9e4_story.html?utm_term=.cf47798fbc84.

Of course, war is not the only time the media got something wrong in a big way. The financial crisis of 2008 was a large stain on the American media, who were blind to the crisis until it was already too late.

Throughout 2006 and 2007, financial wizards like Art Laffer, Mike Norman, and Ben Stein[127] regularly appeared on television reassuring viewers that the economy had never been better. Investors told Americans trusting their expertise to dump their money into the stock market.

As *The Washington Post* put it, the business press never conveyed a real sense of alarm until institutions began to collapse.[128] Then managing editor for *Fortune* Andy Serwer told *The Washington Post* that he felt it wouldn't have mattered if they did because people would have ignored them.

Even after it was obvious that the economy was in free fall and that investors should be panicking about how to protect themselves during the collapse, some media personalities continued to try and prop up failing financial institutions.

On March 6, 2008, Jim Cramer, one of America's most prominent business analysts, told his viewers that he believed in the financial institution Bear Stearns. "I believe in the Bear franchise...at $69 (a share) I'm not giving up (on Bear Stearns)."[129] Just a few days later on March 11, a man named Peter wrote asking if he should take his money out of Bear Stearns to which Cramer said, "No! No! No! Bear Stearns is fine. Do not take your money out. Bear Stearns is not in trouble...That's just being silly. Don't be silly."[130] By March 16, Bear Stearns stock

---

127   "Peter Schiff was Right," YouTube video, December 30, 2013, https://www.youtube.com/watch?v=sgRGBNekFIw.

128   Steve Schifferes and Richard Roberts, *The Media and Financial Crises: Comparative and Historical Perspective*, (London: Routledge, 2014) p.xxvi.

129   "Jon Stewart slams Jim Cramer" YouTube video, January 8, 2014, https://www.youtube.com/watch?v=NkytKDzCEeU

130   "Mad Money Host Jim Cramer: Don't Be Silly On Bear Stearns" YouTube video, March 28, 2013https://www.youtube.com/watch?v=V9EbPxTm5_s

fell by over 85 percent and was acquired by JP Morgan Chase for $2 per share.

The media did everything they could to assure anxious Americans that the world wasn't collapsing. MSNBC's Ali Velshi admitted that during production meetings they would examine wording to minimalize the severity of the market.[131] It was as if a monsoon was coming and the weatherman told you to carry an umbrella on your way to work.

When it turned out that twice in a single decade, the American media failed to accurately hold Wall Street and Washington accountable and warn citizens of the oncoming crisis, Americans started surrendering their faith in the media. According to Gallup, it was during that time period between 2002 and 2008 that faith in the media fell by double digits.[132]

Most recently, the media has endorsed a woke progressive view of racial injustice that sees discrimination everywhere. Georgia State University PhD student Zach Goldberg researched the number of news articles mentioning certain topics on race and immigration[133] and found that around 2010, the media increasingly featured "woke" terminology and subject matters at an alarming pace.

The number of news articles mentioning diversity and inclusion increased by about 1,500 percent between 2010 and 2018; the term whiteness was used around five hundred times

---

131   Richard Perez-Pena, "Amid Market Turmoil, Some Journalists Try to Tone Down Emotion." *The New York Times*. September 21, 2008. https://www.nytimes.com/2008/09/22/business/media/22press.html

132   Art Swift, "Americans' Trust in Mass Media Sinks to New Low." *Gallup*, September 14, 2016, https://news.gallup.com/poll/195542/americans-trust-mass-media-sinks-new-low.aspx

133   Zach Goldberg, "1/n Spent some time on LexisNexis over the weekend. Depending on your political orientation, what follows will either disturb or encourage you. But regardless of political orientation, I'm sure we can all say 'holy fucking shit.'" May 28, 2019, https://twitter.com/ZachG932/status/1133440945201061888

in 2010 and over two thousand times in 2018; critical race theory had under one hundred mentions in 2010 but over three hundred in 2018; unconscious bias went from being used around one thousand times in 2014 to about six thousand times in 2018, white privilege was used 250 times in 2012 and over two thousand times in 2018; systemic racism was mentioned about 100 times in 2012 and over two thousand times in 2018. *The New York Times* was especially guilty of this radicalization on the subject race increasing their usage of the term's discrimination, people of color, social justice, diversity, and racism by over 300 percent over the course of a few years. By 2018, the term whiteness and racism were used in nearly two percent of all *New York Times* articles.

This move toward woke journalism had an effect on the readers' overall perception of discrimination in America. Data collected by the American National Election Studies (AMNES) showed that readers of *The New York Times* are more likely to perceive an increase in discrimination against blacks and women in society.[134, 135] Media consumption has a long history of affecting the outlook of discrimination in America; a 2007 study found that Americans, especially minorities, were more likely to believe that police brutality an epidemic if they consumed a large amount of network news.[136]

It's arguable that America has become more woke because the elite institutions like the media have been pushing that narrative on the American public.

---

134   Zach Goldberg, "This might be relevant insofar as a) perceptions of the prevalence of discrimination among liberals saw tremendous increases across this period, and b) there's a robust relationship between NYT readers and perceiving more discrimination." May 30, 2019, https://twitter.com/ZachG932/status/1134336204340678656

135   Zach Goldberg, May 30, 2019, https://twitter.com/ZachG932/status/1134336408498397189

136   Kenneth Dowler and Valerie Zawilski, "Public perceptions of police misconduct and discrimination: Examining the impact of media consumption." *Journal of Criminal Justice*, March-April 2007. p. 193–203.

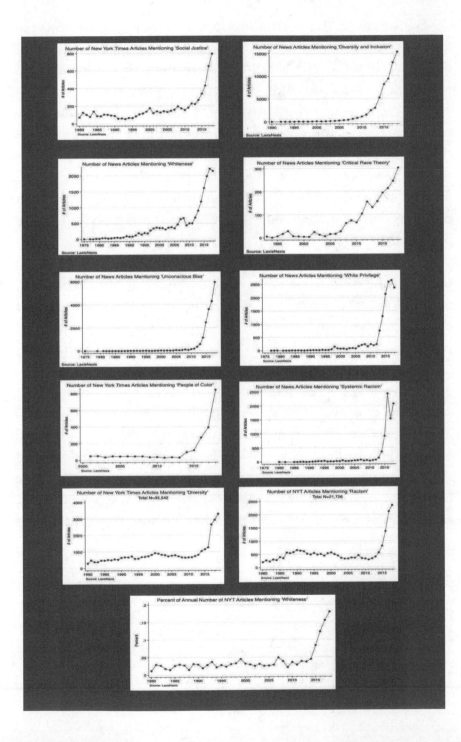

For decades, the media has been more concerned about salvaging their narratives than focused on relaying facts to citizens. They created a bubble of respectable opinions and they almost always worked only within those confines.

So, it comes as no surprise that people in the media were fully unaware of the growing national populist uprising across the world. It's even less surprising that most mainstream news outlets promoted negative news stories about the movement's leading figures, political parties, and ideas because not only did it represent a challenge to the institutions they worked to protect, but also an affront to their cosmopolitan values.

In the same way that Velshi said that his media outlet purposefully tried to downplay the language about the severity of the 2007 financial crisis, many media outlets do the exact opposite when discussing the repercussions of national populists' election victories. When Haider's Freedom Party came in second place in the Austrian election in 2000, *The New York Times* urged President Clinton to recall their ambassador from the country.[137] Indian writer Kapil Komireddi said in May 2019 that if Narendra Modi was re-elected, he would take India to a dark place.[138] When discussing the first round of the French election results, the Spanish paper *ABC* ran a headline, "France, between the centrism of Macron and the radicalism of Le Pen."[139] The day after Bolsonaro won the first

---

137   "An Unwelcome Austrian Government" *The New York Times,* February 4, 2000, https://www.nytimes.com/2000/02/04/opinion/an-unwelcome-austrian-government.html

138   Kapil Komireddi, "Five more years of Narendra Modi will take India to a dark place." *The Guardian,* May 21, 2009, https://www.theguardian.com/commentisfree/2019/may/21/five-more-years-narendra-modi-india-dark-place

139   Matt Fidler, "'Historique': how the media reported the French election- in pictures." *The Guardian,* April 24, 2017, https://www.theguardian.com/world/gallery/2017/apr/24/historique-how-the-media-reported-the-french-election-in-pictures

round of the presidential election, columnist Bernardo Mello Franco wrote in the Brazilian newspaper *O Globo*, "the election rewarded ultraconservatism, truculent discourse, and religious fundamentalism. The bully pulpit has grown and promises to become more powerful."[140]

The same fear that the media should have used to warn their audience about the ongoing failures of the neoliberal world order, was reserved for national populists.

It's a tragedy given the importance of the role the media should play in a civil society. Unfortunately, the current model set up in the United States and most of the West has caused division, social anxiety, and mass distrust. To have a better functioning country, we'd need a more honest news industry.

CHAPTER 3

FOREIGN POLICY BLOWBACK

ONE OF THE biggest misconceptions about national populism is that it's just occurring because of countries' internal struggles between the classes and a backlash against demographic changes. That couldn't be further from the truth. National populism, like most other political movements, doesn't exist in a bubble. What happens in one country affects its neighbors and sometimes causes a surge of national populism.

In the late stage of neoliberalism, globalists have thrust the United States and its allies into a series of military conflicts with the long-term goal of spreading liberal democracy throughout the developing world. This exploration into nation-building across the globe cost the United States trillions of dollars and thousands of lives, while simultaneously causing political blowback in the West that helped advance national populist ideas.

The United States has been at war for most of its history, American wars can be broken down into three categories: wars that are a part of the civic religion like the Civil War or World

61

War II that had near-universal consensus,[141] wars of expansion like the Mexican-American war, which gave the US control of vast amounts of new territory, and finally, wars for liberalism like Vietnam and Afghanistan. The latter has taken a toll on voters and their commitment to Pax Americana.

National populists, like most Americans, want a realist foreign policy, which means one that does not give out war guarantees to every country on Earth and maintains more than eight hundred bases in more than seventy countries[142] around the world. Instead, they want a more restrained foreign policy and a government that nation builds at home instead of using resources on military adventurism.

For more than twenty years, Americans voted in four back-to-back presidential elections for candidates that promised to reduce our global footprint, end wars, and focus more on the homeland. Yet despite these elections, America's governing class' revolving door of military experts, and the military-industrial complex—which profits immensely off of the US' foreign policy—has kept America in a state of permanent war.

Europe has also experienced a rise of national populism as a result of America's overextended foreign policy, but it hasn't been as a direct result of their countries fighting wars, although some nations like Britain and Poland have aided the American war efforts. Their continent has been inundated with refugees who have been displaced by wars involving Western governments. That includes efforts by both Americans and

---

141   United States Holocaust Memorial Museum, "How did Public Opinion About Entering World War II Change Between 1939 and 1941?" https://exhibitions.ushmm.org/americans-and-the-holocaust/us-public-opinion-world-war-II-1939-1941

142   David Vine, "Where in the World Is the U.S. Military?" *Politico Magazine*, July/August 2015, https://www.politico.com/magazine/story/2015/06/us-military-bases-around-the-world-119321

Europeans to topple dictators in nations like Libya and Syria as well as their efforts to keep the peace in nations like Bosnia.

These military conflicts that displaced millions of people and created waves of refugees washing on Europe's shore led to the rise of national populist parties in Germany, Italy, Austria, and Switzerland.

AMERICA'S ENDLESS WARS

America has been at war for most of history. It has fought in wars that became part of its civic religion, wars of expansion, and lastly, wars for liberalism.

This chapter will only focus on the last type because it is partially responsible for the rise of national populism.

Since the end of the Cold War, America has been a country in search of an identity. For over a century, America's identity was intrinsically attached to westward expansion, industrialization, and imperialism. During several periods including the mid-19th century, the turn of the 20th century, and between the two World Wars, America also flirted with a certain degree of noninterventionism and looking inward.

The Japanese bombing of Pearl Harbor in 1941 changed all that forever. America allied with the USSR and Great Britain to fight and defeat the Axis powers. In the aftermath of that war, the US and the USSR engaged in a half-century-long Cold War and the nuclear arms race. When the Berlin Wall fell in 1989 and the Soviet Union broke apart two years later, America was left as the world's sole superpower. A nation that had no more giants to conquer, no morale mission to give the nation purpose.

So, when President George H. W. Bush began creating the idea of a post-Cold War America, he decided that the country would not return to any semblance of a pre-World War II nation. In his address to Congress on September 11, 1990, H.

W. Bush mapped out a new world order[143] that America would be responsible for a world freer from the threat of terrorism… an era in which the nations of the world, east and west, north and south, can prosper and live in harmony. He said it was the job of America and the world to defend common vital interests, support the rule of law, ease trade restrictions, and stand up against aggression.

America's new normal was to engage in conflicts to protect global law and order and expand neoliberalism. The sons and daughters of America's shores would die to promote freedom in Somalia, Iraq, and Afghanistan. This is the new manifest destiny and national identity, that the American elites thought up.

It was a Wilsonian vision of America, the progressive view that policymakers in Washington could form a more perfect union on a global scale. Critics from both the left and the right panned Bush's speech and future vision of the US.

"In 1915, the U.S. was weaker militarily than Britain and Germany but had become the world's strongest country economically…Today, the U.S. remains the strongest military power but lags behind Europe and Japan in key industries. With a decaying infrastructure and educational system and soaring public and private debt, the U.S. could fall behind even further," warned progressive writer John Judis in *The New York Times*.[144]

Nationalist conservatives like Samuel Huntington and Pat Buchanan also scoffed at Bush's plans for the country.

Yet, their voices were eclipsed by neoconservatives and globalists like Charles Krauthammer who insisted the world was unipolar, the center of the world is an unchallenged

---

143   President George W.H. Bush, Address Before a Joint Session of the Congress on the Persian Gulf Crisis and the Federal Budget Deficit, Washington D.C., September 11, 1990.

144   John B. Judis, "George Bush, Meet Woodrow Wilson." *The New York Times*, November 20, 1990, https://www.nytimes.com/1990/11/20/opinion/george-bush-meet-woodrow-wilson.html

superpower, the United States, attended by its Western allies.[145] The neocons foresaw Pax Americana, a world at peace provided by the Treasury of the United States and the blood of the American military.

George H. W. Bush was just a one-term president, but his successors Bill Clinton, George W. Bush, and Barack Obama all continued his legacy to some degree. Carrying out missions to liberalize developing countries, former communist governments, and states with authoritarian leaders. Like most policies pushed by the ruling class of America, this was done without the consent of the American people. All three presidents campaigned as foreign policy realists who wouldn't make it their job to remake the world, but all of them ended up doing just that.

Clinton campaigned on "it's the economy, stupid," promising to that if elected he would differ from Bush Sr. by focusing on domestic issues such as healthcare and increasing wages.[146] He even vowed to cut defense spending because the Cold War was over and spend the money on social programs. The idea was so outrageous to Cold Warriors and neoconservatives that former President Richard Nixon wrote an op-ed in *The New York Times* opposing the cuts.[147]

Yet when he entered the Oval Office, all the promises he made to the American people were left at the door. While

---

145   Charles Krauthammer, "The Unipolar Moment." *Foreign Affairs,* January/February 1990, https://www.foreignaffairs.com/articles/1991-02-01/unipolar-moment

146   Michael Kelly, "The1992 CAMPAIGN: Democrats—Clinton and Bush Compete to Be Champion of Change; Democrats Fight Perception of Bush Gain." *The New York Times,* October 31, 1992, https://www.nytimes.com/1992/10/31/us/1992-campaign-democrats-clinton-bush-compete-be-champion-change-democrat-fights.html

147   Richard Nixon, "Save the Peace Dividend." *The New York Times,* November 19, 1992, https://www.nytimes.com/1992/11/19/opinion/save-the-peace-dividend.html

Clinton did slash defense spending in his first term by about 15 percent,[148] it wasn't nearly as dramatic as the cuts he promised by President Clinton and his then secretary of defense Leslie Aspin. Over the five fiscal years from 1994 to 1998, the Clinton administration spent $1.3 trillion on Pentagon spending.

Despite the cuts to spending, Clinton engaged in military adventurism around the world. He expanded NATO to include Poland, Hungary, and the Czech Republic and for a time, he continued America's humanitarian mission in Somalia that ended with the death of eighteen American soldiers. Clinton also spent billions of peace dividends meant for Americans on missions to Haiti, Saudi Arabia, Kuwait, Bosnia, the former Yugoslavia, a second mission in Somalia, and Kosovo. Clinton also occasionally launched missiles into Iraq, Afghanistan, and Sudan.[149]

Clinton imposed harsh food sanctions on Iraq that starved nearly half a million Iraqi children to death. Osama bin Laden cited these sanctions as one of the reasons to declare war against the United States.[150]

The president that promised to reinvest peace dividends on social programs to help poor Americans was spending billions of dollars annually on peacekeeping missions around the world.

Perhaps one of Clinton's worst foreign policy decisions was when his administration allowed them to bill the Pentagon for

---

148   Lawrence J. Korb, Laura Conley, and Alex Rothman, "A Return to Responsibility." The Center for American Progress, July 14, 2011, https://www.americanprogress.org/issues/security/reports/2011/07/14/10016/a-return-to-responsibility/

149   Lynn Wooley, "Bill Clinton and the Decline of the Military" *Human Events,* December 21, 2006, https://humanevents.com/2006/12/21/bill-clinton-and-the-decline-of-the-military/

150   Osama bin Laden, "Declaration of War against the Americans Occupying the Land of the Two Holy Places." *Al Quds Al Arabia,* August 1996, https://is.muni.cz/el/1423/jaro2010/MVZ203/OBL___AQ__Fatwa_1996.pdf

the cost of these mergers and acquisitions.[151] These mergers meant that there were fewer defense companies absorbing a larger share of government contracts. Companies like Lockheed Martin are now so big that they have the ability through their huge government connections to make it very difficult for any future Congress to slash defense spending. That all happened under Clinton.

George W. Bush was a lot like Clinton in the respect that he promised voters a humble foreign policy and attacked the Clinton administration over their efforts to nation-build.

Even before the terrorist attacks on September 11, 2001, it looked like Bush would never deliver on those promises. From the start of his administration, he filled his cabinet with war hawks and neocons like Dick Cheney, Donald Rumsfeld, Paul Wolfowitz, Douglas Feith, and John Bolton—a group of people Colin Powell described as "fucking crazies!"[152] With men like that running the administration, there's very little chance that America was going to pursue a humble foreign policy even if 9/11 had not happened.

After September 11, the neocons running the White House had carte blanche to commit America to fight their wars to liberalize the world. Along the way, they even converted Bush to acceptance and support of the broader neoconservative worldview.

Bush's second inaugural might as well have been his baptism where the president fully embraced a neoconservative ideology.

---

151   Lawrence J. Korb, "Merger Mania: Should the Pentagon Pay for Defense Industry Restructuring?" *Brookings Institute,* June 1, 1996, https://www.brookings.edu/articles/ merger-mania-should-the-pentagon-pay-for-defense-industry-restructuring/

152   Martin Bright, "Colin Powell in four-letter neo-con 'crazies' row." *The Guardian,* September 11, 2004, https://www.theguardian.com/media/2004/ sep/12/Iraqandthemedia.politicsphilosophyandsociety

"So, it is the policy of the United States to seek and support the growth of democratic movements and institutions in every nation and culture, with the ultimate goal of ending tyranny in our world," Bush said to the American public, "The great objective of ending tyranny is the concentrated work of generations. The difficulty of the task is no excuse for avoiding it. America's influence is not unlimited, but fortunately for the oppressed, America's influence is considerable, and we will use it confidently in freedom's cause."[153]

In that speech, the same president who attacked the Clinton administration for the efforts in nation-building and promised a humble foreign policy betrayed everything he promised his voters in 2000. Bush vowed that generations of Americans would spend their blood and treasure fighting for the freedom of people on foreign land that did not ask for it, did not want it, and in many cases would hate America for imposing it on them. Bush described Iraq, Iran, and North Korea as the axis of evil and neoconservatives used the term 'Islamofascism' to describe the ideology they were opposing.

This choice of language signified that the war on terror was a religious war to the neoconservatives. It was no longer about preventing another 9/11, but a holy war against evil itself.

The Republican Party and conservative movement especially became drunk on this ideology. Their ideologic hubris infected nearly the entire conservative movement during this time period. Prominent conservative writers advocated for war across the world: *National Review*'s Jonah Goldberg wrote that America should colonize Africa,[154] Norman Podhoretz

---

153   President George W. Bush, Second Inaugural Address, Washington D.C., January 20, 2005.

154   Jonah Goldberg, "A Continent Bleeds." *National Review,* May 3, 2000, https://www.nationalreview.com/2000/05/continent-bleeds-jonah-goldberg/

authored an op-ed titled "The Case for Bombing Iran,"[155] and David Frum wrote that any Republican opposing the Iraq War was an unpatriotic conservative.[156]

Those unpatriotic conservatives who vocally opposed the invasion of Iraq like Pat Buchanan, Robert Novak, Justin Raimondo, Llewellyn Rockwell, and Samuel Francis were marginalized by mainstream Conservative Inc. To be part of the Republican Party during the age of Bush, you needed to subscribe to the war party mentality.

Nearly everything the neoconservatives promised the American public about the Iraq War turned out to be untrue: Saddam did not have stockpiles of weapons of mass destruction;[157] Americans were not greeted as liberators;[158] insurgency was not in its last throes,[159] rebuilding Iraq did not cost American taxpayers only $1.7 billion,[160] Iraq did not help al-Qaeda[161] and by May 1, 2001, the mission was not accomplished.[162]

---

155   Norman Podhoretz, "The Case for Bombing Iran." *Commentary Magazine,* June 2007, https://www.commentarymagazine.com/articles/the-case-for-bombing-iran/

156   David Frum, "Unpatriotic Conservatives," *National Review,* March 25, 2003, https://www.nationalreview.com/2003/03/unpatriotic-conservatives-david-frum/

157   "Report: No WMD stockpiles in Iraq," CNN, October 7, 2004, http://edition.cnn.com/2004/WORLD/meast/10/06/iraq.wmd.report/

158   "Transcript for September 14" *NBC News: Meet the Press,* September 14, 2003, http://www.nbcnews.com/id/3080244/ns/meet_the_press/t/transcript-sept/

159   "CNN Larry King Live Interview with Dick Cheney, Lynne Cheney." CNN, May 30, 2005, http://transcripts.cnn.com/TRANSCRIPTS/0505/30/lkl.01.html

160   Joseph Stiglitz and Linda Bilmes, *The Three Trillion Dollar War,* W.W. Norton & Company Inc. (New York City 2008).

161   Eliot A. Cohen, "World War IV" *The Wall Street Journal,* November 20, 2001, https://www.wsj.com/articles/SB1006219259392114120

162   Catherine Lucey, "Bush was haunted by his own 'Mission Accomplished.'" *The Boston Globe,* April 14, 2018, https://www.bostonglobe.com/news/nation/2018/04/14/bush-was-haunted-his-own-mission-accomplished/E73SdIkXxBfUGsbyXv7ISI/story.html

The lies, falsehoods, and visions of a new world order cost America more than 36,000 dead and wounded and $2 trillion.[163][164]

While the plans surrounding the invasion and occupation of Iraq had their shortcomings, the problem ultimately was with the neoconservative foreign policy. It is impossible to export democracy to people who are not willing to accept it. A 2019 study published in *Nature Human Behavior* found that cultural changes lead to democracy rather than the neoconservative philosophy that forcing democratic institutions on people will lead to changes in the culture. The presence of democratic institutions did not predict any substantive changes in the measured cultural values, the study found. These results hold accounting for other factors, including gross domestic product per capita and non-independence between nations due to shared cultural ancestry. Cultural values lead to, rather than follow, the emergence of democracy.[165]

Americans had reservations about several military interventions including Clinton's engagements in Haiti, Bosnia, Kosovo, Liberia, and Somalia.[166] However, Americans overwhelmingly supported the war in Afghanistan and Iraq when they started.[167,168] Their shell shock over the 9/11 attacks and

163   United States. U.S. Department of Defense. "Casualty Status." Washington, December 9, 2019, https://www.defense.gov/Newsroom/Casualty-Status/

164   Daniel Trotta, "Iraq war costs U.S. more than $2 trillion: study" Reuters, March 14, 2013. https://www.reuters.com/article/us-iraq-war-anniversary-idUSBRE92D0PG20130314

165   Damian J. Ruck, et al., "The Cultural Foundations of Modern Democracies." *Nature News*, Nature Publishing Group, December 2, 2019, https://www.nature.com/articles/s41562-019-0769-1

166   Richard Eichenberg, *Victory Has Many Friends U.S. Public Opinion and the Use of Military Force, 1981–2005*, Tufts University (Medford 2005).

167   Frank Newport, "Seventy-Two Percent of Americans Support War Against Iraq." *Gallup.com*, October 21, 2019, https://news.gallup.com/poll/8038/seventytwo-percent-americans-support-war-against-iraq.aspx

168   David W. Moore, "Eight of 10 Americans Support Ground War in Afghanistan." *Gallup.com*, November 28, 2019, https://news.gallup.com/poll/5029/eight-americans-support-ground-war-afghanistan.aspx

fears of terrorism drove their support for the Bush doctrine, but as the war continued year after year, the American public soured on Bush and his war.

They voted for a Democratic Congress in 2006 and in 2008, elected Barack Obama, who like Bush and Clinton before him, ran as a peace candidate who opposed the Iraq War since its beginning—unlike his neocon opponents Hillary Clinton and John McCain.

Quickly after he was elected, Obama echoed the beliefs of George W. Bush with a speech in the Grand Hall of Cairo University, "I do have an unyielding belief that all people yearn for certain things: the ability to speak your mind and have a say in how you are governed; confidence in the rule of law and the equal administration of justice; government that is transparent and doesn't steal from the people; the freedom to live as you choose. These are not just American ideas; they are human rights. And that is why we will support them everywhere."[169]

Needless to say, that's not what all people believe; that is the incoherent ideology of neoconservatives, neoliberals, and globalists and has led to two decades of war, military intervention, and nation-building. Humans are naturally tribal and are in a constant struggle for power and security; they value those bonds over the hollow principles of humanistic brotherhood.

Just like Clinton and Bush, Obama backtracked on his commitments to end the wars and pull back from his predecessors' assault on civil liberties. Obama's administration increased the surveillance on American citizens, outpaced Bush on targeted killings using drone strikes,[170] supported a fail-

---

169 The White House Archive "Remarks by the President at Cairo University."Obama Whitehouse Archive, June 4, 2009, https://obamawhitehouse.archives.gov/the-press-office/remarks-president-cairo-university-6-04-09

170 Jennifer Williams, "From Torture to Drone Strikes: The Disturbing Legal Legacy Obama Is Leaving for Trump." *Vox*, January 11, 2017, https://www.vox.com/policy-and-politics/2016/11/14/13577464/obama-farewell-speech-torture-drones-nsa-surveillance-trump

ed surge in Afghanistan,[171] overthrew Gaddafi in Libya turning it into a failed state, removed troops from Iraq only to send them to fight ISIS,[172] funded organizations affiliated with al-Qaeda,[173] was complicit in a Saudi-led genocide in Yemen,[174] and ran a covert CIA operation to overthrow the government of Syria.[175]

After nearly a quarter of a century of the American people electing presidents who campaigned against nation-building and war, the United States had commitments to defend more than sixty countries in case of an invasion and had hundreds of military bases around the globe.

By 2016, Americans had enough of the neocons, the wars, and the nation-building.

A Pew Research poll taken in May 2016 found that a plurality of Republicans and Independents believed the United States did too much to try and help solve world problems.[176] That same poll found that 57 percent of Americans including 62 percent of Republicans wanted the world to deal with their

---

171   Rajiv Chandrasekaran, "The Afghan Surge Is Over." *Foreign Policy,* September 25, 2012, https://foreignpolicy.com/2012/09/25/the-afghan-surge-is-over/

172   Mark Thompson, "Number of U.S. Troops in Iraq Keeps Creeping Upward." *Time,* April 18, 2016, https://time.com/4298318/iraq-us-troops-barack-obama-mosul-isis/

173   Sam Westrop, "Exclusive: Obama Administration Knowingly Funded a Designated Al-Qaeda Affiliate." *National Review,* July 25, 2018, https://www.nationalreview.com/2018/07/obama-administration-al-qaeda-affiliate-knowingly-funded/

174   Micah Zenko, "Happy Anniversary to America's Shameful Travesty of a War in Yemen." *Foreign Policy,* May 27, 2017, https://foreignpolicy.com/2017/03/27/happy-anniversary-to-americas-shameful-travesty-of-a-war-in-yemen/

175   Mark Mazzetti and Ali Younes, "C.I.A.Arms for Syrian Rebels Supplied Black Market, Officials Say." *The New York Times,* June 26, 2016, https://www.nytimes.com/2016/06/27/world/middleeast/cia-arms-for-syrian-rebels-supplied-black-market-officials-say.html

176   "Widespread Uncertainty About America's Place in the World." *Pew Research Center for the People and the Press,* September 18, 2018, https://www.people-press.org/2016/05/05/1-americas-global-role-u-s-superpower-status/

own problems and 69 percent believed the US should concentrate more on their own national problems. Nearly one in three Trump supporters even soured on NATO, saying it had been bad for the US.

The elites were so tone-deaf to this shift among voters that they believed Trump destroyed his campaign by attacking the legacy of George W. Bush and the Iraq War during a South Carolina Republican debate.[177]

During that debate, Trump launched into a series of condemnations against neocons and the legacy of George W. Bush. Trump called the Iraq War a big, fat mistake and said Bush lied to launch the invasion.[178] Although establishment figures in the GOP circled the wagons to support Bush and the war, even veterans, who make up a huge portion of the South Carolina Republican voting bloc, were beginning to think that the war was a mistake.[179]

According to one poll on the 2016 primary election, veterans favored the two most anti-war candidates running for office—Senator Bernie Sanders and Trump in their respected parties.[180]

In their endless pursuit of liberal hegemony, the war party of Bush, Clinton, Bush, and Obama helped create the political

---

177   John McCormack, "South Carolina Voters Angered by Trump's Claim That Bush Lied to Start Iraq War." *Washington Examiner,* February 17, 2016, https://www.washingtonexaminer.com/weekly-standard/south-carolina-voters-angered-by-trumps-claim-that-bush-lied-to-start-iraq-war

178   Allen Cooper, "Trump, Jeb Bush Clash over George W. Bush." *USA Today,* February 14, 2016, https://www.usatoday.com/story/news/politics/onpolitics/2016/02/13/trump-bush-debate/80361688/

179   Kim Parker and Ruth Igielnik, "Majorities of U.S. Veterans, Public Say the Wars in Iraq and Afghanistan Were Not Worth Fighting." *Pew Research Center,* July 10, 2019, https://www.pewresearch.org/fact-tank/2019/07/10/majorities-of-u-s-veterans-public-say-the-wars-in-iraq-and-afghanistan-were-not-worth-fighting/

180   George R. Altman and Leo Shane III, "Military Times Survey: Troops Back Donald Trump, Bernie Sanders for President." *Military Times,* August 8, 2017, https://www.militarytimes.com/news/2016/03/14/military-times-survey-troops-back-donald-trump-bernie-sanders-for-president/

movement that nominated and then elected Trump. For more than two decades, voters cast ballots for the candidate who promised to forge a new normal and focus on domestic policy instead of foreign intervention. The entrenched bureaucracy and military-industrial complex refused to allow voters' wishes, so in the end, they just decided to go with the man who would blow up the entire system if it meant ending the wars for liberalism.

GADDAFI'S REVENGE

National populism in Europe also experience a surge because of the Western countries' military adventurism, but it was much different than the one experienced in America.

Because of its geographical position, it's generous welfare states, and a political class that sought to remake the continent, Europe was the prime location for refugees. To wealthy Europeans living in gated communities and detached from the middle and working classes, the influx of these refugees was an opportunity to show compassion, and in some cases, it allowed them to prove to the world that Europe had evolved past its history of wars and prejudice. Middle and working-class Europeans didn't feel the same, as they had to deal with the economic and social burden of taking waves of poor people from vastly different cultures, some of whom had criminal intentions.

After experiencing the cost of neoliberal compassion, European voters in country after country turned to national populist candidates.

The tiny country of Switzerland experienced this during the late '90s as it had to grapple with hundreds of thousands of refugees fleeing Yugoslavia and Kosovo. A series of ethnic wars produced a massive wave of refugees into Central Europe. Between 1992 to 1995, Switzerland took over 24,000 Bosnian refugees.[181] When the Kosovo War began in 1998 between Yugoslavia and Kosovo separatists backed by NATO, over 850,000 Kosovo Albanians were displaced. [182] Switzerland took in over 53,000 Kosovar refugees in response, the highest of any country per capita in Western Europe.[183]

The flood of refugees came at a large financial and social cost to Switzerland. At the time, the Swiss economy was not in great shape: they had a record-level 7 percent unemployment rate[184] and the thousands of people settling into the country every month did not make the situation easier.

Economics aside, there was also a cultural and criminal aspect to the wave of refugees that put Swiss voters on edge. Immigrants from Yugoslavia were not new to Switzerland; they had been coming over for decades as low-skilled workers. Culturally, however, many of them were Muslim and very difficult to integrate into Swiss society. The addition of tens of thousands more through the refugee program furthered cultural anxiety. Yugoslavians remain one of the least popular immigrant groups in Switzerland—along with Turks, Arabs, and Germans.[185]

181   Switzerland. Federal Department of Justice and Police FDJP, Swiss Agency for Development and Cooperation, *The population of Bosnia and Herzegovina in Switzerland*, October 2014, https://www.bundespublikationen.admin.ch/cshop_mimes_bbl/2C/2C59E545D7371EE495A4A6B21623F42A.pdf

182   Mirka Krasniqi, "Like the Syrians, I Fled My Country. Here's What You Don't Understand about Refugees." *The Washington Post*, March 1, 2019, https://www.washingtonpost.com/posteverything/wp/2015/09/18/like-the-syrians-i-fled-my-country-heres-what-you-dont-understand-about-refugees/?utm_term=.da01a5ecec54

183   Lulzim Cota, "Serbs Now Kosovo Refugees." UPI, June 12, 2000, https://www.upi.com/Archives/2000/06/12/Serbs-now-Kosovo-refugees/1518960782400/

184   Elizabeth Olson, "Right-Wing Political Party Leads in Swiss Elections, Endangering 40-Year Coalition." *The New York Times*, October 25, 1999, https://www.nytimes.com/1999/10/25/world/right-wing-political-party-leads-swiss-elections-endangering-40-year-coalition.html

185   Marc Helbling, "Why Swiss-German dislike Germans." (presentation, Swiss Political Science Association, University of Geneva, January 8, 2010)

Part of the reason that the Swiss people had such a negative opinion of immigrants and refugees from Yugoslavia, especially from Albania, is because they had much higher levels of criminality than native Swiss. A 2010 study conducted by the Federal Statistical Office found that young men who immigrated from Bosnia and Herzegovina, Croatia, and Macedonia had a crime rate about 230 percent higher than native Swiss, while young men from Serbia and Montenegro were about 310 percent higher.[186]

In the 1999 federal election, the national populist Swiss People's Party (SVP) led by Christoph Blocher campaigned on reforming the asylum laws that had flooded Switzerland with refugees. He also rallied around a message of protecting the Swiss identity, opposing its membership into the United Nations and the EU, reducing the number of foreign residents, protecting jobs for the Swiss people, and rejecting multiculturalism.[187]

This message of nationalism resonated throughout the country; not only did Blocher do well in the SVP's strongholds in the suburbs of Zürich, but also among voters who had typically opposed the SVP, including white-collar voters, self-employed professionals, and those living in the French-speaking parts of the country.[188]

After all the votes were counted, the SVP won the largest number of votes in Switzerland with 22.6 percent. In the following election in 2003, the SVP became the largest political party in Switzerland for the first time in history and continues to hold a plurality of seats in the National Council to this day.

---

186   "Neie Statistik: Tamilen Sind Krimineller Als Ex-Jugoslawen." *Tages-Anzeiger,* September 10, 2010, https://www.tagesanzeiger.ch/schweiz/standard/ Neue-Statistik-Tamilen-sind-krimineller-als-ExJugoslawen/story/27784193

Swiss voters' demands for tighter asylum laws didn't end with those two elections; they voted in favor of amendments to their constitution in 2006 by a margin of 68 to 32 percent and again in 2013 by an even larger margin of 79 to 21 percent.[189]

Swiss citizens also voted for a referendum during the height of the refugee crisis to streamline the process, cut down on wait time, and offer free legal advice from those fleeing Syria.[190] They also voted less than a month later to give the SVP the largest proportion of the vote that any single party has obtained since Switzerland's creation of proportional representation in 1919.[191]

With an even greater share of the vote, the SVP passed further restrictions for asylum seekers in December of 2018.[192]

The Swiss experience with a massive wave of refugees should have been a warning sign to leaders around Europe. Despite compassionate Europeans desire to help those in a less fortunate situation than themselves, too many refugees created a national populist backlash. The largest party in Switzerland swung from the pro-European and anti-capitalist Social Democratic Party to the national populist SVP in a matter of eight years.

It also should have warned against destabilizing poor countries in the surrounding areas. The civil war led by

189   "Switzerland Votes to Tighten Asylum Law" *Deutsche Welle,* June 9, 2013, https://www.dw.com/en/switzerland-votes-to-tighten-asylum-law/a-16869512

190   Brenna Hughes Newghaiwi, "Switzerland Offers Europe Lessons on Handling Asylum Seekers." Reuters, September 21, 2015, https://www.reuters.com/article/us-europe-migrants-swiss/switzerland-offers-europe-lessons-on-handling-asylum-seekers-idUSKCN0RL0TU20150921

191   Reuters, "Anti-Immigration Party Wins Swiss Election in 'Slide to the Right'." *The Telegraph*, October 19, 2015, https://www.telegraph.co.uk/news/worldnews/europe/switzerland/11939953/Anti-immigration-party-wins-Swiss-election-in-slide-to-the-Right.html

192   "Swiss Change Policy for Returning Refugees." *SWI Swissinfo. ch*, December 12, 2018, https://www.swissinfo.ch/eng/migration_swiss-change-policy-for-returning-refugees/44613688

separatists in Yugoslavia and Kosovo led to the destabilization and a mass exodus of refugees to wealthier countries, thus causing the rise of national populism in Central Europe. It seems like a simple enough understanding of the way of the world to the average person.

Yet it came as a total surprise to the political elite that NATO allies intervening in the Libyan Civil War and America funding rebel groups in Syria could create another refugee crisis and national populist uprising like in Switzerland. Only this time, the European refugee crisis would lead to a national populist revolution on steroids.

The chain of events that would lead to the 2015 European refugee crisis started with the Arab Spring in the winter of 2010 when a man named Mohamed Bouazizi set himself on fire to protest the government of Tunisia. Protests hit nearly every country in the Middle East and North Africa. They ranged from minor demonstrations and concessions by the government, as was the case in Saudi Arabia to full out civil wars and coups d'état in Egypt, Yemen, Algeria, Tunisia, Iraq and, most importantly, Syria and Libya.

Libya's civil war began to unfold on February 15, 2011, when protestors demanded that the nation's long-reigning dictator Muammar Gaddafi step down from power. Two days later, protestors held a Day of Revolt and Gaddafi responded by having his military and police murder more than a dozen of them.[193]

As the days passed, protests continued and turned increasingly violent as Gaddafi ordered his artillery, helicopter

---

193   "Libya: Benghazi Clashes Deadly – Witnesses." *BBC News*, February 18, 2011,
        https://www.bbc.com/news/world-africa-12506787

gunships, and security forces to kill protestors.[194] By February 20, protestors started capturing military barracks as members of Gaddafi's army began turning on the dictator. The civilian death toll continued to climb by the end of the first week as Gaddafi ordered airstrikes on funeral processions.

Gaddafi began giving speeches on state television vowing to fight to the death[195] as he desperately clung to power. Rebels began taking control of eastern Libya and in the suburbs of Tripoli.

With the body count rising and Gaddafi vowing to fight to the bitter end, the EU called for an investigation by the UN Security Council over human rights violations. Just two days later, the UN Security Council unanimously passed Resolution 1970 on February 26, condemning Gaddafi's use of lethal force and imposing sanctions on the country.[196]

On February 27, US Secretary of State Hillary Clinton announced that the US would offer any kind of assistance to help the rebels overthrow Gaddafi.[197] The following day, British Prime Minister David Cameron proposed a no-fly zone over Libya to prevent Gaddafi's air force from killing civilians.[198] By March 1, Australian Minister of Defense Stephen Smith also

---

194 Nick Meo, "Libya Protests: 140 'Massacred' as Gaddafi Sends in Snipers to Crush Dissent." *The Telegraph*, February 20, 2011, https://www.telegraph.co.uk/news/worldnews/africaandindianocean/libya/8335934/Libya-protests-140-massacred-as-Gaddafi-sends-in-snipers-to-crush-dissent.html

195 Andrew England and Hebah Saleh, "Defiant Gaddafi vows fight to death," *The Financial Times*, February 23, 2011, https://www.ft.com/content/5b307dd4-3e9d-11e0-9e8f-00144feabdc0?ftcamp=rss#axzz1Eil3i6Ng

196 United Nations Security Council, *Resolution 1970*, February 26, 2011, https://www.icc-cpi.int/NR/rdonlyres/081A9013-B03D-4859-9D61-5D0B0F2F5EFA/0/1970Eng.pdf

197 "Rebels Move in on Tripoli," *News Core*, February 2011, https://www.news.com.au/world/rebels-move-in-on-tripoli/news-story/ef7bc30d58348145f5423cf3c4f857be

198 Alistair MacDonald, "Cameron Doesn't Rule Out Military Force for Libya," *The Wall Street Journal*, March 1, 2011, https://www.wsj.com/articles/SB10001424052748704615504576172383796304482

weighed in that Australia was considering a military option against Gaddafi.[199]

Gaddafi's forces-built momentum over the next two weeks, regaining rebel-controlled towns in eastern Libya. By March 17th Libyan forces began to close in on Benghazi, one of the rebels' strongholds.

Fearing that a massacre was imminent, a coalition of NATO allies led initially by France[200] began attacking Gaddafi's forces around Benghazi. On March 23, NATO allies including the US, UK, Canada, Italy, Denmark, and Norway launched Operation Unified Protector, creating a no-fly zone and arms embargo on Libya.

The series of attacks on Gaddafi's forces were able to cripple them and gave the rebels an upper hand. The attacks continued even after Gaddafi's forces no longer posed a threat to civilians in Benghazi. Though they insisted the mission was about saving the lives of civilians, it was very clear that they would stop short at nothing but regime change.

A 2016 examination conducted by the House of Commons' bipartisan Foreign Affairs Committee found that the NATO allies' premise for the military intervention was based on faulty information and no one in the government carried a proper inquiry to look at the claims that Gaddafi was preparing to genocide his own people. "We have seen no evidence that the UK Government carried out a proper analysis of the nature of the rebellion in Libya," the report stated. "UK strategy was founded on erroneous assumptions and an incomplete understanding of the evidence."[201]

---

199   Adam Gartrell, "Rudd Ramps up Call for Libya No-Fly Zone," *The Age*, February 28, 2011, https://www.theage.com.au/national/rudd-ramps-up-call-for-libya-no-fly-zone-20110301-1bccl.html

200   Jonathan Marcus, "Libya: French Plane Fires on Military Vehicle," *BBC News*, March 19, 2011, https://www.bbc.co.uk/news/world-africa-12795971

201   The United Kingdom, House of Commons: Foreign Affairs Committee, *Libya: Examination of intervention and collapse and the UK's future policy options*. September 6, 2016.

The report found that although Gaddafi did kill some civilians, the threat of a massacre was overstated by Western governments and rebel groups and had little intelligence backing up their claims. It also stated that the governments ignored information coming through that these rebel groups had become infiltrated with Islamic extremists and the bombing campaign gave them the opportunity to build an operation in Libya.

While Muammar Gaddafi certainly threatened violence against those who took up arms against his rule, this did not necessarily translate into a threat to everyone in Benghazi, the report stated. In short, the scale of the threat to civilians was presented with unjustified certainty.

It pointed out that in the towns Gaddafi reclaimed from the rebels he hadn't massacred civilians; for example, when Gaddafi forces retook the city of Misrata, just 1 percent of people killed in the battle were women and children.

The report also stated that the allies' mission was clearly to topple Gaddafi and not to just protect civilians. When the French began to attack Gaddafi's troops outside of Benghazi, they retreated forty miles from the city, yet that was the beginning of coalition bombings. If the primary object of the coalition intervention was the urgent need to protect civilians in Benghazi, then this objective was achieved in less than 24 hours, the reported noted.

Certain political figures including US Secretary of State Hillary Clinton, UN Ambassador Samantha Powers, British Prime Minister David Cameron, British Foreign Secretary William Hague, British Defense Minister Liam Fox, French President Nicolas Sarkozy, as well as several others used the opportunity to advance their ultimate goal of regime change. France, in particular, saw it as an opportunity to increase its influence in North Africa and gain a greater share of Libyan oil production.

None of these allied nations had learned any lessons from the War in Iraq or had any thoughts about who would replace Gaddafi. The then US permanent representative to NATO Ivo Daalder and the then supreme allied commander of Europe James Stavridis stated, "NATO's operation in Libya has rightly been hailed as a model intervention."[202]

In August of 2011, rebel forces took control of Tripoli. In October 2011, Gaddafi was found hiding in a drainage pipe and was killed by his captors, who beat, sodomized, and then shot him to death as he begged for his life.[203]

After Gaddafi, Libya became a war-torn nightmare. The nation's GDP dropped from $75 billion in 2010 to just over $41 billion in 2014, and according to the report by the House of Commons, nearly 50 percent of Libya's 6.3 million people had been impacted by the civil war and political instability and 2.4 million required some form of humanitarian assistance.[204] Post-Gaddafi Libya became a safe haven for slavery, ISIS, human smuggling, and arms trading.

The NATO allies turned Libya into a failed state. In 2016, President Obama described the situation in Libya as a shit show.[205]

Yet Libya wasn't the only nation the Western governments were actively pushing for regime change.

---

202   Ivor Daaider, James Stavridis, "NATO's Victory in Libya: The Right Way to Run an Intervention." *Foreign Policy*, March/April 2012, pp. 2-7

203   Martin Chulov, "Gaddafi's Last Moments: 'I Saw the Hand Holding the Gun and I Saw It Fire.'" *The Guardian*, October 20, 2012, https://www.theguardian.com/world/2012/oct/20/muammar-gaddafi-killing-witnesses

204   James Carden, "The UK's Devastating New Report on NATO's Regime Change War in Libya." *The Nation*, September 19, 2016, https://www.thenation.com/article/the-uks-devastating-new-report-on-natos-regime-change-war-in-libya/

205   Tim Walker and Nigel Morris, "Barack Obama says David Cameron allowed Libya to become a 's*** show'" *The Independent*, March 10, 2016, https://www.independent.co.uk/news/uk/politics/barack-obama-says-david-cameron-allowed-libya-to-become-a-s-show-a6923976.html

The Arab Spring also impacted the Syrian government led by Bashar al-Assad. From the very beginning, Western leaders including Obama, Sarkozy, German Chancellor Angela Merkel, and Cameron called on Assad to resign, but of course, he resisted.

A civil war broke out and by the summer of 2012, Obama at the request of Israeli President Benjamin Netanyahu and Jordanian King Abdullah II began a multibillion-dollar covert program to arm and train the Syrian rebels.[206] The operation was given the name Timber Sycamore and it served as the centerpiece for President Obama's strategy for regime change in the country.[207]

The operation was run by the Military Operations Command (MOC) in Jordan, where Americans would train Syrian rebels and the Saudis would supply them with weapons, although that quickly changed and the US started also supplying them with arms.

At first, this was a highly effective operation; the Syrian rebels won a series of battles in Northern Syria, which allowed them to advance deep into the nation's interior. According to one report, rebels trained and armed by Timber Sycamore were responsible for killing or wounding about one hundred thousand soldiers in Assad's military.[208]

---

206   Mark Mazzetti, et al., "Behind the Sudden Death of a $1 Billion Secret C.I.A. War in Syria." *The New York Times*, August 2, 2017, https://www.nytimes. com/2017/08/02/world/middleeast/cia-syria-rebel-arm-train-trump.html

207   Greg Miller and Adam Entous, "Plans to Send Heavier Weapons to CIA-Backed Rebels in Syria Stall amid White House Skepticism." *The Washington Post*, October 23, 2016, https://www.washingtonpost. com/world/national-security/plans-to-send-heavier-weapons-to-cia-backed-rebels-in-syria-stall-amid-white-house-skepticism/2016/10/23/ f166ddac-96ee-11e6-bb29-bf2701dbe0a3_story.html

208   David Ignatius, "What the Demise of the CIA's Anti-Assad Program Means." *The Washington Post*, July 20, 2017, https://www.washingtonpost. com/opinions/what-the-demise-of-the-cias-anti-assad-program-means/2017/07/20/f6467240-6d87-11e7-b9e2-2056e768a7e5_story.html

Problems quickly arose however, as some of the Syria-backed members were allied with the al- Qaeda-linked al-Nusra Front. As the American-backed militants gained ground in Northern Syria, so did the al-Qaeda-backed Islamists. The advancement of al-Nusra became the justification for Putin to begin bombing rebels in Syria.[209]

There were further complications as Jordanians began selling the American weapons that were flooding into their country on the black market.[210] Some of those weapons made it to arms dealers, who sold them to ISIS militants, who then used them to kill American-backed rebels.[211] To say it was a disaster is an understatement.

Syria's civil war became a proxy war for the United States, Russia, and Iran. All sides had vested interest in winning the war, which meant keeping it going and propping up various militias throughout the country, including radical Islamic extremists. The creation of ISIS and its series of military successes only worsened the situation and the war dragged on for over eight years, killing an estimated 470,000 people[212] and turning 5.6 million more into refugees.[213]

Caught in the mix of the Arab Spring, the proxy war in Syria and the failed state in Libya were the millions upon millions

---

209   Zack Beauchamp, "How Russian Bombing Is Changing Syrian War, in 3 Maps." *Vox*, February 16, 2016, https://www.vox.com/2016/2/16/11020140/russia-syria-bombing-maps

210   Arutz, Sheva Staff, "CIA Weapons for Rebels Sold to Arms Dealers." *Israel National News*, https://www.israelnationalnews.com/News/News.aspx/214182

211   Phil Sands, "Death of a Syrian Arms Salesman." *The National*, August 8, 2016, https://www.thenational.ae/world/death-of-a-syrian-arms-salesman-1.144999

212   Priyanka Boghani, "A Staggering New Death Toll for Syria's War – 470,000." *PBS*, February 11, 2016, https://www.pbs.org/wgbh/frontline/article/a-staggering-new-death-toll-for-syrias-war-470000/

213   UNHCR: The United Nations Refugee Agency, *Operational Portal, Refugee Situations*, last updated December 1, 2019, https://data2.unhcr.org/en/situations/syria

of young, poor, and desperate Muslims who saw Europe as an opportunity to start a new life.

Before the Arab Spring, Europeans had been accepting between two and three hundred thousand asylum seekers annually between 2008 and 2012. [214] Illegal border crossing into Europe had been relatively minimal at about 78,000 in the year 2012,[215] in part because of an agreement reached by the Libyan government with Italy to act as a buffer between millions of African refugees and Europe.[216] Italy struck a deal with the dictator in 2004 to accept Africans deported from Italian territories[217] and the EU made an arrangement with Gaddafi in 2008 to offer him $500 million in exchange for keeping migrants out of Europe. All in all, for more than twenty years, Gaddafi received over $5 billion to prevent a migrant crisis and for the most part, he kept his end of the deal.

When Gaddafi was deposed in 2011, the migrants had no one left to stop them and the number of people crossing illegally through Central Mediterranean routes went from forty-five thousand in 2013 to over 170,000 in 2014.

The main port of entry, however, was in Greece. From 2014 to 2015, the number of Syrians displaced by the civil war more than doubled from 1.55 million to 3.9 million[218] and when refugees discovered the fastest way to Europe was through the

---

214 “Asylum statistics” *Eurostat,* last modified May 10, 2019, https://ec.europa. eu/eurostat/statistics-explained/index.php/Asylum_statistics

215 “Migrant Crisis: Illegal Entries to EU at Lowest Level in Five Years,” *BBC News,* January 4, 2019, https://www.bbc.com/news/world-europe-46764500

216 Amanda Sakuma, “How Libya Became the Gatekeeper of Africa's Migrant Crisis.” MSNBC, May 16, 2016, http://www.msnbc.com/specials/ migrant-crisis/libya

217 European Parliament, *European Parliament resolution on Lampedusa,* April 14, 2005, https://www.europarl.europa.eu/sides/getDoc.do?pubRef=-//EP// TEXT+TA+P6-TA-2005-0138+0+DOC+XML+V0//EN

218 “The Dispossessed,” *The Economist,* June 18, 2015, https://www.economist. com/graphic-detail/2015/06/18/the-dispossessed

Eastern Mediterranean route, they began crossing into the country with the aid of human smugglers.

According to the EU, human smugglers made at least five billion dollars in 2015 alone[219] bringing asylum seekers into Europe. Greece's neighbor Turkey turned a blind eye to the whole thing but was very well aware of the billion-dollar human trafficking operation in their country.[220]

Europeans were completely unprepared for the humanitarian and national security crisis at their feet and worked to simply manage rather than curtail the millions of people making their way to Europe.

Then on September 2, pictures of Alan Kurdi, a three-year-old Syrian boy who drowned when he was being illegally transported to Greece, emerged. The picture of the lifeless boy on the beaches of Turkey went worldwide and gave an innocent face to all peoples attempting to cross into Europe. The boy's picture went viral and was splashed on the cover of nearly every major newspaper in the EU. It became a rallying cry that something had to be done to deal with the humanitarian crisis in Syria.

So, in response, politicians did what they do best and overreacted.

On September 5, three days after Kurdi's body was discovered, German Chancellor Angela Merkel announced she was opening her nation's floodgates. The German government would not stop anyone from seeking asylum in their borders. "The right to political asylum has no limits on the number of

---

219   Rick Gladstone, "Smugglers Made at Least $5 Billion Last Year in Europe Migrant Crisis," May 17, 2016, https://www.nytimes.com/2016/05/18/world/europe/migrants-refugees-smugglers.html

220   Patrick Kingsley, "Hiding in Plain Sight: inside the World of Turkey's People Smugglers." *The Guardian*, November 29, 2015, https://www.theguardian.com/world/2015/nov/29/hiding-in-plain-sight-inside-the-world-of-turkeys-people-smugglers

asylum seekers," Merkel said, "As a strong, economically healthy country we have the strength to do what is necessary."[221]

The Austrian chancellor also announced that same day that Austria would assist the migrants, including those that had been held in Hungary, by busing them into Germany.[222] Croatia, which up to that point had refused to build a border wall to protect itself from the waves of migrants,[223] announced that they were ready to help people fleeing violence.[224] Macedonia allowed migrants to have three-day asylum permits to allow them to travel to Germany or Sweden.[225]

Germany's decision to have open borders, however compassionate it seemed at the time, created a crisis of epic proportion. More than 5 million people from the Middle East and Africa made their way to Europe in 2015 and 2016, using both legal asylum applications as well as illegally crossing the border.[226] A poll taken in October of 2015 of seven EU countries found that while most Europeans felt the EU had a duty to help refugees fleeing war, a majority of citizens in France, Italy, Netherlands,

221   "Germany's Angela Merkel Says No Number Limits to Right to Asylum," *Independent,* September 5, 2015, https://www.independent.ie/world-news/germanys-angela-merkel-says-no-numbers-limits-to-right-to-asylum-31504442.html

222   Alison Smale, et al., "Migrants Cross Austria Border From Hungary." *The New York Times,* September 4, 2015, https://www.nytimes.com/2015/09/05/world/europe/migrant-crisis-hungary.html

223   Hina Obavljeno, "Hrvatska Nece Graditi Zidove Za Izbjeglice' Vesna Pusic Iskazala Prezir Prema Madarskom Rjesenju." *Jutarnji.hr,* https://www.jutarnji.hr/vijesti/hrvatska/hrvatska-nece-graditi-zidove-za-izbjeglice-vesna-pusic-iskazala-prezir-prema-madarskom-rjesenju/293875/

224   Siobhan O'Grady, "In Croatia, Migrants Are Welcome Until They're Not." *Foreign Policy,* September 20, 2015, https://foreignpolicy.com/2015/09/17/in-croatia-migrants-are-welcome-until-theyre-not/

225   Associated Press, "Macedonia Allows Migrants to Legitimately Transit Country." *VOA,* June 18, 2015, https://web.archive.org/web/20151119090246/http://www.voanews.com/content/macedonia-migrants-asylum-law/2828577.html

226   UNHCR: The UN Refugee Agency, *Refugee Crisis in Europe,* https://www.unrefugees.org/emergencies/refugee-crisis-in-europe/

UK, and Denmark believed there were already too many immigrants in their country.[227] Even one-third of Germans agreed with that opinion.

In the aftermath of Merkel's announcement, the borders of Greece and Italy were flooded with desperate people from around the third world attempting to make their way to Europe. More than ten thousand people left Turkey for Greece daily.

Some European leaders immediately regretted Merkel's decision and put in place barriers to stop the flow of migrants through their country, threatening the EU's Schengen Agreement. By October 2015, Austria started erecting a border fence with Slovenia[228] and in January began slashing the number of asylum claims, much to the outrage of the EU.[229] Hungary closed its border with Croatia[230] and sealed its border with Serbia with razor wire.[231] In January 2016, Denmark introduced border controls with Germany.[232] The UK built a mile-long border fence across from the French migrant camp in Calais.[233]

---

227 Alberto Nardelli, "Europeans Feel a Duty to Help Refugees – but Not in Their Countries." *The Guardian,* October 30, 2015, https://www.theguardian.com/news/datablog/2015/oct/30/european-attitudes-towards-refugees-poll-eu

228 Nina Lamparski, "Austria to Build Border Fence, Threatening Schengen Zone." *Yahoo! News,* October 29, 2015, https://news.yahoo.com/austria-build-slovenia-border-fence-control-migrant-flow-081818360.html

229 "Migrant Crisis: Austria Asylum Cap Begins despite EU Anger." *BBC News,* February 19, 2016, https://www.bbc.com/news/world-europe-35609823

230 Rick Lyman, "Hungary Seals Border With Croatia in Migrant Crackdown." *The New York Times,* October 16, 2015, https://www.nytimes.com/2015/10/17/world/europe/hungary-croatia-refugees-migrants.html

231 "Hungary Seals Border with Razor Wire." *Euronews,* September 15, 2015, https://www.euronews.com/2015/09/15/hungary-seals-border-with-razor-wire

232 Jakob Stig Jorgensen and Elisabeth Arnsdorf Haslund, "Regeringen Indfører Midlertidig Grænsekontrol Til Tyskland." *Berlingske,* January 4, 2016, https://www.berlingske.dk/politik/regeringen-indfoerer-midlertidig-graensekontrol-til-tyskland

233 "Will New Mile-Long Calais Fence Stop Migrants?" *BBC News,* August 8, 2015, https://www.bbc.com/news/av/world-europe-33833536/will-new-mile-long-calais-fence-stop-migrants

European governments were left attempting to play catch-up, trying to figure out how to process and handle the millions of people arriving at their shore and the millions more who were planning on coming.

NATO allies' decision to intervene in Libya and Syria helped manifest a humanitarian and national security crisis. Add this to the fact that the number of Islamic terrorist attacks attempted or successfully carried out in Europe between 2014 and 2015 increased from two to seventeen and the number of victims killed by Islamic terrorist attacks skyrocketed by more than 350 percent between those two years.[234]

This created an electoral backlash against establishment parties throughout Europe as voters flocked to national populist parties that promised a reduction in immigrants, tighter borders, and a more aggressive stance against terrorism.

In 2016 and 2017, national populist parties made electoral gains in Austria, Germany, Hungary, the Netherlands, France, and most importantly in Italy, where Matteo Salvini turned a separatist party into the largest right-wing party in the nation.

"Italians first," Salvini declared in a television interview just six weeks before the 2018 election.[235] At a campaign stop, he declared that the refugee crisis brought criminals to Italy, "Guys, we have imported a few good people, but there has also been a tide of delinquents and I want to send them home, from the first to the last. We are packed with drug dealers, rapists, burglars— and the League is the solution."[236] Salvini's nearly singular focus

---

234   "EU Terrorism Situation & Trend Report." *Europol*, last updated June 27, 2019, https://www.europol.europa.eu/activities-services/main-reports/eu-terrorism-situation-and-trend-report#fndtn-tabs-0-bottom-2

235   Catherine Edwards, "'Italians First': Italy's Far-Right Leader Echoes Trump in Election Campaign," January 24, 2018, https://www.thelocal.it/20180124/italians-first-far-right-northern-league-matteo-salvini-donald-trump-2018-election

236   James Politi, "Fiery Salvini Forces Anti-Immigrant Tone on Italy Poll Debate." *Financial Times*, March 2, 2018, https://www.ft.com/content/d9b7a876-1d48-11e8-956a-43db76e69936

on immigration and the migrant crisis forced more moderate right-wing parties to also embrace his position.[237]

On March 4, 2018, Salvini's party Lega received 17.35 percent of the vote, quadruple the number from the 2013 election, making it the largest conservative party in Italy.[238] Exit polls showed that unlike other nationalist parties, Lega did better among female voters than male and among voters under thirty than over sixty-five years old.[239]

Italian voters no longer believed that the center-right party Forza Italia that governed Italy from 2006 to 2013 could secure their borders and stop the flood of refugees reaching their shore. A whopping 41 percent of voters who supported Forza Italia in 2013 switched to Lega in 2018, while just 33 percent decided to stick with Forza. Lega became the new center of the political right in Italy.

Salvini has gone on to be one of the biggest headaches for European leaders like France's Emmanuel Macron and presents another challenge to the EU.

What their politicians failed to realize is that they created the opportunity for Salvini to rise in the polls. It's arguable that the migrant crisis that led Salvini to political relevancy was created by the same people who despise him. American and European elites who pushed for foreign policy adventurism in Libya, Syria, and Iraq helped fuel the migrant crisis[240] which helped elevate national populist politicians across Europe.

CHAPTER 4

ILLEGAL IMMIGRATION

ILLEGAL IMMIGRATION AFFECTS nations on every continent on the globe, from the Congolese living illegally in Angola to the Bangladeshis living without documents in India to the Mexican population living in the United States. It is an innate human characteristic for people to move to a place where they perceive they'll be better off. Likewise, humans of all races, creeds, and nationalities expect their governments to protect their interests from noncitizens and foreign governments.

The major difference with illegal immigration across the world is some nations are very proactive in restricting illegal immigration and enforcing the rule of law, while others aren't.

As mentioned above, the African nation of Angola has had a huge illegal alien population mostly coming from the Republic of Congo. Over the years, Angola's government has launched controversial but effective measures that deported hundreds of thousands of illegal aliens in a matter of weeks. Most recently in 2018, when 380,000 Congolese were deported in less than a month.[241] In 2019, they continued their campaign and expelled over 1,400 foreign nationals in a week.[242]

Though Angola has far fewer available resources than most Western nations that have large populations of illegal aliens, they have something most other countries don't: political willpower. Where there's political willpower, illegal immigration can be curbed. Where there's no political resolve, it becomes a crisis as is the case in many Western countries.

One example is America, where illegal immigration has become a multigenerational crisis. America spent about the same amount of money on immigration enforcement since the creation of the Department of Homeland Security in 2003[243] as Angola's entire GDP in 2018 and 2017 combined.[244] Yet America's illegal immigration crisis has only gotten worse.

The American government estimates that there are about 12 million illegal aliens living in the United States,[245] but multiple studies, including ones from Yale and MIT,[246]

---

241 Agence France-Presse, "Angola Says 380,000 Illegal Migrants Exit in Weeks." *Voice of America,* October 21, 2018, https://www.voanews.com/africa/angola-says-380000-illegal-migrants-exit-weeks

242 Angola, Government of Angola, "Over 1,000 illegal immigrants expelled," Luanda, updated January 14, 2019, http://www.angop.ao/angola/en_us/noticias/politica/2019/0/3/Over-000-illegal-immigrants-expelled,f81b4f36-9d3e-4f54-a13f-795a92c750b4.html

243 "The Cost of Immigration Enforcement and Border Security," *Americana Immigration Council,* October 14, 2019, https://www.americanimmigrationcouncil.org/research/the-cost-of-immigration-enforcement-and-border-security

244 "Angola GDP: 161 Billion International Dollars (2018)," *World Economic,* accessed December 17, 2019, https://www.worldeconomics.com/GrossDomesticProduct/Angola.gdp

245 U.S. Government. Department of Homeland Security, "Population Estimates: Illegal Alien Populations Residing in the United States. January 2015," December 2018, www.dhs.gov/sites/default/files/publications/18_1214_PLCY_pops-est-report.pdf

246 Mohammad Fazel Zarandi, Jonathan S. Feinstein, Edward H. Kaplan, "Yale Study Finds Twice as Many Undocumented Immigrants as Previous Estimates," *Yale Insights,* September 24, 2018, https://insights.som.yale.edu/insights/yale-study-finds-twice-as-many-undocumented-immigrants-as-previous-estimates

Bear Stearns[247], and Pulitzer Prize-winning journalists Donald Barlett and James Steele[248] have all estimated that the official number is far too low. They all estimate that the number is probably between the 20 to 30 million range.

Decade after decade, both Democrats and Republicans offered platitudes to voters as promised to fix this problem. The situation continued to get worse until a billionaire from New York offering up some of the most extreme rhetoric on illegal immigration became president because he made his hawkish immigration stance the cornerstone of his campaign.[249] Americans just had enough, and they're not alone.

Illegal immigration brings together a large cross-section of voters because it ignites certain feelings of unfairness and is easy to understand when it comes to the rule of law. Voters are also worried that illegal immigrants are less likely to assimilate and more likely to commit crimes, bring in terrorism, and be dependent on government assistance.

This animosity toward illegal immigration can occur regardless of the population of illegal immigrants living in a country. For example, voters in Chile saw a drastic rise in immigration throughout the 1990s and 2000s.[250] Still, the overall number of foreign-born residents accounted for just 3 percent of the population. Despite the number being relatively low especially

247   Robert Justich and Betty Ng, "The Underground Labor Force Is Rising To The Surface," *Bear Stearns,* January 3, 2005, https://cdn.factcheck.org/UploadedFiles/Bear_Sterns_20_million_illegal.pdf

248   Donald L. Barlett and James B. Steele, "Illegal Aliens: Who Left the Door Open?" *Time,* March 30, 2006, http://content.time.com/time/magazine/article/0,9171,995145,00.html

249   Harry Enten and Perry Bacon Jr., "Trump's Hardline Immigration Stance Got Him To The White House." *FiveThirtyEight,* September 12, 2017, https://fivethirtyeight.com/features/why-polls-showing-daca-as-popular-even-among-republicans-dont-tell-the-whole-story/

250   Juan Landaburu, "El Debate Sobre La Inmigracion Illegal Se Extiende a La Region." *LA NACION,* June 24, 2007, https://www.lanacion.com.ar/el-mundo/el-debate-sobre-la-inmigracion-ilegal-se-extiende-a-la-region-nid920108

in comparison to countries in Europe and America, voters demanded that their government take action against illegal immigrants.[251]

A poll taken in June 2017 found the Chileans soured on President Michelle Bachelet's open borders policy with 57 percent of citizens saying the country should take drastic measures to exclude all illegal immigrants.[252] Chileans' opinion of legal immigrants wasn't much higher, with 40 percent believing that immigrants were taking jobs from natives, 41 percent believing they increased the level of crime, 34 percent believing that immigrants were good for the economy, and only 35 percent of Chileans believed that immigrants improved Chile by bringing new ideas and cultures.

President Bachelet, a member of the Socialist Party, refused to do much on illegal immigration, which led to voters rejecting her party in the 2017 election. Her successor was the more conservative Sebastián Piñera, who campaigned on deporting illegal aliens. Once elected Piñera began deporting more than one thousand Haitians back to their native country on humanitarian flights[253] and began tightening the laws around legal immigration.[254]

Chile's backlash against illegal immigration and their lack of acceptance of legal immigrants underscores the immense conflict immigration presents around the world. Most immigrants both legal and illegal were South American, they spoke the same language, had many similar customs, in some cases, shared a border and still received a political pushback once the population reached a certain threshold.

So, it should come to no surprise that other nations facing illegal immigration from more diverse nations than their host countries experienced a more severe political pushback. This is the case in Australia, Italy, and Israel.

AUSTRALIA

Australia, which has a skills-based legal immigration policy, has experienced waves of asylum seekers and illegal immigrants traveling to the country by boat since the end of the Vietnam War. By the time Middle Easterners started arriving in the early 2000s, Australians tolerance for boat people crumbled. A majority of Australians wanted all boats carrying asylum seekers turned back.[255]

John Howard, a conservative politician leading the right-wing Liberal Party, campaigned on regaining control of Australia's borders and immigration system. This campaign against illegal immigration was credited as the main reason why his party won in November 2001 election.[256] "We will decide who comes to this country and the circumstances in which they come," was his rallying cry at his campaign launch on October 28, 2001.[257]

Under Howard, the Liberal Party passed a bill called the Pacific Solution that made it illegal to enter the country by sea. Boats were stopped at sea and forced to either head back to the ports which they came from, which most of them did, or to go to an offshore camp which would house them while their asylum claims were being processed. Australia sent more than 1,500 asylum seekers to these camps in Papa New Guinea and Naru in 2002 and 2003. The policy was so successful that it deterred a countless number of people from attempting

255   "Migrants Welcome – Unless They're from the Middle East." *The Sydney Morning Herald*, October 3, 2005, https://www.smh.com.au/national/migrants-welcome-unless-theyre-from-the-middle-east-20051003-gdm69u.html

256   Lawson Crescent, "Tampa Affair." *National Museum of Australia*, August 29, 2019, https://www.nma.gov.au/defining-moments/resources/tampa-affair

257   "John Howard's 2001 Election Policy Speech" YouTube video, February 22, 2013, https://www.youtube.com/watch?time_continue=68&v=FxlunUpz-Nc

to illegally make their way into the country. Only 140 asylum seekers reached Australia from 2002 to 2006.[258]

That all changed when Australians voted for the left-wing Labor Party, led by Kevin Rudd, in 2007 and abandoned the Pacific Solution.

The number of boat people landing on Australia doubled in a single year. By 2009 the number crossing into Australia was 400 percent higher than it had been in 2006 and that number tripled to 6,555 the year after, the highest number ever recorded.

Even left-wing members of the Labor Party revolted against their leadership, who had abandoned the offshore camps. The media and voters turned hostile toward the Labor Party, who were blamed for enriching human smugglers. Labor's poll numbers shrunk from 60 percent in December 2009 to just 46 percent in June 2010. [259] At that point, Labor voters had it and Rudd lost his party's leadership to Julia Gillard, who became the nation's new prime minister.

Gillard changed gears, promising to take a more hardline approach to illegal immigration, especially when it came to human smugglers, whom she promised to smash.[260] She tried hard to strike a careful balance between demonizing the smugglers and having sympathy for asylum seekers. It took years before she created one major reform making mainland Australia a migration zone, meaning that even if migrants landed in Australia, they would still be forced into detention

---

258   Parliament of Australia, *Boat arrivals in Australia: a guide to the statistics*. Canberra: Parliament of Australia, January 23, 2014, https://www.aph.gov.au/About_Parliament/Parliamentary_Departments/ Parliamentary_Library/pubs/rp/rp1314/QG/BoatArrivals

259   Joe Kelly, "Archive; Two-party preferred: 2010-2014." *The Australian,* https:// www.theaustralian.com.au/nation/newspoll

260   Reza Hasmath and Jafa McKenzie, "Deterring the 'Boat People': Explaining the Australian Government's People Swap Response to Asylum Seekers." *Australian Journal Political Science 48(4)*, 2013. p. 417–430.

facilities.[261] By that point in 2013, more than twenty thousand migrants were arriving by boat to Australia's shore in a single year.

The new leader of the Liberal Party, Tony Abbott, used Gillard's inability to handle the crisis as well as her new policy known as People's Swap against her in the 2013 election. The People's Swap deal was an agreement between Australia and Malaysia where over a four-year period, Australia would send over eight hundred unprocessed asylum seekers to Malaysia and in return, they would accept four thousand processed refugees.[262] Abbott argued that Gillard had struck terrible deals and that no self-respecting country would allow itself to be a dumping ground for other countries' problems.[263]

Like so many populists, Abbott was able to convey to voters that Australia was being disrespected, taken advantage of and that their leaders had crafted a terrible five-for-one deal.

Voters began to think that for the first time in Australia's history, it was not in control of its own borders and the populist backlash was too much for the Labor Party. Their poll numbers sank and the far-left of their party were dissatisfied with Gillard's handling of the situation. On June 26, 2013, she lost the leadership vote of her party to Rudd, who once again became prime minister.

On September 7, Abbott's Liberal Party and their National Coalition gained eighteen seats in Parliament, becoming the

---

261   Karen Barlow, "Parliament Excises Mainland from Migration Zone."
       ABC News, May 16, 2013, https://www.abc.net.au/news/2013-05-16/
       parliament-excises-mainland-from-migration-zone/4693940
262   Anthea Mulakala, "Understanding the Australia-Malaysia Refugee Swap." The
       Asia Foundation, August 25, 2011, https://asiafoundation.org/2011/08/24/
       understanding-the-australia-malaysia-refugee-swap/
263   Hasmath and McKenzie, "Deterring the 'Boat People': Explaining the
       Australian Government's People Swap Response to Asylum Seekers."
       Australian Journal Political Science 48(4), 2013. p. 424.

RYAN JAMES GIRDUSKY AND HARLAN HILL

governing majority and polls showed that a majority of Australians wanted those arriving by boat to be treated more harshly.[264]

Just eleven days after the election, Abbott's government launched Operation Sovereign Borders (OSB) with the sole goal of stopping the boats. Under OSB, the Abbott government took a zero-tolerance position toward illegal boat arrivals and any asylum seekers who landed on Australia's shore or were caught in Australian waters would have mandatory detention in one of their offshore facilities. Abbott's government also worked with other countries like Indonesia to stop the mass migration of people.

By November 2013, there was a 90 percent reduction in the number of people illegally crossing into Australia by boat.[265] The number of boats that landed in Australia declined from three hundred in 2013 to just one in 2014, and zero arrived in 2015 and 2016.[266]

OMB was a huge success for Abbott's government and increased confidence that the Australian government could control its borders. With illegal immigration wiped out, Australians became more welcoming toward legal immigrants. A study by the Scanlon Foundation found that Australians became more accepting of foreigners, had greater trust in the

264   Philip Dorling, "Australian Want Boat Arrivals Treated More Harshly: Poll." *The Sydney Morning Herald,* January 7, 2014, https://www.smh.com.au/politics/federal/australians-want-boat-arrivals-treated-more-harshly-poll-20140108-30g97.html

265   Andrew Bolt, "Under Abbott, 207 boat people in November. Under Gillard, 2630 boat people last November." *Herald Sun,* November 29, 2013, https://www.heraldsun.com.au/blogs/andrew-bolt/under-abbott-207-boat-people-in-november-under-gillard-2630-boat-people-last-november/news-story/97cbee3870ff947a1d5406de3aa9d843

266   Parliament of Australia, "Boat arrivals and boat 'turnbacks' in Australia since 1976: a quick guide to the statistics." Canberra: Parliament of Australia, January 17, 2017, https://www.aph.gov.au/About_Parliament/Parliamentary_Departments/Parliamentary_Library/pubs/rp/rp1617/Quick_Guides/BoatTurnbacks

government, and an increased sense of patriotism and social cohesion among both the native-born and recent immigrants.[267] The poll also found that more than 35 percent of Australians still wanted the legal levels of immigration reduced.

What most critics of Abbott's OMB policy couldn't understand was that the need to curb illegal immigration has nothing to do with xenophobia or racism and everything to do with trust in their government's ability to protect their sovereignty. A world without borders or with just loose border control is a world with heightened tension and an increased lack of trust.

Abbott's ability to stop boatloads of migrants from coming into his country provided a huge boost to his party. Though he was personally a controversial figure and lost his party's leadership in 2016, his National Coalition would go on to win federal elections in 2016 and 2019. Since OMB was successfully launched, illegal immigration in Australia has held steady at about 60,000 people who entered the country legally and then overstayed their visas.[268][269] The National Coalition has taken up steps to start curbing these illegals as well by pushing landlords, real estate agents, banks, employers, and daycare operators to verify visas and report illegals to the government.

267   David Marr, "Australia in 2014: 'Stop the Boats' Helps Nation Feel Warmer to Immigrants." *The Guardian,* October 28, 2014, https://www.theguardian. com/australia-news/2014/oct/28/-sp-australians-in-2014-a-happy-people-with-a-deep-attachment-to-country-and-culture

268   Sam Duncan, "Over 60,000 Illegal Migrants Are Living in Australia." *Daily Mail,* January 3, 2018, https://www.dailymail.co.uk/news/article-5231989/60-000-illegal-migrants-living-Australia.html

269   Mosiqi Acharya, "60,000 illegal migrants hiding in Australia, claims report." April 1, 2018, https://www.sbs.com.au/language/english/60-000-illegal-migrants-hiding-in-australia-claims-report

ITALY

The former Australian prime minister isn't the only one who saw political success by stopping boats from entering their country. As mentioned in the chapter about foreign policy, Matteo Salvini rose to prominence after Western governments including the United State destabilized North Africa and the Middle East, creating one of the worst refugee crises in history. Salvini was able to make his party, which was formally a secessionist group located only in Northern Italy, the most popular nationwide in less than three years by tackling the issue of illegal immigration.

During the 2018 election, Salvini and his Lega Party were almost laser-focused on the issues of migrants arriving in Italy by boat and deporting half a million illegal immigrants.[270] His national populist rhetoric about putting Italy First and securing their borders resonated with parts of Italy where Lega had traditionally performed very badly.

The migrant situation, however, had turned people against the EU, traditional parties, and establishment politicians.

In 2016, Italy was the leading destination for migrants trying to come to Europe and by 2017, Italy received 67 percent of all the EU's migrants.[271] From 2014 to 2016, more than six hundred thousand migrants washed up on Italy's shore from Africa with most attempting to make their way to Germany.

It overwhelmed tiny towns in Sicily and Southern Italy that were already the most economically depressed areas of the country. Compounding the issue was several refugees committed a series of high-profile killings that rocked the country including

---

270   Nick Squires, "Italian Politician Pledges to Kick out Half a Million Illegal Migrant If Elected Prime Minister." *The Telegraph,* January 23, 2018, https://www.telegraph.co.uk/news/2018/01/23/italian-politician-pledges-kick-half-million-illegal-migrants/

271   "Migration to Europe in Charts." *BBC News,* September 11, 2018, https://www.bbc.com/news/world-europe-44660699

the murders of Ashley Olsen,[272] Vincenzo Solano, and Mercedes Ibáñez,[273] Pamela Mastropietro,[274] Desirée Mariottini,[275] as well as the attempted killing of fifty-one children on board their school bus.[276] There were also a number of high-profile rapes, robberies, and physical assaults that got the attention of the Italian newspapers and social media.

An opinion poll taken by the newspaper *la Repubblica* found that in September 2017, 46 percent of Italians believed migrants represented a threat to their personal security, up from just 26 percent in 2012.[277] A poll in 2018 found that 58 percent of Italians were fearful of migrants[278] and 61 percent of Italians did not feel safe in their city.[279]

A study commissioned by the Confcommercio-Imprese Per l'Italia, in December 2016 found that foreigners committed

272 Nick Squires, "Italian Police Arrest Illegal Immigrant over Murder of American Woman in Florence." *The Telegraph,* January 14, 2016, https://www.telegraph.co.uk/news/worldnews/europe/italy/12097235/Italian-police-reportedly-arrest-man-over-murder-of-American-woman-in-Florence.html

273 Nick Squires, "Murder of Elderly Couple in Sicily Fuels Italy's Growing Anti-Immigrant Sentiment." *The Telegraph,* August 31, 2015, https://www.telegraph.co.uk/news/worldnews/europe/italy/11834743/Murder-of-elderly-couple-in-Sicily-fuels-Italys-growing-anti-immigrant-sentiment.html

274 Oliver Harvey Macerata, "How a Brutal Murder 'Blamed' on an Illegal Immigrant Could See Italy Leave the EU." *The Sun,* March 2, 2018, https://www.thesun.co.uk/news/5706492/pamela-mastropietro-immigrants-italy-leave-eu/

275 "Italy Arrests 3 in Teen's Slaying That Fuels Migrant Debate." AP NEWS, October 25, 2018, https://apnews.com/18055a786dc742a8ae41962ffc7125bc

276 Angela Giuffrida, "Driver in Italy Accused of Setting Fire to School Bus Carrying 51 Children." *The Guardian,* March 20, 2019, https://www.theguardian.com/world/2019/mar/20/driver-arrested-in-milan-after-allegedly-setting-school-bus-on-fire

277 Crispian Balmer, "Rape Cases Fuel Anti-Migrant Angst in Italy Ahead of Election." Reuters, September 13, 2017, https://www.reuters.com/article/us-italy-rapes/rape-cases-fuel-anti-migrant-angst-in-italy-ahead-of-election-idUSKCN1BO23C

278 "Il Quadro politico dopo gli eventi di Macerta," *Politicapp SWG,* February 9, 2018, http://www.swg.it/politicapp?id=hkll

279 "Quasi due terzi dei cittadini si sentono insicuri," *Politicapp SWG,* January 25, 2018, http://www.swg.it/politicapp?id=ijkr

more crimes than native Italians, especially in wealthier regions in Northern Italy with illegal immigrants committing more crimes than legal immigrants. The study also found that the difference in crime rates between native Italians and foreigners leveled off once immigrants successfully assimilated into Italian society.[280]

Salvini was one of the only politicians addressing these issues on the campaign trail with his promise to reinstate law and order won over thousands of new supporters. At an early rally in Rome in 2015, Salvini led an all-out assault against the establishment who were more concerned over what they deemed as a rise of fascism instead of the migrant crisis. "For tender-hearted journalists and leftists, the problem is 10 rightwing kids reading a pamphlet," he said. "For me, the problem is the thousands of illegal immigrants stealing, raping and dealing drugs."[281]

Throughout the campaign, Salvini repeatedly promised voters that he would end the migrant crisis and deport illegal aliens who were making Italy unsafe. "Open doors in Italy for good people and a one-way ticket for those who come to Italy to create commotion and think they will be taken care of. "Send them home" will be one of our top priorities," he said.[282]

Part of his charm was his willingness to go against the grain, speaking to voters with an anti-elitist and politically incorrect vernacular that they understood. "(I'll be eating) six kilos of polenta with ossobuco (tonight)…I won't say salami or pork

---

280   Confcommercio Imprese Per l'Italia, "UNA NOTA DESCRITTIVA SU CRIMINALITÀ E IMMIGRAZIONE." *Ufficio Studi Confcommercio,* (Rome: 2016).

281   Alexander Stille, "How Matteo Salvini Pulled Italy to the Far Right." *The Guardian,* August 9, 2018, https://www.theguardian.com/news/2018/aug/09/how-matteo-salvini-pulled-italy-to-the-far-right

282   Lloyd Johnson, "Italy Vows to 'Send Home' around Half a MILLION Undocumented Immigrants." *Express,* June 1, 2018, https://www.express.co.uk/news/world/968310/italy-news-immigration-send-home-immigrants-eu-matteo-salvini-lega

because some may get offended. Long live sausage! Long live salami! Long live pork, coppa and pancetta," Salvini said to a cheering crowd in the northeastern city of Padua.[283] Though this may seem unimportant, it was a slight against elitists who claimed Italy must change its culture in order to be sensitive to Muslim migrants who, among other things, do not eat pork.

Refusing to be politically correct was an important characteristic of Salvini. He mastered social media, posting on Facebook an average of ten times per day about how the elites were refusing to address mass immigration and the refugee crisis.

"A 25-year-old girl was attacked in the Milan train station, saving herself from RAPE only through use of pepper spray, Salvini wrote on his Facebook. The rapist was arrested today, let's hope this time he finds a judge who keeps him in prison for years. P.S. I am not allowed to tell you that the rapist is Nigerian, an illegal immigrant with a criminal record, or I will be accused of RACISM."

At the same time, Salvini was willing to be as bombastic as possible, Italy's left-wing parties were eating each other alive. The ruling Democratic Party (PD) struck a deal to fund migrant camps in Italy and train members of the Libyan coast guard to stop migrant vessels. The move slightly reduced the number of boats leaving Libya, but not enough to calm Italians' general panic over the situation. At the same time, progressives in Italy's government slammed the move stating it was opposed to their humanitarian values.[284]

Italy's progressive politicians' infighting allowed for Salvini to gain the support of some of their voters who thought their

283   James Politi, "Fiery Salvini Forces Anti-Immigrant Tone on Italy Poll Debate." *The Financial Times,* March 2, 2018, https://www.ft.com/content/d9b7a876-1d48-11e8-956a-43db76e69936

284   Steve Scherer, "Italian Left's Efforts to Stop Migrants May Backfire at Election." Reuters, November 22, 2017, https://www.reuters.com/article/us-europe-migrants-italy/italian-lefts-efforts-to-stop-migrants-may-backfire-at-election-idUSKBN1DM1JA

party's leadership was being too weak on the migration issue. What Salvini understood was that while newspaper editors, academics, and elitists in Rome hated him, the people agreed with his positions on immigration, even if they weren't willing to say so out loud.

Italians had concerns over the direction of the country and where it was going culturally, politically, and economically. Everyday Italians felt that they were becoming divorced from the nation they grew up in. A study released directly after the 2018 Italian national election found that 73 percent of Italians believed that traditional parties and politicians did not care about people like them, 53 percent thought Italy had become weak, and 59 percent said they felt Italian culture was disappearing.[285]

And while most Italians believed in the principles of asylum and a plurality felt warm toward migrants themselves, 57 percent of Italians believed immigration had a negative impact on their country. An additional 42 percent believed that refugees posed a major security threat and 44 percent believed that immigrants were not making-an-attempt to integrate into Italian society. A whopping 40 percent believed that most of the migrants could never integrate because Italian identity was incompatible with Islam.

On election day, Salvini's Lega Party overperformed what pollsters had estimated and received 17.4 percent of the vote becoming the largest right-wing party in Italy. As mentioned in chapter one, Italy's right-wing coalition created a government with the left-wing populist Five Star Movement and Salvini was named Deputy Prime Minister and Minister of the Interior, which put him in charge of displaced persons and internal security.

Salvini was sworn into his new positions on June 1 and began immediately working to fulfill his campaign promises

---

285   Tim Dixon, et al., "Attitudes towards National Identity, Immigration and Refugees in Italy." *More in Common*, (London: 2018).

on immigration. On June 10, Salvini announced that he was closing Italy's ports to nongovernment organizations (NGOs) carrying migrants on boats attempting to dock in the country.[286]

"From today, even Italy is beginning to say no [to migrants]," Salvini tweeted in defiance of the NGOs seeking to bring migrants into his country.[287]

A week later, Salvini proposed conducting a census of Roma people (gypsies) living in Italy to see how many of an estimated 180,000 were capable of being deported, but he received pushback from the prime minister and was ultimately forced to abandon the idea.[288]

By fall, the Council of Ministers and the Italian Parliament approved several pieces of legislation backed by Salvini to better enforce immigration law and deter illegal immigration. The Salvini decree suspended the refugee application to anyone deemed socially dangerous or anyone who had a prior criminal record.[289] That following month, the legislature overwhelmingly passed a bill ending the practice of giving out asylum on humanitarian grounds and increased funding to law enforcement.[290] Weeks later, the Italian government handed

286 Fabio Albanese et al., "Migranti, L'Italia Sfida Malta. Salvini: Chiudiamo I Porti – La Stampa." June 27, 2019, https://www.lastampa.it/cronaca/2018/06/11/news/migranti-l-italia-sfida-malta-salvini-chiudiamo-i-porti-1.35907153?refresh_ce

287 Ibid.

288 Elisabetta Povoledo and Gaia Pianigiani, "Italian Minister Moves to Count and Expel Roma, Drawing Outrage." *The New York Times,* June 19, 2018, https://www.nytimes.com/2018/06/19/world/europe/italy-roma-matteo-salvini.html

289 Angela Giuffrida, "Italian Government Approves Salvini Bill Targeting Migrants." *The Guardian,* September 24, 2018, https://www.theguardian.com/world/2018/sep/24/italian-government-approves-bill-anti-migrant-measures-matteo-salvini

290 Steve Scherer, "Italy's Salvini Gets Win with New Asylum and Security Rules." Reuters, November 29, 2018, https://www.reuters.com/article/us-italy-politics-immigration-security/italys-salvini-gets-win-with-new-asylum-and-security-rules-idUSKCN1NY1JN

another victory to Salvini by refusing to ratify the UN's pact of migration.[291]

Salvini's war against NGOs continued throughout 2019 when the deputy prime minister refused to allow boats filled with migrants to dock in Italy and increased the fine on NGOs that refused to adhere to Italian law to one million Euros.[292] When a thirty-one-year-old German NGO ship captain named Carola Rackete decided to ram police boats and dock anyway, she was arrested and became the main target of Salvini's. When she filed a lawsuit against Salvini for defamation, he stood defiant and tweeted, "She breaks laws and attacks Italian military vessels, and then she sues me. I'm not afraid of the Mafia, let alone a rich and spoiled communist!"[293] By August of 2019, German NGOs announced they were no longer challenging Salvini's policy of closing ports off to migrants, choosing instead to bring them to Malta.[294]

His refusal to back down only cemented his support among Italian citizens, who began to flock to Salvini throughout the end of 2018 and the beginning of 2019. A poll taken in January 2019 found that a majority (51 percent) of Italians agreed with Salvini's approach of preventing any boats from landing on Italian shores.[295]

291   Associated Press, "The Latest: Italy Bows out of Meeting on UN Migration Pact." *Fox News,* November 28, 2018, https://www.foxnews.com/world/the-latest-italy-bows-out-of-meeting-on-un-migration-pact

292   Crispian Balmer, "In New Migrant Standoff, Italy's Salvini Blocks Two NGO Boats." Reuters, August 13, 2019, https://www.reuters.com/article/us-europe-migrants-italy/in-new-migrant-standoff-italys-salvini-blocks-two-ngo-boats-idUSKCN1V315R

293   Chris Tomlinson, "Arrested Migrant Ferry Captain to Sue Salvini for Sander." *Breitbart,* July 7, 2019, https://www.breitbart.com/europe/2019/07/07/arrested-migrant-ferry-captain-to-sue-salvini-for-slander/

294   Bartolo Dall, "Alan Kurdi, L'Ong Si Arrende a Salvini: 'Portiamo I Migranti a Malta'." *Il Giornale,* August 2, 2019, http://www.ilgiornale.it/news/cronache/long-si-arrende-salvini-portiamo-i-migranti-malta-1735304.html

295   Nando Pagnoncelli, "Migranti, Un Italiano Su Due per Lo Stop Agli Sbarchi." *Corriere Della Sera,* January 12, 2019, https://www.corriere.it/politica/19_gennaio_11/migranti-italiano-due-lo-stop-sbarchi-d357d924-15e0-11e9-9cd3-6f68d3bb44a0.shtml

After years of politicians unable to deliver on their campaign pledges, Salvini was a breath of fresh air. He was one of the few Italian politicians who could take credit for delivering on his promise to cut down on migrants entering Italy. Only 964 migrants arrived in Italy during the month of September 2018, the first time less than a thousand migrants arrived in a single month in over four years. A mere 2,755 migrants arrived in Italy from January 1 to July 1, 2019, a monumental reduction from the year prior, when 18,645 arrived between January to August 2018.[296, 297]

By the end of July, Salvini's party was the most popular in Italy, with pollsters stating that nearly 39 percent of Italian voters would support Lega in the next election.

Italy's populist coalition government collapsed in August 2019, yet Salvini's immigration agenda was so popular that the Five Star Movement's Luigi Di Maio demanded that any new government must maintain Salvini's security decree.[298]

ISRAEL

It wasn't all migrants arriving by boat that triggered a national populist backlash; Israel experienced a wave of illegal immigrants coming from Africa in the mid-to-late 2000s and

---

296   Adriano Bosoni, "When It Comes to EU Migration Policies, Italy Won't Go Down Without a Fight." *Stratfor*, July 9, 2019, https://worldview.stratfor.com/article/when-it-comes-eu-migration-policies-italy-won-t-go-down-without-fight-mediterranean-libya-europe

297   United Nations International Organization for Migration, "Mediterranean Migrant Arrivals Reach 58,158 in 2018; Deaths Reach 1,514." *The UN Migration Agency*, August 3, 2018, https://reliefweb.int/report/italy/mediterranean-migrant-arrivals-reach-58158-2018-deaths-reach-1514

298   AFP, "Italie: Le Mouvement 5 Etoiles Pose Ses Conditions a La Naissance Du Nouveau Gouvernement." *Franceinfo*, August 30, 2019, https://www.francetvinfo.fr/monde/italie/crise-politique-en-italie/italie-le-mouvement-5-etoiles-pose-ses-conditions-a-la-naissance-du-nouveau-gouvernement_3597013.html#xtor=CS2-765-[twitter]-

early 2010s that caused Israel to build a wall along their border with Egypt.

Throughout the early 2000s, Israel experienced a small but steady number of illegal aliens entering their country with the hopes of improving their financial situation. For the most part, the Israeli government turned a blind eye, given that the figures were so low.[299] Prime Minister Ariel Sharon floated the idea of building a barrier on part of the border to stop Palestinians from moving between the two countries to bring in contraband, especially weapons.[300]

In January 2007, a terrorist crossed over from Egypt and blew himself up at a bakery in the city of Eilat, killing three people and awakening Israeli citizens to the growing threat of their porous border.

By 2010, the increased threat of terrorism and the rising number of illegal aliens crossing into Israel started a major backlash and pushed politicians to embrace Sharon's idea of a border wall. Illegal immigration soared during this time period; according to Israel's Interior and Justice Departments, 26,635 Africans illegally immigrated to the Jewish State by July 2010.[301] That number ballooned to sixty thousand by 2012,[302] with most being refugees from the war-torn countries of Sudan and Eritrea.[303] Although the number was relatively low, making

---

299   David Mac Dougall and Josef Federman, "African Migrants in Israel Have Little Hope." *San Diego Tribune,* January 7, 2014, https://www.sandiegouniontribune.com/sdut-african-migrants-in-israel-have-little-hope-2014jan07-story.html

300   Tim Butcher, "Sharon Presses for Fence across Sinai." *The Telegraph,* December 7, 2005, https://www.telegraph.co.uk/news/worldnews/middleeast/1504945/Sharon-presses-for-fence-across-Sinai.html

301   Irial Glynn Kleist, History, Memory and Migration: Perceptions of the Past and the Politics of Incorporation, Palgrave Macmilan, (New York: 2012) p. 169.

302   Joel Greenberg, "In Israel, African migrants face backlash," *The Washington Post,* June 23, 2012, https://www.washingtonpost.com/world/africa/in-israel-african-migrants-face-backlash/2012/06/23/gJQAwLSvxV_story.html

303   Nehemiah Strassler, "Refugees, no infiltrators." *Haaretz,* September 24, 2012, https://www.haaretz.co.il/opinions/letters/1.1223407

up less than 5 percent of Israel's population, Netanyahu's government didn't allow the numbers to spike further before taking bold action.

On January 12, 2010, the Israeli government approved the construction of two fences on seventy-five miles of the Egyptian border.[304] Construction started that November but given the immense number of Africans moving through the area, the Israeli government upgraded the wall across 245 miles of the Egyptian border with radar and motion detectors. This idea was inconceivable just a few years prior when Sharon was in office.

While the wall was under construction, Israel had to decide how they would handle the approximately sixty thousand illegal immigrants living in the country. While the Israeli government insisted they were economic migrants looking for work or, as some in Netanyahu's administration called them, infiltrators, international organizations like the United Nations insisted that 90 percent were genuine refugees Under the United Nations Convention relating to the Status of Refugees, which Israel is a signatory of, Israel could not forcibly remove refugees to a place of persecution.[305] Without the ability to deport them, the Israeli government held most of them without a long-term status. Israel has a slow and strict refugee policy, much more stringent than countries in North America and Europe: of the 13,764 Sudanese and Eritreans who applied for refugee status, only ten were formally given that designation.

With most illegal aliens sitting in limbo, many migrated to South Tel Aviv, which caused a near-instant backlash among residents who saw their arrival in the thousands correlate with a rising crime rate. Israelis began calling South Tel Aviv,

---

304   "Israel Approves Egypt Border Fence." *Express UK,* January 11, 2010, https://
       www.express.co.uk/news/world/151030/Israel-approves-Egypt-border-fence
305   "Illegal Migrants & Refugees in Israel." *The Jewish Federation of North
       America,* February 2018, https://cdn.fedweb.org/fed-42/2212/
       Migrants%2520to%2520Israel%2520-%2520Full%2520Background%2520Br
       iefing%2520February%25209%25202018.pdf

where many migrants resided, Soweto which was the site of an uprising in South Africa.[306]

Residents of South Tel Aviv's fear of migrants bringing crime was not unfounded. According to government data, there was a 23 percent increase in crimes committed by foreigners from 2011 to 2012 just as the number of illegal aliens crossing into Israel was hitting its apex.[307] The number of cases where crimes were committed by foreigners increased from 1,779 in 2006 to approximately 3,500 in 2015. Half of these new criminal cases opened against African migrants were in Tel Aviv. This rise in crime was evident to voters; a 2015 survey conducted by the Tel Aviv police found that just 38 percent of South Tel Aviv residents felt safe walking outside their homes at night.[308]

The rise in crime created a ripple effect throughout Israel for years to come, even in the traditionally liberal areas of the country. Nearly two-thirds of Israelis supported a plan to deport Sudanese and Eritreans to safe third countries like Rwanda. [309] While for some, Israel's identity as a Jewish state plays a factor in their belief of restricting immigration, even a majority of Israeli Arabs and 25 percent of voters who supported left-wing parties agreed with the plan to deport refugees.

By 2018, a Pew Research poll found that Israel had become the Western country most opposed to taking in refugees fleeing war and violence, even more so than Japan, Hungary, Russia,

---

306   Isabel Kershner, "Crackdown on Migrants Tugs at Soul of Israelis," *The New York Times,* June 18, 2012, https://www.nytimes.com/2012/06/18/world/middleeast/crackdown-on-african-immigrants-tugs-at-israels-soul.html?module=inline

307   Omri Ephraim, "Police: 23% increase in foreign crime," *National Ynet,* March 19, 2012, https://www.ynet.co.il/articles/1,7340,L-4204802,00.html

308   Israel Gideon, et al., "Why Israel's Border Fence Worked," *Mida,* February 21, 2017, https://mida.org.il/2017/02/21/israels-border-fence-worked/

309   Lahav Harkov, "Two-Thirds of Israelis Favor Deporting African Migrants, Polls Finds," *The Jerusalem Post,* February 8, 2018, https://www.jpost.com/Israel-News/Two-thirds-of-Israelis-favor-deporting-African-migrants-poll-finds-540960

Poland, and Italy.[310] Furthermore, a whopping 73 percent of Israelis told Pew they preferred if their country took fewer or no new immigrants at all.[311]

With the political winds at their back, the Israeli government completed its border wall with Egypt in December of 2013 at a cost of $450 million to taxpayers.[312] They even went on to expand the project before it was finished and increased the size of the border fence in particular areas with a high volume of illegal immigrants, increasing the height from about sixteen feet to roughly twenty-six feet high.[313]

The border barrier between Israel and Egypt led to almost an immediate reduction of illegal immigration coming from Africa. According to government statistics, the number of refugees coming from Africa decreased by 99 percent in the first year alone, from 9,570 Africans crossing during the first six months of 2012 to just thirty-four crossing in the first six months of 2013.[314] That number dropped further to just sixteen border crossings once an upgraded border wall was completed in 2016.

---

310   Phillip Connor, "Europeans Support Taking in Refugees – but Not EU's Handling of Issue." *Pew Research Center,* https://www.pewresearch.org/fact-tank/2018/09/19/a-majority-of-europeans-favor-taking-in-refugees-but-most-disapprove-of-eus-handling-of-the-issue/

311   Ariel David, et al., "73 Percent of Israelis Want Fewer or No New Immigrants, Finds Global Pew Poll." *Haaretz,* December 12, 2018, https://www.haaretz.com/israel-news/73-percent-of-israelis-want-fewer-or-no-new-immigrants-finds-global-pew-poll-1.6740736

312   Gidon Ben-zvi, "Israel Completes 245 Miles, NIS 1.6 Billion Security Fence Along Sinai Border with Egypt." *The Algemeiner,* December 4, 2013, http://www.algemeiner.com/2013/12/04/245-mile-1-6-billion-shekel-security-fence-between-israel-and-sinai-completed/

313   Anna Ahronheim, "Israel Completes Heightened Egypt Border Fence," *The Jerusalem Post,* January 18, 2017, https://www.jpost.com/Israel-News/Israel-completes-heightened-Egypt-border-fence-478840

314   Maayana Miskin, "New Data Shows 99% Drop in Illegal Entry." *Israel National News,* February 7, 2013, http://www.israelnationalnews.com/News/News.aspx/169521#.UeXqBUB15DQ

Israel's border wall became the idolized by national populists around the world, with leaders like Donald Trump, Viktor Orbán, and Narendra Modi all vying to build their own version of Israel's border wall. In the case of Orbán, the erection of his border wall led to an even more drastic decrease of migrants flowing into Hungary. After the barrier was completed in October 2015,[315] the number of illegal migrants apprehended crossing into his country declined from 138,396 in September 2015 to just 315 in November 2015.[316]

With the crisis of illegal border crossing behind them, Netanyahu's government focused on removing the sixty thousand African refugees living in Israel.

Unable to send them back to Sudan and Eritrea, Israel began the process of shipping them to safe third countries like Rwanda or Uganda. In order to speed up the process, Netanyahu announced on January 3 that each of the 38,000 remaining illegal aliens still living in Israel would be offered a grant of $3,500 and a plane ticket back to Africa or face imprisonment in an Israeli cell.[317]

Every country must guard its borders, Netanyahu said while announcing the plan. The infiltrators have a clear choice— cooperate with us and leave voluntarily, respectably, humanely and legally, or we will have to use other tools at our disposal, which are also according to the law.[318]

---

315   Rick Lyman, "Hungary Seals Border With Croatia in Migrant Crackdown." *The New York Times*, October 16, 2015, https://www.nytimes.com/2015/10/17/world/europe/hungary-croatia-refugees-migrants.html?_r=0

316   "Elfogott Migránsok Száma - Dátum Szerinti Lekérdezés." Rend rségnél Szolgálni es Vedunk, last updated November, 2015, https://archive.is/J9O0y

317   Jeffrey Heller, "Israel Offers to Pay African Migrants to Leave, Threatens Jail." Reuters, January 6, 2018, https://www.reuters.com/article/us-israel-migrants/israel-offers-to-pay-african-migrants-to-leave-threatens-jail-idUSKBN1ES0UY

318   Isabel Kershner, "Israel Offers African Migrants a Choice: Ticket Out or Jail." *The New York Times*, January 4, 2018, https://www.nytimes.com/2018/01/04/world/middleeast/israel-africans.html

THE UNITED STATES

A large wave of illegal immigration creates social distrust between citizens and their government, believing that they have lost control of administering their borders and the ability to enforce their nation's laws. When long periods go by when illegal immigration is never enforced, it cements those beliefs into the voters' minds and erodes respect in the nation-state as an institution.

However, when governments find ways to stop illegal immigration, enforce their laws, and deport aliens who entered their territory without consent, it can lead to a huge boost to governing parties as it did in Italy, Australia, and Israel.

Lega, Likud, and the Liberal Party of Australia were rewarded politically for being able to do what so few elected officials are able to do in the West: keep their promise and restore a sense of fairness in the system. It gave confidence to voters and won over even some converts who were worried about terrorism, crime, and the slow erosion of their sovereignty.

Which brings us to America, a nation with all those promises but no Modi, Salvini, Abbott, Netanyahu, or Orbán to fix them.

As opposed to all the nations mentioned above, America has been dealing with waves of illegal immigration for decades, and it has become a multigenerational crisis that presidents have failed to fix. As each president kicked the can further down the road and vacated their constitutional responsibility to defend the borders of the US, the illegal alien population rose to between 3 and 6 percent of the nation's population (depending on whose estimates you believe.)

Illegal aliens in America now have political interest groups fighting for protected status, the erosion of America's borders, and special protections not even given to foreigners legally residing in the country.

Somewhere between President's Eisenhower strict enforcement of illegal immigration and Reagan's 1986 amnesty, the

American government surrendered on enforcing immigration law.

No single president was responsible for the lawless invasion and open disregard of America's immigration laws by millions of foreigners and yet none made it a primary goal to seal America's borders. Had any president from Carter to Obama done just that, there's a possibility the American public may have never voted for Donald Trump. Rather than looking to enforce the law and stop illegal immigration, most American presidents looked to pass amnesties to reward their illegal behavior.

In 1986, when Ronald Reagan passed the first large-scale amnesty of its kind, it was supposed to be a one-time fix[319] in exchange for increased immigration enforcement.[320] The enforcement never came, but several amnesties followed in the years after Reagan's amnesty, including an amnesty for 578,000 people in 1994, a rolling extension of the 1994 amnesty in 1997, the Nicaraguan Adjustment and Central Americans Relief Act for one million Central Americans also in 1997, the Haitian relief act for 125,000 Haitians, an amnesty in 2000 for 400,000 illegal aliens who missed out on the 1986 amnesty, and the LIFE amnesty for 900,000 illegal aliens also given out in the year 2000.[321]

There was never an amnesty large enough to satisfy the cheap labor lobby or open borders advocates. All these amnesties did was encourage more illegal immigration from people across the world who believed they could live in the shadows, have American children through the birthright citizenship,

---

319   United States Senate, *Congressional Record- Senate*, October 17, 1986, https://archive.org/stream/congressionalrec132munit#page/n257/mode/2up

320   Robert Pear, "The Immigration Bill: Step by Step." *The New York Times*, October 21, 1986, https://www.nytimes.com/1986/10/21/us/washington-talk-the-immigration-bill-step-by-step.html

321   Michelle Malkin, "No More Illegal Alien Waivers." *Real Clear Politics*, December 3, 2010, https://www.realclearpolitics.com/articles/2010/12/03/no_more_illegal_alien_waivers_108138.html

and hold their breath until the next amnesty was drummed up by legislators in Washington. Harvard PhD Karl Eschbach testified to Congress that amnesties, incentivize other ineligible unauthorized immigrants to remain in the United States with the hope that they will be the beneficiaries of a future adjustment of status.[322]

Other protections offered by Congress including the Williams Wilberforce Trafficking Victims Protection Reauthorization Act passed in 2008 led to a surge of unaccompanied minors.[323] Human smugglers made billions of dollars[324] getting minors across the border because Congress passed a bill to grant them special protections.

While Americans wanted to be compassionate, they did not support policies that rewarded illegal border crossings. President Obama's executive order to protect illegal aliens who came to the US as children (DACA) as well as their parents (DAPA) were extremely unpopular with Americans at the time they were enacted. An NBC/*Wall Street Journal* poll taken in 2014 found that just 38 percent of Americans supported Obama's executive order that shielded millions of illegal immigrants from deportation.[325]

By 2014, after decades of failed enforcement measures and several efforts by the political class to enact a series of amnesties,

---

322   Ian Smith, "Yes, Amnesty Encourages More Illegal Immigration." *National Review,* August 11, 2015, https://www.nationalreview.com/2015/02/defying-common-sense-immigration-ian-smith/

323   CatalinaAmuedo-Dorantes and Thitima Puttitanun, "Was DACA Responsible for the Surge in Unaccompanied Minors," *International Migration/Volume 55, Issue 6,* October 16, 2017, https://onlinelibrary.wiley.com/doi/full/10.1111/imig.12403

324   Victoria A. Greenfield, et al., "Human Smuggling Operations from Central America to the United States," *RAND Corporation,* April 22, 2019, https://www.rand.org/pubs/research_briefs/RB10057.html

325   "NBC/WSJ Poll: Nearly Half Opposed Executive Action on Immigration." *NBC News,* June 11, 2015, https://www.nbcnews.com/politics/first-read/nbc-wsj-poll-nearly-half-oppose-executive-action-immigration-n251631

a majority of Americans—including Democrats—supported doubling the number of border agents and building a seven hundred-mile fence along the Mexican-American border.[326] Even when pollsters mentioned that those security measures would come at a $46 billion cost, a majority of Americans, including 43 percent of Democrats, still supported it.

Building a barrier on the border wasn't unique to Trump; American presidents going back to Jimmy Carter[327] have supported some kind of fencing along the heavily trafficked areas of the border. The most successful fence pre-Trump a triple-sided border fence in the San Diego area of California. A government study found that border apprehensions declined by 76 percent from the time it was constructed in 1992 to 2004.[328] In 2006, Congress voted to build seven hundred miles of San Diego-like fencing across the border. The Secure Fence Act of 2006 received bipartisan support including one-third of House Democrats[329] and nearly 60 percent of Senate Democrats including then senators Hillary Clinton and Barack Obama.[330]

An Associated Press/Ipsos poll found that voters supported the border fence by a slim 49 to 48 percent margin, but an

326   Sean Sullivan and Scott Clement, "Senate Immigration Plan Wins Majority Support from Public," *The Washington Post*, April 28, 2019, https://www.washingtonpost.com/news/the-fix/wp/2013/07/18/senate-immigration-plan-wins-majority-support-from-public/

327   "A History of the Southern Border," *The Week*, February 2, 2019, https://static1.squarespace.com/static/52eec360e4b0c81c80749630/t/5c609e6cf4e1fc3c525db0db/1549835884843/AoW+1819_23+Border+History.pdf

328   Cindy Carcamo, "Border Wall Built in 1990s Cut Illegal Immigration, but It Also Brought Problems for Small Town." *The Los Angeles Times*, March 9, 2018, https://www.latimes.com/local/california/la-me-jacumba-border-fence-20180309-htmlstory.html

329   United States Congress, "Final Vote Results for Roll Call 446: Secure Fence Act," *United States House*, September 14, 2006, http://clerk.house.gov/evs/2006/roll446.xml

330   United States Senate, "Roll Call Vote 109th Congress – 2nd Session Vote Summary," *United States Senate*, September 29, 2006, https://www.senate.gov/legislative/LIS/roll_call_lists/roll_call_vote_cfm.cfm?congress=109&session=2&vote=00262

NBC News/*Wall Street Journal* poll from June 2006 found that Americans were more likely to vote for a candidate who supported building a fence than one who didn't support it by a twenty-four-point margin. Despite having mixed feelings on the fence, a supermajority of Americans wanted more to be done to curb illegal immigration, a Quinnipiac University poll found that 71 percent wanted Congress to do more to stop the flow of illegal aliens.[331]

Despite voters' hopes, more would not be done.

The following year, Democrats took over Congress and passed a law authored by Republican Senator Kay Bailey Hutchinson that allowed the Department of Homeland Security (DHS) not to build fencing in areas, that the use or placement of such resources is not the most appropriate means to achieve and maintain operational control over the international border at such location.[332]

So, of the proposed seven hundred miles of double-layered fencing that was originally proposed by Congress, just fourteen miles had tertiary pedestrian fencing and only thirty-six miles had secondary fencing. Nearly half of all fencing was just vehicle fencing, which migrants could easily hop over on their way to the US.[333]

The only time immigration enforcement was discussed after the Secure Fence Act of 2006 was in a context of how it could be part of a comprehensive immigration package that included rewarding illegal aliens. In lieu of understanding

---

331 "Immigration." *PollingReport.com,* April 2010, https://www.pollingreport.com/immigration4.htm

332 Editorial Board, "How Congress Prevented Border Fence Law's Implementation," *Investors' Business Daily,* November 12, 2015, https://www.investors.com/politics/editorials/congress-prevented-border-fence-law-implementation/

333 "The Current State of the Border Fence," *Fair US,* May 2019, https://www.fairus.org/issue/national-security/current-state-border-fence

Einstein's definition of insanity, nearly all Republicans and every Democrat who ran for president in 2008, 2012, and 2016 supported some type of amnesty for illegal aliens. Politicians would debate how a mass amnesty would increase national GDP, help corporations find more labor and would be the humanitarian thing to do, all the while leaving out of that conversation how it would affect the American worker.

A 2012 report in the *Cato Journal* published by the libertarian Cato Institute, which advocates for mass immigration and amnesty, admitted that amnesty would have a negative effect on the wages of native workers. The report, written by a senior economist at the Federal Reserve Bank of Dallas and a professor from Agnes College, found that low-skilled native workers and new legal immigrants would suffer if an amnesty included newly arrived immigrants. Ultimately, native workers and legal immigrants would possibly be pushed out of the job market and be forced to get a higher-skilled occupation.[334]

Finding higher-skilled occupations sounds simple in theory, but in real terms, it would create economic havoc on millions of families across the US.

If newly legalized immigrants move out of ethnic enclaves or into higher-skilled occupations or better jobs, those movements are likely to affect natives and other immigrants, the report stated. Labor market outcomes may worsen for natives and other immigrants if newly legalized immigrants compete with them for jobs. If the immigrants who adjust status are long-term US residents, they are more substitutable for native workers than newly arriving immigrants, which heightens the labor market effect. Competing native workers and other immigrants may choose to move or switch occupations in response.

---

334   Pia Orrenius and Madeline Zavodny, "The Economic Consequences of Amnesty for Unauthorized Immigrants," *The Cato Journal*, (Washington DC: 2012) p. 94, 96.

The report also stated that any form of amnesty would also bear a huge financial burden on state and local governments in places with large populations of illegal aliens due to the fact that they would be eligible for more types of welfare programs.

Most attempts to calculate the net fiscal impact of unauthorized immigrants conclude that they pay less in taxes than they receive in services, on average…legalizing the undocumented population is likely to aggravate the gap between revenues and outlays. The fiscal burden would be particularly heavy for state and local governments, which bear a large share of costs for most means-tested transfer programs, in the medium run. In the long run, the federal government would bear more costs as legalized immigrants age into Social Security and Medicare eligibility.

Politicians' concerns weren't working-poor Americans or the towns and small cities throughout the country that would falter as a consequence of amnesty. Republicans did all they could to cater to big business that wanted an endless supply of cheap labor and Democrats all but gave up on immigration enforcement to win favor from ethnic lobbies and woke white liberals.

Which is why Trump was able to move through the Republican primary so seamlessly—because he was in a league of his own on national populist issues like immigration. After Trump won the presidency, Democrats became even more hardened on their woke views of race and immigration, completely abandoning almost all forms of immigration enforcement that they endorsed in the past and that most Americans still support. This include:

- 73 percent of Americans believed it was important to prevent unqualified illegal aliens from receiving welfare benefits; 58 percent of Democrats agreed.

- 68 percent of Democrats opposed sending previously deported illegal aliens who have re-entered the country to prison; 46 percent of Americans agreed.[335]

- 60 percent of Democrats supported free healthcare for illegal immigrants; 33 percent of Americans agreed. [336]

- 58 percent of Democrats opposed adding a citizenship question to the US Census; 33 percent of Americans agreed.

- 58 percent of Americans believe increasing deportations should an important goal; 41 percent of Democrats agreed. [337]

- 45 percent of Democrats supported decriminalizing the border; 27 percent of Americans agreed.

- 43 percent of Democrats supported abolishing ICE; 25 percent of Americans agreed.[338]

- 42 percent of Americans believed controlling and reducing illegal immigration was a top foreign policy goal; 20 percent of Democrats agreed. [339]

335   Zach Goldberg, Twitter, "Just since January of 1995, we have arrested more than 1,700 criminal aliens and prosecuted them on federal felony charges because they returned to America after having been deported," August 22, 2019 11:40 AM, https://twitter.com/ZachG932/status/1164608224701685764

336   NPR/PBS/Marist Poll, *News Hour/Marist Poll National Tables,* July 15–17, 2019, http://maristpoll.marist.edu/wp-content/uploads/2019/07/NPR_PBS-NewsHour_Marist-Poll_USA-NOS-and-Tables_1907190926.pdf#page=3

337   Zach Goldberg, Twitter Post, "They're also less likely to see preventing welfare abuse among immigrants as an important goal," July 5, 2019 2:16 PM, https://twitter.com/ZachG932/status/1147253037360189440/photo/1

338   Li Zhou, "Most Americans Oppose Abolishing ICE," *Vox,* July 11, 2018, https://www.vox.com/2018/7/11/17553330/abolish-ice-poll

339   Dina Smeltz, et, al., "America Engaged, American Public Opinion and US Foreign Policy," *2018 Chicago Council Survey,* 2018, https://www.thechicagocouncil.org/sites/default/files/report_ccs18_america-engaged_181002.pdf

- 37 percent of Americans believed that a large number of immigrants and refugees coming into the US posed a threat; 20 percent of Democrats agreed. [340]

- 36 percent of liberals opposed deporting illegal aliens who had been convicted of committing crimes; 19 percent of Americans agreed. [341]

While an evolution toward woke politics was responsible for a great deal of this, partisan politics also played a role in Democrats' embrace of more open-border immigration policies. Support among Democrats for building a barrier on the border dropped significantly after then-candidate Trump endorsed the idea. Support for a wall dropped from an average of 44 percent in late 2015 to 12 percent by early 2019. [342]

The candidates for the 2020 Democratic nomination were so extreme on the issue of immigration that leading figures in the Democratic Party including former Democratic Senate Majority Leader Harry Reid, [343] the Center for American Progress, [344] former Obama aide David Axelrod, [345] and *New York Times* opinion

---

340   Ibid. p. 24

341   ORC International Poll, "Interviews with 1,025 adult Americans," *CNN poll,* March 17, 2017, http://i2.cdn.turner.com/cnn/2017/images/03/17/rel4g.- .immigration.pdf

342   Emily Ekins, "Americans Used to Support a Border Wall. What Changed Their Minds?" *Cato Institute,* January 15, 2019, https://www.cato.org/publications/ commentary/americans-used-support-border-wall-what-changed-their-minds

343   Cameron Joseph, "EXCLUSIVE: Harry Reid: 'Of Course' Medicare for All and Decriminalizing Border Crossings Are Bad Ideas." *Vice,* August 20, 2019, https://www.vice.com/en_us/article/ywadgw/exclusive-harry-reid-of-course- medicare-for-all-and-decriminalizing-border-crossings-are-bad-ideas

344   Scott Bixby, "Think Tank to Dems: Trump's Immigration Message Is Winning." *The Daily Beast,* July 22, 2019, https://www.thedailybeast.com/ center-for-american-progress-warns-dems-trump-is-winning-the-immigration- messaging-war?ref=home?ref=home?ref=home

345   Brie Stimson, "Axelrod Warns Medicare-for-All, Immigration Proposals Unpopular with Voters." *Fox News,* July 31, 2019, https://www.foxnews. com/politics/former-obama-aide-warns-dems-medicare-for-all-immigration- proposals-unpopular-with-democratic-voters

writers like Tom Friedman[346] all warned them they were distancing themselves too much to the average voter and it could cost them the general election against Trump. Despite calls to back down from those positions, the candidates only became more emboldened.

Without a Democratic Party working toward enforcing immigration law, Americans were stuck with only the Republicans and President Trump's administration to enforce the laws from 2016 onwards.

Trump offered strong rhetoric on the campaign trail, promising to enforce the laws, end illegal immigration, and build a wall along the border. It was music to the ears of millions of voters who saw their nation's laws being openly ignored and politicians advocating for special rules for law-breakers. Unfortunately, his efforts were thwarted for most of his first term as president by the Republicans in Congress, rogue district court judges, and his own staff.

Congressional Republicans offered no help to Trump when it came to changing immigration laws to close loopholes for illegal immigrants or alter the legal immigration system. Under Speaker Paul Ryan, who like his mentor Jack Kemp, supported mass immigration and amnesty, Congress did not close any loopholes or fund a border wall.[347] Despite the fact that voters handed Republicans the Congress and the Presidency, congressional Republicans insisted there was nothing they could do to deliver on immigration for the American public.

So, for two years, they focused on delivering corporate tax cuts and a rollback of business regulations that helped their

---

346   Thomas L Friedman, "Trump's Going to Get Re-Elected, Isn't He?" *The New York Times,* July 16, 2019, https://www.nytimes.com/2019/07/16/opinion/trump-2020.html?action=click&module=Opinion&pgtype=Homepage

347   Tara Golshan, "Paul Ryan Really Wishes the House Speaker Would Fix Immigration and the Debt." *Vox,* November 29, 2018, https://www.vox.com/2018/11/29/18118216/paul-ryan-regrets-immigration-debt

donors. It wasn't like they exactly had a lot of pushback from Trump's staff inside the White House.

Trump fired the chairman of his transition team, Governor Chris Christie, soon after he was elected due to a personal grudge between the New Jersey governor and the president's son-in-law.[348][349] Without a formal plan of how to hire the most competent staff that would be able to deliver on the president's campaign promises, staffers like Reince Priebus, Trump's first Chief of Staff, flooded the administration with personnel who despised Trump and worked tirelessly to halt his national populist agenda. So many members of Trump's staff weren't on board with the promises he made to voters that it was astounding. Among these rogue staff members was Trump's first legislative affairs director, Marc Short, who was paid over a million dollars to work against Trump during the election.[350] He misled the president on key pieces of immigration legislation[351] and didn't do any arm-twisting to push the president's immigration agenda through Congress.[352] There was also Trump's

---

348   Mary Louise Kelly. "Chris Christie: There Is No One With More Influence Over Trump Than Jared Kushner." *NPR*, January 29, 2019, https://www.npr.org/2019/01/29/689388865/chris-christie-there-is-no-one-with-more-influence-over-trump-than-jared-kushner

349   Aaron Blake, "Analysis: Ivanka Trump and Jared Kushner Are a Case Study in Why Nepotism Is Problematic." *The Washington Post*, March 12, 2019, https://www.washingtonpost.com/politics/2019/03/12/ivanka-trump-jared-kushner-are-case-study-why-nepotism-is-problematic/

350   Richard Eskow, et al., "Marc Short: Koch Dark-Money Operative Is Trump's Liaison to Congress." *Truthout*, January 24, 2017, https://truthout.org/articles/marc-short-koch-dark-money-operative-is-trump-s-liaison-to-congress/

351   Neil Munro, "Seven Ways Marc Short Stalled Donald Trump's Immigration Reforms." *Breitbart*, February 19, 2019, https://www.breitbart.com/politics/2019/02/19/seven-ways-marc-short-stalled-donald-trumps-immigration-reforms/

352   Matthew Nussbaum, et al., "Trump's Man on the Hill Tries Not to Make Promises He Can't Keep on Immigration," *POLITICO*, February 10, 2018, https://www.politico.com/story/2018/02/10/immigration-legislation-house-marc-short-398994

personal assistant Madeleine Westerhout, who cried in grief the night Trump was elected.[353] There were even low-level staffers including members of his office personnel like Courtney Mullen, who threw an End of the World party the night after Trump clinched the GOP nomination.[354]

Without help from Congress or a functioning White House, many of Trump's key immigration promises went unfulfilled, border apprehensions spiked to over one hundred thousand per month by March 2019,[355] and some of Trump's earliest supporters began abandoning him.

Realizing his avenues to institute change through Congress were limited, especially since Democrats won the House in 2018, the Trump administration forced rule changes out of existing regulations. Unbeknownst to most voters, there are a plethora of tough immigration laws already on the books that just haven't been properly enforced by past presidents. Though Congress could help the president by passing new laws, there's plenty at the executive branch's disposal to enforce immigration laws. Toward the third year of Trump's presidency, he began to cracking down on illegal immigration and pushing immigration enforcement through rule changes rather than working with Congress.

In 2019 alone, the Trump administration moved to end the Flores Settlement Agreement,[356] created a safe third country

353 Daniel Lippman, "Trump's Personal Assistant Fired after Comments about Ivanka, Tiffany." *POLITICO*, August 30, 2019, https://www.politico.com/story/2019/08/30/trumps-personal-assistant-fired-ivanka-tiffany-1479226

354 Steve Nelson, "White House Personnel Office Described Trump GOP Nomination as 'End of the World'." *The Washington Examiner*, March 23, 2019, https://www.washingtonexaminer.com/news/white-house/white-house-personnel-official-described-trump-gop-nomination-as-end-of-the-world

355 United States U.S. Customs and Border Protection, "Southwest Border Migration FY 2020," *U.S. Customs and Border Protection*, last modified December 9, 2019, https://www.cbp.gov/newsroom/stats/sw-border-migration

356 Katie Reilly and Madeleine Carlisle, "Trump Administration's Move to End Flores Agreement Rejected." *Time*, September 30, 2019, https://time.com/5657381/trump-administration-flores-agreement-migrant-children/

agreement with Guatemala,[357] ended in-person interpreters at immigration hearings,[358] instituted a policy that forced asylum seekers to remain in Mexico during their immigration proceedings which helped weed out phony asylum claims,[359, 360] expedited removal of illegal aliens who couldn't prove that they had been in the US continuously for two years,[361] limited asylum claims based on family relations,[362] and changed the public charge rule that barred legal immigrants from obtaining green cards if they used specific types of welfare programs over a certain period of time.[363]

These rule changes increased enforcement, caused border apprehensions to plummet, and moved the ball forward on long-term solutions to America's broken borders. As Trump began to incrementally make changes and enforce the law, fe-

357   Kirk Semple, "The U.S. and Guatemala Reached an Asylum Deal: Here's What It Means." *The New York Times,* July 29, 2019, https://www.nytimes.com/2019/07/28/world/americas/guatemala-safe-third-asylum.html

358   Tal Kopan, "Trump Administration Ending in-Person Interpreters at Immigrants' First Hearing." *San Francisco Chronicle,* July 3, 2019, https://www.sfchronicle.com/politics/article/Trump-administration-ending-in-person-14070403.php

359   Julian Aguilar, "Expansion of 'Remain in Mexico' Policy Brings Tension, Fear to Border Cities," *The Texas Tribune,* July 3, 2019, https://www.texastribune.org/2019/07/03/expansion-remain-mexico-policy-brings-tension-fear-border-cities/

360   Molly Hennessy-Fiske and Wendy Fry, "Stymied by U.S. Asylum Policies, Many Migrants on the Border Are Heading Home." *Los Angeles Times,* August 4, 2019, https://www.latimes.com/world-nation/story/2019-08-03/stymied-by-u-s-asylum-policies-many-migrants-on-the-border-are-heading-home

361   Jasmine Aguilera, "What to Know About DHS' New Expedited Removal' Rule." *Time,* July 23, 2019, https://time.com/5632671/undocumented-immigrants-expedited-removal/

362   Ted Hesson and Josh Gerstein, "DOJ Restricts Asylum Claims Based on Family Relations." *POLITICO,* July 29, 2019, https://www.politico.com/story/2019/07/29/doj-asylum-claims-family-relations-1624028

363   Aaron Rupar, "Why the Trump Administration Is Going after Low-Income Immigrants, Explained by an Expert," *Vox,* August 12, 2019, https://www.vox.com/2019/8/12/20802613/trump-public-charge-immigration-rule-change-explained-marielena-hincapie

deral judges issued a series of nationwide injunctions to stop him. Using the power of the judiciary, they acted as the last line of obstruction against Trump's agenda. Judges, mostly appointed by Democrat presidents, issued more nationwide injunctions on Trump than had been placed on the first forty US presidents combined.[364]

So, momentum continues to go in the right direction so long as Trump is president, but he's still a long way from achieving the victories he promised his voters. Illegal border crossings are still higher than they were under most of Obama's presidency, and illegal aliens continue to ignore federal immigration law, with the number of illegal aliens skipping their court date doubling from 2013 to 2017.[365] Most horrifying of all is the fact that the next Democrat president will almost surely be forced into a position of not enforcing immigration law at all.

Although Democrats continue to embrace the ideology of open borders and fret over what will happen to illegal aliens who are forced to respect the US' immigration laws, they should be more concerned over what the American people will do if Trump fails to deliver like Abbott, Salvini, and Netanyahu. It's very much possible that the next person the American people turn to will be more hawkish on controlling the border and have the political wherewithal to actually get it done.

CHAPTER 5

LEGAL IMMIGRATION

IMMIGRATION IS THE single biggest motivating factor leading to the national populist revolution across the world. While it is not the only issue, it is the universal unifying element that has been rousing the masses on every continent against globalism. Immigration is the single most important issue facing democracies across the world because it affects all other foreign and domestic policy.

If immigration is done correctly, it can enrich a society's culture, stimulate its economy, and better the lives of its citizens. If it's done haphazardly, it can increase economic frustrations, fuel cultural anxiety, drastically change a nation's politics, and eat away at social capital. It is uniquely complicated because it can never be fully reversed and is entirely tied to the character of anthropological features of both the host nation and the newly received immigrants.

A nation can come back from many failed policies: a lost war, an economic recession, and a devaluation of currency. Yet a country can never come back from an immigration policy that exacerbates human beings' tribal instincts and erodes their cultural and national character.

A nation's choice of what kind of immigration policy it's pursuing today is undeniably linked to that country's political, cultural, and economic destiny. Harvard Professor Nathan Nunn said, "The primary thing that migrants brought with them is themselves...along with the settlers (and migrants) also came their beliefs and values regarding freedom, liberty, equality, and the appropriate role of government."[366]

It's understandable that for millions of people, dialogue centered around immigration policy is tethered to their emotions. A majority of people who are reading our book are either immigrants or the descendants of immigrants. That is especially true of people living in the Americas, all of whom are either the descendants of indigenous tribes, settlers, slaves, or immigrants, with the latter making up the largest portion of the population.

For Americans especially, immigration has been romanticized with the images of 19th and early 20th-century European immigrants looking at the Statue of Liberty as they enter the new world in search of freedom. More recently, it's been portrayed by stories of Asian or Hispanic immigrants waiting decades to enter the US only to take a menial labor job just with the hopes of creating a better life for their families. Europeans have also been barraged with stories of refugees fleeing oppressive regimes that threaten their lives and those of their loved ones.

Lost in these narratives is the question of how a nation's immigration policy is beneficial to citizens already living in that country. The governing elite treats the effects of immigration on

---

366   Nathan Nunn, "Culture and the Historical Process," *National Bureau of Economic Research*, (Cambridge: 2012).

the native population of most Western societies as inconsequential, yet they are—in many respects—what's driving the current rebellion against neoliberalism across the world.

In most countries, people very clearly want lower levels of immigration and some type of assimilation by their new citizens. Voters in Western democracies have been signaling to this message to their governing class for decades.

The demand for reforming immigration in Western countries is stronger now than it has been in over a century. An unlikely reason for this is because the internet and social media have increased the visibility of the effects of mass immigration across the West. Incidents like the Muslim grooming gangs in the UK, terrorist attacks in France, the New Year's Eve rapes committed by migrants in Germany, MS-13 gangs in the US, and the tens of thousands of migrant boats in Australia are no longer isolated incidents, the West is very aware that on every continent, their culture is being changed by mass immigration. People living thousands of miles from each other all feel mutually under attack as the descendants of the European continent and Western civilization. This global declining demographic awareness has lent itself to increasing racial anxieties even where racial diversity isn't very strong. We're going coin this phenomenon as Western degeneration awareness, the fact that Western people are becoming alert to the fact that the elites of their country are supporting policies that are irrevocably altering their societies without their consent and their only course of action is to support national populist parties.

That's why national populist parties are succeeding in countries like Hungary, Finland, and Poland which have a very small foreign-born population and have been basically immune from the wave of Islamic terrorist attacks that have swept through Europe. Westerners across the world are aware that their demographic future may look nothing like their past and it is causing warranted concerns, anger, anxiety, and fear.

This trend of demanding lower levels of immigration started long before the creation of the internet, the European refugee crisis, or any other recent events. Polls have shown that people across the globe have demanded lower levels of immigration for quite some time, but politicians in the governing elite have refused to comply.

Standing in the way of a more restrictive immigration policy is the destructive forces of corporate giants and the dueling ideologies of neoliberalism and woke progressivism. The ruling class is married to these ideas and special interest groups either because they believe in the ideology of open borders and racial justice or because they financially benefit from mass immigration.

Neoliberalism, which is the ideology practiced by a majority of the elites especially in center-right and center-left parties, holds that the world should be more interconnected and interdependent. Neoliberals have benefited from globalization more than any other segment of society, so they overly value the merits of international organizations like the UN and NATO, trade deals, and the cheap labor that comes from mass immigration. Neoliberals believe that without their ideology and its adherents, the world is a dark and dangerous place. Although they benefit from living in stable Western nations, they don't value Western culture, and they believe that people are interchangeable as long as they hold the same values.

To neoliberals, any debate on immigration must be on their terms, regardless of the fact that many of their chief points are clichés and straw man arguments. Those include the views that diversity is a strength, America is a nation of immigrants, immigrants do the jobs citizens won't do, those who question mass immigration have racist motives, Hispanics are natural Republicans, parties and politicians who want to restrict immigration are far-right, a moderate approach to immigration is amnesty for illegals and increasing legal immigration, and so forth.

American neoliberals hold that any immigration policy must conform to Emma Lazarus's poem that's featured on the Statue of Liberty.

Beside neoliberals are indoctrinated progressives, who have become radicalized on the issue of race and, by proxy, immigration. The new left centered in major cosmopolitan areas have experienced what *Vox* writer Matthew Yglesias defined as a great awokening[367] where white liberals have moved so far to the left on questions of race and racism that they are now, on these issues, to the left of even the typical black voter.

An overwhelming 87 percent of white liberals in America believe that increasing the number of people from different races, ethnic groups, and nationalities make the country a better place—more than any other racial identity group, including blacks and Hispanics. The ANES 2018 Pilot Survey found that white liberals were the only racial group in America to have a negative feeling of warmth toward their own racial and ethnic in-group members. In other words, while blacks will have positive feelings toward other blacks, Asians to Asians, Hispanics to Hispanics, white liberals have a negative reaction toward fellow white people.

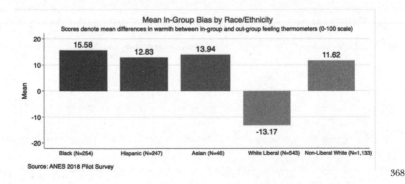

Mean In-Group Bias by Race/Ethnicity
Scores denote mean differences in warmth between in-group and out-group feeling thermometers (0-100 scale)

Source: ANES 2018 Pilot Survey

368

---

368   Zach Goldberg, "America's White Saviors." *Tablet Magazine,* June 6, 2019, https://www.tabletmag.com/jewish-news-and-politics/284875/americas-white-saviors

Believing that diversity is always good and having warm feelings toward out-groups over in-groups obviously affects the way white liberals feel about immigration policy. Polling data from 1965 showed that less than 10 percent of white liberals supported increasing legal immigration; that number doubled in the late 2000s and early 2010s and rapidly increased to over 50 percent by 2018.[369]

Studies showed that white liberal Democrats are more concerned with issues of race, immigration, and identity even more than nonwhites, who were more interested in issues like jobs and taxes.[370] These opinions weren't just for highly educated Democrats living in urban areas. Even working-class white Democrats' opinions on race and immigration were far to the left of Independents and Republicans who shared their economic interests.[371] These factors have made the Democrat Party radicalized on the subject.

Any attempt to reform immigration in a way that would reduce the number of nonwhites coming into the US would clearly not be a desirable outcome because they have higher feelings of empathy for nonwhites over whites. Such thinking is why liberals in America have such a negative reaction to Trump whenever he even attempted to alter the nation's immigration laws: to them, it's a matter of orthodoxy and not policy. It's not a question of how many immigrants a country takes in per

---

369   Ibid.

370   Thomas Edsall, "The Democratic Party Is Actually Three Parties." *The New York Times,* July 24, 2019, https://www.nytimes.com/2019/07/24/opinion/2020-progressive-candidates.html?fbclid=IwAR1MYNYUJYRaRwD6AyJQuRrK1BROxkCafgFQG7tihbCKCHP963hBls2ZAHo

371   Thomas Edsall, "There Are Really Two Distinct White Working Classes." *The New York Times,* June 26, 2019, https://www.nytimes.com/2019/06/26/opinion/pelosi-white-working-class.html?rref=collection%2Fbyline%2Fthomas-b.-edsall&action=click&contentCollection=undefined&region=stream&module=stream_unit&version=latest&contentPlacement=1&pgtype=collection

year and how they affect the native population, but instead a question of whether or not they're a secularly moral person. The Democratic Party's position on immigration has become centered on the ideology of white saviors and their woke orthodoxy, which is as sacrosanct to them as the Holy Trinity is to Catholics.

Left-wing parties were also motivated politically to embrace mass immigration due to the fact that immigrants and their descendants vote heavily for left-wing parties like Labour in the UK and the Democrats in the US.

For example, in the 2016 election, Hillary Clinton beat Trump in the popular vote by 2.87 million votes. This became a regular talking point on the left to justify that Clinton should have been president instead of Trump; however, according to exit polls, Trump beat Clinton by a margin of 49 to 45 percent among native-born Americans. Clinton made up for this loss by winning naturalized immigrants by a margin of thirty-three points.[372]

While talking heads have blamed Trump for the growing shift among immigrants toward the Democrat Party, those trends predate his presidency. Analysis conducted by these authors found that Democrats steadily increased their share of the vote in eighty of the 109 counties[373] that transformed from majority white in 2000 to majority minority in 2018.

Counties in Georgia were especially affected as they went from majority white and supporting former President George W. Bush by over 60 percent of the vote in 2000 to becoming minority-majority and supporting Obama and Clinton in

---

[372]   "National President Exit Polls," CNN, November 23, 2016, https://www.cnn.com/election/2016/results/exit-polls

[373]   Jens Manuel Krogstad, "Reflecting a Demographic Shift, 109 U.S. Counties Have Become Majority Nonwhite since 2000." *Pew Research Center,* August 21, 2019, https://www.pewresearch.org/fact-tank/2019/08/21/u-s-counties-majority-nonwhite/

2012 and 2016. The only areas that became significantly more Republican were rural ones where a majority of the immigrant population were noncitizens and came to work in agriculture or the food industry. Places like Titus and Calhoun, Texas; Eddy, New Mexico; Telfair, Georgia, and Cherokee, Oklahoma voted more for Trump as a protest to mass immigration that changed their communities.

US County	2016 Trump Victory Margin	2000 Bush Victory Margin
Titus County, Texas	+41.5%	+24.5%
Eddy County, New Mexico	+41.3%	+18.1%
Calhoun County, Texas	+36.5%	+14.5%
Telfair County, Georgia	+29.9%	−2.4%
Cherokee County, Oklahoma	+27.5%	−2.4%

Democrats almost willingly abandoned these communities as they saw their future in the urban diversity of megacities, not in the working-class Rust Belt of their past. Democrats were not alone in this belief.

The same is true for the UK's Labour Party, which in 2018 found itself losing its hold on working-class parliamentary seats but for the first time ever won every seat in hub cities like Bristol, Cardiff, Leeds, Sheffield, and Manchester as young voters and ethnic minorities flocked to Jeremy Corbyn's party.[374]

Neoliberals and woke progressives have made immigration restriction a taboo subject to most centrist parties, with few exceptions like the Social Democrats in Denmark and the Labour Party of New Zealand, all of whom took hawkish immigration policies either during their campaign or after they were elected in 2019.

Elite institutions that pride themselves on not being associated with their fellow working-class citizens have equally become engulfed in the great awokening. For example, the phrase melting pot is considered a microaggression by the administrators in the University of California system[375] and the term illegal immigrant has been banned from major news outlets like *USA Today*, *The Los Angeles Times*, and *The Associated Press* since 2013.[376] This divide on immigration has only steepened the divide between coastal anywheres and rooted somewheres.

Politically, the left-wing parties' ambition to get diversity at all costs and the right-wing parties' need to deliver their vision of globalism that benefited their economic class fueled much-needed energy behind national populist parties.

It's arguable that had the traditional center-right and center-left neoliberal parties not been so rigid in their need to defend of globalism, politicians like Salvini, Trump, and Le Pen wouldn't have catapulted toward the top of the polls. Their refusal to negotiate on this issue allowed national populists to argue that their nation was ruled by a distant governing class that didn't care about people like them.

IMMIGRATION: SAFE, LEGAL, AND RARE

Voters inclined to support national populists on the subject of illegal immigration believe that the ruling elite have abdicated their responsibility to defend their nation's sovereignty, enforce their laws, and control their borders. Illegal immigration has been responsible for national populist uprisings across the world.

Legal immigration, however, is a much more important issue when it comes to the rise of national populism. It is the

---

375 Robby Soave, "The University of California's Insane Speech Police." *The Daily Beast*, June 22, 2015, https://www.thedailybeast.com/ the-university-of-californias-insane-speech-police?ref=home

376 Emily Guskin, "Illegal, 'Undocumented,' 'Unauthorized': News Media Shift Language on Immigration." *Pew Research Center*, June 17, 2013, https:// www.pewresearch.org/fact-tank/2013/06/17/illegal-undocumented-unauthorized-news-media-shift-language-on-immigration/

defining issue that separates most national populist parties from other center-right alternatives. National populists across the globe desire an immigration policy that mirrors the way Democrats in America felt about abortion in the mid-'90s when President Bill Clinton said it should safe, legal, and rare.[377]

Immigration is one of the issues that is both politically and socially divisive, where the anywheres and the somewheres have drastically different opinions over the effects immigration is having on their country and the appropriate levels their nation should be absorbing.

A 2017 survey by Chatham House on ten EU countries (Austria, Belgium, France, Germany, Greece, Hungary, Italy, Poland, Spain, and the UK) found that 57 percent of elites believed immigration had been good for the country, but only 25 percent of the public felt the same way. While 58 percent of the elites felt that immigration enhanced their nation's cultural life, only 32 percent of the public felt this way. The elites are also less likely to believe that mass immigration has brought crime or put a strain on social services.[378]

That's really where the divide over immigration lies: the elite and the people differ on how immigration benefits their nation's culture, strains social services, has negative economic repercussions on workers, and if they bring crime. College-educated cosmopolitans live in a far different reality than that of those without college educations living in the suburbs and small towns, and this trend has been going on for decades.

In the United States, polls consistently showed for over forty years, Americans wanted their politicians to decrease legal immigration levels. The Gallup survey, for example, showed that

---

377   Hillary Clinton, *Living History*, Simon & Schuster (New York: 2003) p.431.

378   Thomas Raines, et al., "The Future of Europe: Comparing Public and Elites Attitudes." *Chatham House*, September 5, 2019, https://www.chathamhouse.org/publication/future-europe-comparing-public-and-elite-attitudes

a majority or plurality of Americans has supported reducing immigration levels nearly every year from 1971 to 2015. [379] During that entire time, politicians in both parties increased legal immigration; the US foreign population ballooned from 9.6 million to 42.4 million over that period.[380]

The tricky thing about polls when it comes to immigration is that most Americans don't know how many legal immigrants come into the country every year. So, when a Harvard/Harris poll in 2018 asked people what their ideal number of immigrants annually would be, only 19 percent said that the US should import one million immigrants or more annually, which about the current number. A majority, 54 percent, said they prefer 500,000 or less, which would be about a 50 percent reduction in overall numbers.[381] Another poll from 2018 conducted by the Public Religion Research Institute has similar findings, with 51 percent of Americans supporting restricting the level of legal immigration.[382]

One thing above all others is clear: Americans have believed for a long time that the immigration system is broken, and they've known that it didn't need a couple of quick fixes but a complete overhaul. A 2007 *New York Times* poll found that 89 percent of Americans believed the US immigration

379   Jeffrey M. Jones, "New High in U.S. Say Immigration Most Important Problem." *Gallup*, October 7, 2019, https://news.gallup.com/poll/259103/new-high-say-immigration-important-problem.aspx

380   Jie Zong and Jeanne Batalova, "Frequently Requested Statistics on Immigrants and Immigration in the United States," *Migration Policy Institute*, April 14, 2016, https://www.migrationpolicy.org/article/frequently-requested-statistics-immigrants-and-immigration-united-states-5

381   "Monthly Harvard-Harris Poll: January 2018 Re-Field," *Harvard Harris*, January 20, 2018, http://harvardharrispoll.com/wp-content/uploads/2018/01/Final_HHP_Jan2018-Refield_RegisteredVoters_XTab.pdf

382   Daniel Cox, et al., "Partisan Polarization Dominates Trump Era: Findings from the 2018 American Values Survey," *PRRI*, October 29, 2018, https://www.prri.org/research/partisan-polarization-dominates-trump-era-findings-from-the-2018-american-values-survey/

system needed to be completely rebuilt or fundamentally changed.[383] The poll also found that 72 percent of Americans wanted either some restrictions on who could enter the US or a full immigration moratorium. Just 24 percent wanted no restrictions at all on immigration.

This desire of voters to reduce legal levels of immigration wasn't confined to the US; countries with fairly low foreign-born populations like Brazil wanted to see the numbers decrease as well. A 2018 poll of Brazilians found that 67 percent wanted to reduce legal immigration despite the fact that just 4 percent of people living in Brazil were foreign-born. An Ipsos study found that 35 percent of Brazilians believed there were too many immigrants in their country.[384]

In most countries, a majority or plurality of voters with large national populist parties or leaders believe the population of immigrants is far too high, including 66 percent of Italians, 61 percent of Belgians, 53 percent of French, 53 percent of Indians, 50 percent of Germans, 48 percent of Americans, 48 percent of Swedes, 46 percent of Hungarians, and 44 percent of New Zealanders.

The political elite in Europe and the US saw the rising tide of opposition to mass immigration and paid lip service to voters' concerns with promises that they would fight multiculturalism, reduce immigration levels, and end illegal immigration. Yet these proved to be empty promises as time and time again, voters went to the polls hoping that their government would lower immigration levels and despite their wishes, neoliberals continued to flood their countries with foreigners.

---

383   "Immigration Reform," *CBS News/New York Times*, May 24, 2007, https://www. cbsnews.com/htdocs/pdf/052407_immigration.pdf

384   "Global Views on Immigration and the Refugee Crisis," Ipsos, July 8, 2017, https://www.ipsos.com/sites/default/files/ct/news/documents/2017-09/ Global%20%40dvisor_Immigration_Slides%20-%20US%20Deck%20FINAL. pdf

This gave openings to candidates like Pat Buchanan, Jean-Marie Le Pen, Pauline Hanson, Jörg Haider, and Pim Fortuyn to make an impact in their respected countries. Some won and some lost, but they moved the needle and showed that the establishment parties were vulnerable on the subject of immigration.

In succession, three things happened that would move national populists from the fringe of the political arena to their current place at the center. First, the establishment in most countries failed to do anything meaningful on the subject of immigration, which eroded trust in democratic institutions because the governing class was too attached to ideology and special interests; secondly, social media and the internet brought attention to Western degeneration awareness; and lastly, national populist parties started to moderate their tone and image.

It was much easier for French citizens to vote for a Marine Le Pen who embraced gays and moved away from topics like the Holocaust and the Algerian War than it was for them to vote for her father who seemed set on being portrayed as a national villain. The same is true with Donald Trump, who held an LGBTQ+ flag at a rally and talked about protecting gays and lesbians from Islamic extremists. Matteo Salvini saw the same phenomenon in Italy as he moved Lega away from being a separatist movement in the north to being a national party.

Even a nation like Sweden, which has a long and rich tradition of being tolerant and open to diversity, saw a major backlash by voters who tired of mass immigration. By the 2010s, these voters moved their support from both the center-right Moderate Party and the center-left Social Democrat Party toward the national populists Swedish Democrats, a party that decades in the past had been considered the home of white nationalists until four Gen-Xers led by Jimmie Åkesson[385] cleaned house and moved the party away from the extremists.[386]

These events allowed voters in country after country to cast their fears of being affiliated with far-right organizations and support outsiders advocating for their interests on immigration and against globalization. For a long time, the media and the establishment pushed the voters those to the side as fringe, racist, or insignificant until their numbers were too large that they could no longer be ignored.

As mentioned above, the entire debate on immigration is centered around the subjects of culture, economics, and crime. They are what's fueling almost the entire national populist movement.

CULTURE, IDENTITY, AND SOCIAL COHESION

Of all the changes brought on by mass immigration, the transformation of a nation-state's culture seems to have the most profound political effect in moving voters toward national populist parties.

Human beings, regardless of color or creed, are naturally tribal and cling to a common culture as part of their identity. Institutions use a common culture as a way to form social cohesion and build social capital that allows societies to engage with one another, build trust, and it is the bedrock of most democratic systems. If people feel like their shared culture and

---

385   Laila Ø. Bakken, Fra kjelleren til Riksdagen, Norsk Rikskringkasting AS, September 26, 2010, https://www.nrk.no/urix/fra-nazimarsj-til-riksdagen-1.7304305

386   Jens Rydgren, et al., "Radical right-wing voters from right and left: Comparing Sweden Democrat voters who previously voted for the Conservative Party or the Social Democratic Party." *Scandinavian Political Studies/Volume 42, issue 3–4,* July 21, 2019, https://onlinelibrary.wiley.com/doi/full/10.1111/1467-9477.12147

beliefs are under assault and that their institutions have either failed or abandoned them, they can revert back to being tribal.

This is the state of many Western societies as demographic changes brought on by mass immigration are vastly altering nations' ethnic composition, straining the foundation of many institutions and eroding social cohesion.

Too often, analysts, politicians, and economists speak of immigrants and immigration as merely a numbers game of how to increase GDP or alter the labor pool. Culture, identity, and national borders are secondary thoughts to neoliberals and the consequences of altering them have gone without proper analysis. As the Catholic Cardinal Robert Sarah put it, neoliberalism promotes a mixing that is designed to erode the natural borders of homelands and cultures and leads to a post-national and one-dimensional world where the only things that matter are consumption and production.[387] Social science and learned experience tell us that human beings, however, are not just units of the economy and changes because of mass immigration come at huge social costs.

The increased diversity brought on by mass immigration has changed the fabric of many societies in multidimensional ways. Some of those have been welcomed by most people; for example, the increased options in areas of food, art, and architecture are generally appreciated. However, while diversity is the spice of life, in excess it can also breed social isolation. Professor at Harvard Robert Putnam wrote in his 2006 essay E Pluribus Unum: Diversity and Community in the Twenty-First Century that over generations, diversity is a good thing, but in the short-term, it could be extremely detrimental for

---

387   Staff Reporter, "Cardinal Sarah: Every Nation Has a Right to Distinguish between Refugees and Economics Migrants." *The Catholic Herald*, October 24, 2017, https://catholicherald.co.uk/news/2017/10/24/cardinal-sarah-every-nation-has-a-right-to-distinguish-between-refugees-and-economic-migrants/

social cohesion and erodes social capital. People are less likely to engage with each other, trust each other, and maintain community institutions.[388]

The Social Capital Community Benchmark Survey conducted in 2000 found that greater diversity not only caused a lack of trust among people of different races, nationalities, and ethnicities, it also created a lack of trust in homogeneous groups. Other international studies have also found that greater ethnic diversity not only reduces social capital but also decreases the amount people want to invest both personally and financially in public goods.[389, 390, 391, 392, 393]

American Millennials and Generation Z are the most diverse and progressive generations in their country's history, and yet according to a Pew Research study from 2019, they are the least trusting of society and each other, with 60 percent of those under thirty years old stating most people can't be trusted and 71 percent believing most people would take advantage of you if they got a chance.[394] This is a much different opinion than older and less diverse generations, who are far more trusting of people.

---

388   Robert Putnam, "E Pluribus Unum: Diversity and Community in the Twenty-first Century," *Scandinavian Political Studies/ Volume 30, Issue 2,* June 15, 2007.

389   James M. Poterba, "Demographic Structure and the Political Economy of Public Education." *Journal of Policy Analysis and Management/ Volume 6, Issue 1,* December 7, 1998.

390   Alesina, Alberto, and Eliana La Ferrara. "Who Trusts Others?" *Journal of Public Economics 85,* 2002, p. 207–34.

391   Andrew Leigh. "Trust, Inequality and Ethnic Heterogeneity." *The Economic Record. 82.,* 2006, p. 268–280.

392   Rachel Pennet, "Diversity, Trust and Community Participation in England." Home Office, 2005.

393   Peter Dinesen, Merlin Schaeffer, and Kim Sønderskov, "Ethnic Diversity and Social Trust: A Narrative and Meta," *Analytical Review,* (2019).

394   John Gramlich, "Young Americans Are Less Trusting of Other People – and Key Institutions – than Their Elders." *Pew Research Center,* August 6, 2019, https://www.pewresearch.org/fact-tank/2019/08/06/young-americans-are-less-trusting-of-other-people-and-key-institutions-than-their-elders/

The feeling of widespread social isolation has become commonplace across Western societies and while immigration is not the only factor for this growing alienation, other societal and technological changes are also to blame, it certainly plays a part.

A 2016 PRRI/*The Atlantic* survey found that 48 percent of white working-class voters felt like things have changed so much that I often feel like a stranger in my own country. A smaller but sizable 26 percent of white college-educated voters felt the same.[395] When asked if the American way of life needed to be protected from foreign influence, 68 percent of the white working class and 44 percent of college-educated whites agreed. Among black Americans, the number was identical to working-class whites: 48 percent felt like they were strangers in their own country.[396] A plurality of Americans believed that new immigrants were a threat to traditional American customs and values, with 62 percent of white working-class voters agreeing with that opinion.

Which is why they gravitated to Trump's message of Make America Great Again and his campaign promises to Build That Wall, ban Muslims from immigrating to America, demand immigrants obtain an ideological certificate to ensure they share a mutual love for the county, end birthright citizenship, create a merit-based immigration system, and reduce the overall number of legal immigrants brought to the US every

---

395   Daniel Cox, et al., "Beyond Economics: Fear of Cultural Displacement Pushed the White Working Class to Trump," *PRRI,* May 9, 2017, https://www.prri.org/research/white-working-class-attitudes-economy-trade-immigration-election-donald-trump/

396   Emily Badger, "Estranged in America: Both Sides Feel Lost and Left Out." *The New York Times,* October 4, 2018, https://www.nytimes.com/2018/10/04/upshot/estranged-america-trump-polarization.html

year.[397] This hawkish position on immigration and defending American culture allowed Trump to have his own path to the Republican nomination, with 60 percent of primary voters who said immigration was their most important issue casting their ballots for him.[398]

This feeling of estrangement and anger over mass immigration played into Trump's favor and brought an impressive loyalty to Trump among his base. Nearly two-thirds of Trump voters and half of all working-class white voters and 27 percent of college-educated whites believed that the 2016 election was the last chance to save America.[399]

A study by the International Organization for Migration found that the year prior to the election, a plurality of Americans demanded that their leaders reduce immigration levels. Over 40 percent of Americans wanted to immigration numbers reduced, while only 23 percent wanted them increased, which was much higher than the global average.[400]

The feeling of social isolation due to mass immigration wasn't unique to Americans. A 2016 YouGov poll found that citizens of Western Europe were also increasingly feeling that the high level of foreigners living in their country after the refugee crisis was making them feel like strangers in their homeland.[401]

---

397   "Immigration Reform That Will Make America Great Again," *DonaldJTrump. com,* August 16, 2015, https://assets.donaldjtrump.com/Immigration-Reform-Trump.pdf

398   Harry Enten and Perry Bacon Jr., "Trump's Hardline Immigration Stance Got Him to The White House." *Five Thirty Eight,* September 12, 2017, https://fivethirtyeight.com/features/why-polls-showing-daca-as-popular-even-among-republicans-dont-tell-the-whole-story/

399   Betsy Cooper, et al., "Nearly One in Five Clinton Voters Say Husband or Partner Didn't Vote." *PRRI,* December 1, 2016, https://www.prri.org/research/prri-atlantic-poll-post-election-white-working-class/

400   Neli Esipova, et al., "How The World Views Migration," *International Organization of Migration,* 2015.

401   Matthew Smith Lead, "37% Of Britons Say Immigration Has Meant That Where They Live Doesn't Feel Like Home Any More." *YouGov.* December 5, 2016, https://yougov.co.uk/topics/politics/articles-reports/2016/12/05/many-europeans-say-immigration-has-meant-they-dont

The poll found that 52 percent of Italians, 47 percent of French, 44 percent of Germans, 38 percent of Spanish, 37 percent of Brits, 36 percent of Dutch, and 33 percent of Swedes felt they were a stranger in their own country. Countries with more controlled levels of immigration including Denmark and Poland had lower levels of citizens feeling estranged.

A study of five democracies found that workers who voted for national populist parties and candidates like Marine Le Pen in France or Geert Wilders in the Netherlands were driven by the desire to reduce the influence of immigration on their culture and voice their disapproval of the political establishment. Workers who were anxious about immigration were seven times more likely than those who were not to vote for national populists.[402]

An Ipsos-MORI global survey showed that citizens in every country that experienced a surge of national populism over the last few years had a negative opinion about the impact of immigrants on their nation.[403] The countries with the most amount of people willing to say immigrants had a very positive or fairly positive impact on their societies were Indians (44 percent) and Brits (40 percent) and the countries where they were least likely to say that were Hungary (5 percent) and Italy (10 percent).

Furthermore, a large majority or plurality of citizens agreed with the statement, "Immigration is causing my country to change in ways that I don't like" including 63 percent of Italians, 49 percent of French and Indians, 46 percent of people living

---

402   Daniel Oesch, "Explaining Workers' Support for Right-Wing Populist Parties in Western Europe: Evidence from Austria, Belgium, France, Norway, and Switzerland." *International Political Science Review*, 2008, p.349–373. https://journals.sagepub.com/doi/pdf/10.1177/0192512107088390

403   "Global Views on Immigration and the Refugee Crisis," Ipsos, September 2017, https://www.slideshare.net/IpsosMORI/global-views-on-immigration-and-the-refugee-crisis-79730333/1

in Spain and the US, 45 percent of Germans and Australians, 44 percent of Swedes, and 43 percent of Brits.

Anyone who understood the sociological effects of mass immigration could see that coming. While Westerners feel responsible to take in foreigners fleeing from violence and war, they desire an immigration policy that brings in people from similar backgrounds to their own who can assimilate into society.

A university study from 2008, about a decade before the largest wave of national populist parties, examined dozens of immigration surveys in twenty-five countries in Europe, Canada, Australia and America found that most people in countries like Poland, Italy, Denmark, Australia, Sweden, and Germany believed immigrants should be religiously homogenous to their host country. Meaning that they should share basic Christian values. Furthermore, in nearly every country that was examined, citizens felt that immigrants should have a cultural homogeneity. America stood as the most accepting of diversity, but still, about 40 percent agreed that immigrants should share similar traditions and cultures and nearly 80 percent believed immigrants should speak English.[404]

Citizens of host nations demanding more cultural and religious homogeneity should not be confused with them having a racial preference. Every nation sampled in that study found that only a minority of people wanted their immigrants to be exclusively white. Meaning that people didn't care about an immigrant's race as much as they did about their ability to assimilate culturally into society.

This desire on the part of European countries to only take in people with similar backgrounds especially affected their opinions of their countries taking in large populations of Muslims. A study by the Chatham House in 2017 found that

---

404   Jack Citrin and John Sides, "Immigration and the Imagined
        Community in Europe and the United States." *Political Studies: 2008
        Volume 56,* 2008, p. 33-56.

a plurality or majority of people in ten European countries believed that all immigration from mainly Muslim countries should be stopped, including 64 percent of Belgians, 53 percent of Germans, 58 percent of Greeks, 41 percent of Spanish, 61 percent of French, 51 percent of Italians, 65 percent of Austrians, 47 percent of Brits, 64 percent of Hungarians, and 71 percent of Poles.[405]

The keyword in that survey was stopped, not reduced or slowed down. Large majorities of Europeans across the continent wanted no more Muslim immigration.

Americans, though more favorable to immigrants than Europeans, also said that the US was taking in too many immigrants from certain places like Latin America and Arab countries.[406]

All of these trends were well before the wave of nationalist victories that followed Brexit and politicians in the West began reading the tea leaves. National populists saw a series of small victories, like when the Danish People's Party became part of a coalition government in 2001 by promising voters they'd reduce immigration numbers when Geert Wilders's Party for Freedom entered the Dutch Parliament in 2006 on a platform of stopping the influence of Islam in the Netherlands, and when the Swedish Democrats entered the Riksdag in 2010 on a platform of stopping immigrants from raiding the welfare state. There was no denying that a movement was happening on the right.

As the governing class began understanding that voters were lashing out at mass immigration, some of them began changing their rhetoric on immigration. Senator John McCain, who had a long track record of supporting mass immigration

405   Matthew Goodwin, et al., "What Do Europeans Think
       About Muslim Immigration?" *Chatham House*, December 7,
       2018, https://www.chathamhouse.org/expert/comment/
       what-do-europeans-think-about-muslim-immigration
406   "Huddled Masses: Public Opinion & the 1965 U.S. Immigration Act
       blog." *Roper Center*, July 10, 2015, https://ropercenter.cornell.edu/blog/
       huddled-masses-public-opinion-1965-us-immigration-act-blog

and amnesty, campaigned for president on a platform that included build the dang fence, a promise he never prioritized in the Senate.[407] In the early part of the 2010s, German Chancellor Angela Merkel, French President Nicolas Sarkozy, and British Prime Minister David Cameron all declared that multiculturalism had failed.[408]

To show they were serious, Sarkozy would go on to introduce a burqa ban[409] and Cameron promised, though never delivered on, reducing net immigration into the UK.[410] Merkel continued her rhetoric against multiculturalism even as she opened the doors to over a million refugees, saying it was a grand delusion and demanding that Syrians assimilate.[411]

Aside from the change in rhetoric, policy stayed much the same and mass immigration continued with little reason or support among Europeans. One of the biggest advocates behind this rapid demographic change was Cameron's predecessor.

Former prime minister, Tony Blair vastly increased the number of migrants immigrating to the UK from 326,100 in 1997 to 582,100 in 2004[412] and framed it around the need

---

407   Jane C. Timm, "Far Right to McCain: 'You Said Build the Dang Fence, Where's the Fence?'" *NBC News*, February 26, 2013, http://www.nbcnews.com/id/50874570/t/far-right-mccain-you-said-build-dang-fence-wheres-fence/

408   Tom Heneghan, "Sarkozy Joins Allies Burying Multiculturalism." Reuters, February 11, 2011, https://www.reuters.com/article/us-france-sarkozy-multiculturalism-idUSTRE71A4UP20110211

409   "Nicolas Sarkozy: Burqa Not Welcome in France." *The Telegraph,* June 22, 2009, https://www.telegraph.co.uk/news/worldnews/europe/france/5603070/Nicolas-Sarkozy-burqa-not-welcome-in-France.html

410   "Immigration Policy 'Hasn't Worked so Far', Says David Cameron." *BBC News,* October 6, 2015, https://www.bbc.com/news/uk-politics-34453674

411   Ryan Grenoble, "Angela Merkel Calls Multiculturalism 'A Grand Delusion'." *HuffPost,* December 15, 2015, https://www.huffpost.com/entry/angela-merkel-germany-multiculturalism_n_566f2e15e4b0fccee16f7757

412   Will Somerville, "The Immigration Legacy of Tony Blair." *Migration Policy,* July 19, 2019, https://www.migrationpolicy.org/article/immigration-legacy-tony-blair

for his country to make macroeconomic gains. Despite the narrative created by the government at the time, former Blair advisor Andrew Neather admitted in 2009 that the reason the former prime minister increased immigration was mostly politically motivated. Blair wanted to alter the ethnic character of the UK and rub the Right's nose in diversity.[413]

Blair got both his wishes. British cities like Birmingham, Leicester, Luton, and Slough all become minority-majority, and white Britons became a minority for the first time ever in London. These new immigrants ended up being solid voters for Blair's party, with about 77 percent voting Labour in 2015 and 2017.[414]

Even famed British comedian John Cleese noticed the change, tweeting in 2019, "Some years ago I opined that London was not really an English city any more. Since then, virtually all my friends from abroad have confirmed my observation, so there must be some truth to it...I note also that London was the UK city that voted most strongly to remain in the EU."[415]

Yet this vast ethnic change due to mass immigration did not come without a political blowback for the political elite and liberals. According to Professor Matt Goodwin, support for Brexit was stronger in areas that during the preceding decade

---

413   Tom Whitehead, "Labour Wanted Mass Immigration to Make UK More Multicultural, Says Former Adviser." *The Telegraph*, October 23, 2009, https://www.telegraph.co.uk/news/uknews/law-and-order/6418456/Labour-wanted-mass-immigration-to-make-UK-more-multicultural-says-former-adviser.html

414   Nicole Martin and Omar Khan, "Ethnic Minorities at the 2017 British General Election," *RunnyMede*, February 2019.

415   John Cleese, Twitter, "Some years ago I opined that London was not really an English city any more. Since then, virtually all my friends from abroad have confirmed my observation. So there must be some truth in it...I note also that London was the UK city that voted most strongly to remain in the EU," May 28, 2019 10:21 PM, https://twitter.com/JohnCleese/status/1133604249693110272

had experienced rapid inward migration, such as the coastal town of Boston in Lincolnshire. Between 2001 and 2011, the percentage of people in Boston who had been born outside Britain increased fivefold, to over 15 percent…Three-quarters of people in Boston voted for Brexit.[416] In addition to native Brits fueling a backlash against mass immigration, about one-third of ethnic minorities ended up supporting the Leave campaign during Brexit, far more than had ever voted for the Tories.

Brexit owes a large part of its success to neoliberals like Blair who turned immigration into a focal point over the decision of whether or not to stay in the European Union. A study by the International Organization for Migration found that nearly 70 percent of Brits wanted immigration reduced prior to the vote for Brexit. About three in four voters in Britain who worried about how immigration was changing their country voted for Brexit.[417]

While the demographic and cultural shifts in Europe seem severe, they pale in comparison to the change undergone in the US since the mid-1960s, when Congress voted to change America's longstanding immigration policy.

The current immigration system in the US has caused a more significant ethnic change than any other country because a majority of immigrants (60 percent) receive family-based visas. This means these immigrants are not required to have any special skill or unique talents before receiving a visa to the US; they just needed to be related to someone already here. Aside from chain migration, America's policy of birthright citizenship incentivizes people to illegally enter the US and give birth, making the child an automatic citizen. The whole family can then anchor themselves to that child and eventually

---

416   Matthew Goodwin and Roger Eatwell, National Populism, the revolt against liberal democracy, Pelican (London, 2018), p. 166.
417   Ibid. p. 29

make their way to the US legally; that's where the term anchor baby comes from.

Different nationalities tend to bring more family members through chain migration than others; the average legal Mexican immigrant brings in the highest amount on average, generally sponsoring about 6.38 members of his family.[418] Immigrants from Mexico, China, India, and the Philippines account for 66 percent of all family-based immigration into the US as of 2017.[419]

This policy has led to the largest peacetime demographic change in world history. Europeans and Canadians went from 84 percent of the immigrant population in 1960 to 14 percent in 2013 while the number of Latin American and Mexican immigrants expanded from 10 percent to 52 percent during that same time. During that period, the number of immigrants also quadrupled.[420]

The American people never consented to this massive demographic transformation of their country. It was brought about as a result of the 1965 Immigration Act that abolished the national origins quota system that had been in effect for generations and reduced the overall number of immigrants coming to the US after the great wave of German, Italian, and Jewish immigrants of the late 19th and early 20th century.

At the time, opponents of the bill were mocked for raising a concern about how the legislation would affect immigration patterns over the long-term. Their worries were scoffed out by

---

418   Jessica M. Vaughm, "Immigration Multipliers: Trends in Chain Migration," *Center for Immigration Studies,* September 27, 2017, https://cis.org/Report/Immigration-Multipliers

419   Jens Manuel Krogstad and Ana Gonzalez-Barrera, "Key Facts about U.S. Immigration Policies and Proposed Changes." *Pew Research Center,* May 17, 2019, https://www.pewresearch.org/fact-tank/2019/05/17/key-facts-about-u-s-immigration-policies-and-proposed-changes/

420   "Modern Immigration Wave Brings 59 Million to U.S." *Pew Research Center's Hispanic Trends Project,* June 19, 2018, https://www.pewresearch.org/hispanic/2015/09/28/chapter-5-u-s-foreign-born-population-trends/

the bill's supporters like Senator Ted Kennedy, who told them there was no way this would alter the ethnic makeup or vastly increase the population of the US.

"First, our cities will not be flooded with a million immigrants annually. Under the proposed bill, the present level of immigration remains substantially the same. (sic) Secondly, the ethnic mix of this country will not be upset. Contrary to the charges in some quarters, [the bill] will not inundate America with immigrants from any one country or area, or the most populated and deprived nations of Africa and Asia. In the final analysis, the ethnic pattern of immigration under the proposed measure is not expected to change as sharply as the critics seem to think."[421]

Other supporters of the bill like Senator Daniel Inouye said the total number of potential immigrants would not change very much and Republican Senator Hiram Fong predicted that the people from (Asia) will never reach one percent of the US population.

Of course, all of those things happened in those senators' lifetimes. Not to be outdone in the bad predictions department, Teddy's brother, Senator Robert Kennedy, predicted a total of five thousand immigrants from India would arrive in the US after the bill's passing. He was only off by 100,000 percent. He also predicted that immigration would be limited to 10 percent of the total population in any given year, yet Mexican immigration regularly reached over 20 percent in the following decades.[422, 423]

---

421   Peter J. Duignan, "Making and Remaking America: Immigration into the United States." *The Hoover Institute,* September 15, 2003, https://www.hoover.org/research/making-and-remaking-america-immigration-united-states

422   Tom Gjelten, "How the Immigration Act of 1965 Inadvertently Changed America." *The Atlantic,* October 2, 2015, https://www.theatlantic.com/politics/archive/2015/10/immigration-act-1965/408409/

423   Ben Johnson, "The High Price Today of Immigration Reform in 1965." *Front Page Mag,* December 2002, https://historynewsnetwork.org/article/1175

The American people were neither prepared for nor wanted an influx of the world's poor who had a radically different culture. At the time the 1965 Immigration Act was passed, Americans said they preferred immigrants from Canada, the UK, Scandinavia, Germany, and Ireland and would not like to see immigrants from Russia, Asia, the Middle East, Mexico, and Latin America.[424] The results of the 1965 Immigration Act were contrary to the wishes and wants of the American people.

Each president after the passing of the 1965 bill only continued to increase the flow of immigrants—primarily from Latin America—into the US because they viewed it as good for the economy and believed diversity was a strength. The sheer volume of people put severe strains on local communities across the country, and some underwent extreme demographic changes. For example, the town of Hazelton, Pennsylvania was almost completely non-Hispanic white for its entire history; in 2000 the Hispanic population had grown to 2.15 percent according to Census records, but after nearly a decade of Bush's immigration policy, the city became 37.3 percent Latino by 2010.[425] President Obama continued those policies, and by 2017, Hazelton was a majority Hispanic community.[426]

This type of rapid ethnic change where the Hispanic population was ballooning in relative proportions to the rest of America created a hostile reaction by white Americans[427] who were not

---

424   "Huddled Masses: Public Opinion & the 1965 U.S. Immigration Act blog." *Roper Center,* July 10, 2015, https://ropercenter.cornell.edu/blog/huddled-masses-public-opinion-1965-us-immigration-act-blog

425   "Hazleton, Pennsylvania Population: Census 2010 and 2000 Interactive Map, Demographics, Statistics, Quick Facts," *Census Viewer,* date accessed December 18, 2019, http://censusviewer.com/city/PA/Hazleton

426   United States Department of Commerce, "Quick Facts Hazelton City, Pennsylvania," *U.S Census,* 2018, https://www.census.gov/quickfacts/fact/table/hazletoncitypennsylvania/PST045218

427   Daniel J. Hopkins, "Politicized Places: Explaining Where and When Immigrants Provoke Local Opposition," *The American Political Science Review. Volume 104, No 1,* February 2010. p. 40-60.

prepared for this type of cultural change. It broke down trust, ended societal norms, and created a deep-seated desire for change that culminated in the election of Donald Trump.

It also led to a political change in America as Hispanics tended to be more liberal and register Democrat, support a bigger government with more social services, favor gun control, support raising the minimum wage, support the government curbing free speech, and favor government-run healthcare.[428, 429, 430, 431, 432]

A majority of foreign-born Hispanics viewed themselves as separate from typical Americans which is understandable, but even a third of second-generation and a quarter of third-generation Hispanics still felt the same.[433] That means it could take nearly a century for most current Hispanics to feel assimilated as typical Americans.

The US Census predicts that white Americans will be a minority for the first time in their country's history, which excites woke progressives and the neoliberals. But is America's transition toward Brazil really a good thing? Harvard scholars Steven Levitsky and Daniel Ziblatt argued in their book *How*

428   Taylor, Paul, et al., "V. Politics, Values, and Religion." *Pew Research Center's Hispanic Trends Project,* February 6, 2014, https://www.pewresearch.org/hispanic/2012/04/04/v-politics-values-and-religion/?src=prc-number

429   "Chapter 9: Social and Political Views." *Pew Research Center's Religion & Public Life Project,* August 6, 2018, https://www.pewforum.org/2014/05/07/chapter-9-social-and-political-views/

430   Mark Hug Lopez, et al., "Latinos' Views on Marijuana, Gun Control, Abortion and Minimum Wage." *Pew Research Center's Hispanic Trends Project,* October 16, 2014, https://www.pewresearch.org/hispanic/2014/10/16/chapter-2-latinos-views-on-selected-2014-ballot-measure-issues/

431   Hart Research Associates, "How Will Healthcare Impact The 2018 Latino Vote?" *Unidos US,* "September 26, 2018, http://publications.unidosus.org/handle/123456789/1886

432   Emily Ekins, "The State of Free Speech and Tolerance in America." *Cato Institute,* November 1, 2017, https://www.cato.org/survey-reports/state-free-speech-tolerance-america

433   Paul Taylor, et al., "II. Identity, Pan-Ethnicity and Race." *Pew Research Center's Hispanic Trends Project,* May 15, 2012, https://www.pewresearch.org/hispanic/2012/04/04/ii-identity-pan-ethnicity-and-race/

Democracies Die that there has never been an example in history of a successful multiracial democracy where the once-majority group has become a minority.

So, America is hurtling toward a future that has been disastrous for every other nation that has ever ended up with a similar fate, but why? Because Congress lied while passing an immigration bill and future politicians were either drunk on their own ideology or indebted to special interests who paid for their seats in Congress in exchange for cheap labor? Who knows, maybe America just has special dirt that will ensure it doesn't end up like Lebanon, which endured a civil war when Muslims began outnumbering Christians, but it's a gamble most Americans never wanted to bet.

As these demographic changes have become more profound in the US and Europe, Western degeneration awareness is now expanding to countries like Australia[434] and Canada[435] who already have a merit-based immigration policy and to this point have been fairly immune to national populism. As of the writing of this book, those respected countries are taking vastly different approaches to immigration.

In March 2019, Australia's Liberal Coalition (a center-right governing coalition) voted to reduce legal immigration from 190,000 to 160,000.[436] It also tied immigration to several more work requirements and barred new arrivals from moving into cities to ease congestion and reduce housing prices for middle-

434   Helen Davidson, "Almost Half of Australians Believe Immigration Should Be Reduced, Polls Find." *The Guardian,* May 2, 2019, https://www.theguardian.com/world/2019/may/02/almost-half-of-australians-believe-immigration-should-be-reduced-poll-finds

435   Angela Johnston, "'Thin Veneer of Tolerance': Most Canadians Oppose Accepting More Refugees, Poll Suggest." *CBC News,* July 3, 2019, https://www.cbc.ca/news/canada/manitoba/refugees-tolerance-1.5192769

436   Katharine Murphy, "Coalition's Permanent Migration Cap Revealed as Morrison Launches Population Policy." *The Guardian,* March 19, 2019, https://www.theguardian.com/australia-news/2019/mar/20/coalitions-permanent-migration-cap-revealed-as-morrison-launches-population-policy

class families.[437] It was a drop in the bucket, but it signaled to Australians that the government understood their frustrations and was trying to respond to them.

Canada was a whole different story. Under Prime Minister Justin Trudeau, immigration increased from 310,000 annually to 340,000[438] in 2017, despite the fact that 63 percent of Canadians opposed the plan.[439] In response to Trudeau's willingness to ignore the will of the voter, citizens of Quebec voted in 2018 for a national populist party who promised, among other things, to reduce immigration into the province.

The Coalition Avenir Québec (CAQ) won an astounding 75 seats in the Quebec National Assembly, allowing them to form a government without any coalition partners. Among the promises made by the CAQ's leader François Legault was to reduce legal immigration by 20 percent and pass a values and language test to anyone seeking a Quebec selection certificate. It passed most of those promises into law the following year, along with a burqa ban in government buildings.[440,441]

---

437   Colin Packham, "Australia Cuts Annual Immigrant Cap, Puts Key Cities off-Limits to Some." Reuters, March 20, 2019, https://www.reuters.com/article/us-australia-politics-immigration/australia-cuts-annual-immigrant-cap-puts-key-cities-off-limits-to-some-idUSKCN1R10A5

438   Monique Scotti, "Canadian Government Wants 310,000 Immigrants in 2018, 340,000 a Year by 2020." *Global News,* November 1, 2017, https://globalnews.ca/news/3836805/340k-immigrants-per-year-by-2020-government-unveils-new-immigration-targets/?utm_expid=.kz0UD5JkQOCo6yMqxGqECg.0&utm_referrer=https%3A%2F%2Fcapforcanada.com%2F63-of-canadians-do-not-want-increase-in-immigration-trudeau-ups-quota-to-340000-annually%2F

439   The Canadian Press, "Report on Federal Politics." *Leger,* June 16, 2019, https://leger360.com/wp-content/uploads/2019/06/Federal-Politics-June-2019-Canadians-Opinion.pdf

440   "Legault Year One: How CAQ Has Transformed Quebec so Far." *The Globe and Mail,* July 11, 2019, https://www.theglobeandmail.com/canada/article-quebec-francois-legault-caq-year-one-explainer/

441   Ingrid Peritz and Daniel Leblanc, "Quebec Announces Reduced Immigration Targets, Fuelling Tension with Ottawa." *The Globe and Mail,* December 5, 2018, https://www.theglobeandmail.com/canada/article-quebec-announces-reduced-immigration-targets-fuelling-tensions-with/

The rise of national populism in Canada and Australia shows that no nation is immune to it and the battles of culture and identity are in every nation's future unless the establishment parties start making immediate concessions.

WELFARE

Cultural issues aside, the other fear held by voters is that migrants drain social services and depress wages for native-born workers and recent immigrants, especially those without an advanced degree. This is a belief is broadly held across the world, but especially in places with generous welfare policies like Europe, the US, and Canada.

The most important fact about immigrants that often goes unnoticed is that they're not all the same. Pundits and politicians will often lump them in together as if it's a bag of fruit at a wholesale store; even if you only need one, you have to take buy several dozen.

Some immigrants have enormously economically successful stories, while others prove to be a drain on the welfare state and stagnate wages in certain industries.

Well-respected macroeconomist Garett Jones has noted that wealthy, democratic, and free-market-oriented countries would benefit in the long-term economically by absorbing immigrants who come from countries with high SAT scores. SAT is an acronym for countries that have a long history as nontribal states, worked in agriculture for several thousand years, and have developed most of the world's past technological progress. Nations with high SAT scores are usually more economically successful, have more successful societies, and, in most cases, are demographically made up of the descendants of East Asia and Europe.

This is an important caveat because when media outlets talk about immigrants, they usually don't differentiate nation of origin and there is a big difference. Americans will see stories with headlines like "Majority of America's Billion-Dollar Startups Have an Immigrant Founder"[442] and readers are left to their own devices to imagine which immigrants they're talking about. Readers are free to imagine that refugees from Central America are working to create the next Google or Apple, but in fact, nearly all of the immigrants mentioned in the article are the descendants of East Asians, Europeans, or Sephardic Jews.[443]

Low-skill immigrants from typically low SAT scoring countries present different issues. Natives and other recent immigrants without advanced degrees view them as economic competitors that keep their wages stagnant while those in the middle class and even upper-middle-class believe they absorb a significant amount of social services.

For decades, pundits and politicians have said those beliefs are unwarranted in most cases despite a plethora of news stories where immigrants commit welfare fraud,[444] take public benefits,[445] and occupy jobs that would have otherwise gone to native workers.[446] Yet the governing class has refused to take these concerns seriously and pushed voters in countries throughout

---

442   Stuart Anderson, "55% Of America's Billion-Dollar Startups Have An Immigrant Founder." *Forbes,* February 4, 2019, https://www.forbes.com/sites/stuartanderson/2018/10/25/55-of-americas-billion-dollar-startups-have-immigrant-founder/#2b3f4dcd48ee

443   Stuart Anderson, "Immigrants and Billion-Dollar Companies," *National Foundation for American Policy,* October 2018, https://nfap.com/wp-content/uploads/2019/01/2018-BILLION-DOLLAR-STARTUPS.NFAP-Policy-Brief.2018-1.pdf

444   United States Immigration and Customs Enforcement, "Guatemalan Illegal Alien Residing in Iowa Sentenced for Benefit Fraud." *U.S. Immigration and Customs Enforcement,* May 31, 2019, https://www.ice.gov/news/releases/guatemalan-illegal-alien-residing-iowa-sentenced-benefit-fraud

445   Steven A. Camarota and Karen Zeigler, "63% Of Non-Citizens Households Access Welfare Programs." *Center for Immigration Studies,* November 20, 2018, https://cis.org/Report/63-NonCitizen-Households-Access-Welfare-Programs

446   Dan Mihalopoulos, "At Major Northwest Side Bakery, Labour Issues Pit Blacks vs. Hispanics." *Chicago Sun Times,* February 16, 2018, https://chicago.suntimes.com/2018/2/16/18355997/at-major-northwest-side-bakery-labor-issues-pit-blacks-vs-hispanics

North America and Europe into the arms of national populist parties.

THE UNITED STATES

Americans have a romantic notion of immigrants as hard workers who come to the country for a better life and assimilate in the ways their ancestors did. Right or wrong, this is the feelings many Americans have when it comes to immigration. Two areas where they have the greatest negative reactions toward immigrants is in the subjects of immigrants competing with low-skilled Americans for jobs and using welfare benefits.

Polling in the US is a little dated, but at the time former President George W. Bush was pushing comprehensive immigration reform, that included an amnesty for over 10 million immigrants as well as an expansion of legal immigration, voters believed immigrants were a net negative economically. A majority of Americans believed that immigrants were a burden to the welfare state, competed for jobs, and didn't contribute as much in taxes as they took in public services.[447]

Voters had even stronger negative feelings toward illegal aliens. A 2010 CBS/*New York Times* poll found that 74 percent of Americans, including 64 percent of Democrats, 86 percent of Republicans, and 76 percent of Independents, believed that illegal immigrants weakened public services.[448] As of 2013, a majority of Americans wanted an immigration policy that altered the number of low-skilled immigrants that came into the US depending on the health of the nation's economy.[449]

---

447   Ruy Teixeria, "What the Pubic Really Wants on Immigration." *Center for American Progress,* June 27, 2006, https://cdn.americanprogress.org/wp-content/uploads/kf/TEIXEIRAJUNEPOOL-FINAL.PDF

448   Randal C. Archibold and Megan Thee-brenan, "Polls Shows Most in U.S. Want Overhaul of Immigration Laws." *The New York Times,* May 3, 2010, https://www.nytimes.com/2010/05/04/us/04poll.html

449   https://www.pollingreport.com/immigration2.htm

As is basically always the case, voters didn't get the reforms they wanted. Politicians, especially Republicans, spent the better part of four decades keeping the flow of low-skilled immigrants steady because it helped their corporate donors who benefited from cheap labor. Republicans manufactured the narrative that immigrants were just doing the jobs that Americans wouldn't do. This was their excuse decade after decade for cheap labor and the slogan doing the jobs Americans won't do stuck. A majority of Americans believed that there simply wasn't an American who would work in certain select fields like housekeeping, taxi driving, and agriculture work.

Foreign labor has become part of the lifeblood for certain industries like big tech, agriculture, and construction.

Despite the slogan that immigrants do the jobs Americans won't do and decades of mass low-skilled immigration, as of 2018, the majority of the labor force in nearly every low-skilled industry is American born. Immigrants, both legal and illegal, only make a majority of six civilian occupations according to Census Data. A majority of maids, meat processors, ground workers, construction labor, and janitors are not native-born Americans.[450]

Before Democrats decided to become the party of woke white cosmopolitan liberals, they spent generations as the party of the American worker. Politicians like Barbara Jordan and activists like Cesar Chavez advocated for greater restrictions on immigration in order to protect the wages of union workers, recent immigrants, and minorities, especially blacks.

In the mid-'90s, President Bill Clinton endorsed recommendations outlined in Representative Barbara Jordan's commission on immigration, which would among other things

---

450   Steven A. Camarota, "There Are No Jobs Americans Won't Do." *Center for Immigration Studies,* August 26, 2018, https://cis.org/Report/There-Are-No-Jobs-Americans-Wont-Do

reduce legal immigration from 830,000 to 550,000 annually.[451] The biggest opponent to this modest reduction didn't come on the left, but instead on the right.

It was self-described conservatives who were usually on the side of mass immigration because it favored the business lobby. Republican commentators like William Bennett and Bill Kristol and Congressmen like Jack Kemp, Sam Brownback, Dick Chrysler, and House Majority Leader Dick Armey[452] all worked to sabotage any meaningful immigration reform that would have reduced legal numbers. In the end, all they managed to pass was enforcement measures against illegal immigration; legal immigration ended up increasing over the next decade.

The only other time the United States was even close to passing meaningful immigration reform that would have reduced the number of legal immigrants coming into the country was blocked by Speaker Paul Ryan,[453, 454] a Republican who worked for and admired Jack Kemp, the man who help stop immigration reform in the '90s.

When it comes to how mass immigration affects the wages of native-born Americans and recent immigrants, there have been many studies by economists that have produced a wide array of results. Studying the flow of people in and out of the labor market is very complex and difficult to measure, given there

---

451   John M. Goshko, "Immigration Initiatives Ride Wave of Anxiety Over Illegals." *The Washington Post,* July 2, 1995, https://www.washingtonpost.com/archive/politics/1995/07/02/immigration-initiatives-ride-wave-of-anxiety-over-illegals/8a59d9d2-cdb8-4f33-abe4-77e7e6adbddd/?noredirect=on

452   Daniel Tichenor, *Dividing Lines: The Politics of Immigration Control in America,* Princeton University Press (Princeton, 2002). p. 283.

453   Neil Munro, "Goodlatte: House Leadership Blocked Trump-Backed Immigration Reform." *Breitbart,* December 6, 2018, https://www.breitbart.com/politics/2018/12/05/goodlatte-house-leadership-blocked-trump-backed-immigration-reform/

454   Jack Crowe, "Ken Cuccinelli Blames Paul Ryan for Lack of Progress on Immigration Reform." *MSN.com,* August 22, 2019, https://www.msn.com/en-us/news/politics/ken-cuccinelli-blames-paul-ryan-for-lack-of-progress-on-immigration-reform/ar-AAGbK3e

are multiple variables affecting the results of different studies. Still, a consensus exists by many economists that immigration affects Americans differently based on their level of skill, with recent immigrants and high school dropouts being the most vulnerable populations to an influx of low-skilled immigrants.

Harvard Professor George Borjas who has been studying immigration for over thirty years wrote in 2016, "Wage trends over the past half century suggest that a 10 percent increase in the number of workers with a particular set of skills probably lowers the wage of that group by at least 3 percent. Even after the economy has fully adjusted, those skill groups that received the most immigrants will still offer lower pay relative to those that received fewer immigrants."[455]

That means the laws of supply and demand also affect labor. Too much labor in any given sector of the economy or any one location depresses wages. For instance, a study by Borjas showed that when Miami received an influx of over a hundred thousand mostly non-high school-educated Cubans over a short period of time in 1980, wages for non-Hispanic men without a high school degree dropped by between 10 and 30 percent.[456, 457] Overall, Borjas insists that the effects of mass low-skilled immigration reduce the wages of native-born high school dropouts by 2 to 5 percent.[458]

---

455   George J. Borjas, et al., "Yes, Immigration Hurts American
       Workers." *POLITICO Magazine*, September/October 2016,
       https://www.politico.com/magazine/story/2016/09/
       trump-clinton-immigration-economy-unemployment-jobs-214216

456   John Dorschner, "Wages for Native-Born Miami Workers Took a Hit from Mariel
       Boatlift, New Study Says." *Miami Herald,* July 20, 2017, https://www.miamiherald.
       com/news/local/community/miami-dade/article162683083.html

457   George J. Borjas, et al., "Job Vacancies, the Beveridge Curve, and Supply
       Shocks: The Frequency and Content of Help-Wanted Ads in Pre- and Post-
       Mariel Miami." *The National Bureau of Economic Research,* revised August 2019.

458   George Borjas, "Immigration and the American Worker." *Center
       for Immigration Studies*, April 9, 2013, https://cis.org/Report/
       Immigration-and-American-Worker

Borjas's studies have come under criticism by many economists who insist there is no data to prove that mass immigration effectively lowers the wages of Americans. Other studies have found that increasing the labor supply by 1 percent negatively affects the wages of black high school dropouts by 1.7 percent and all high school dropouts by between .3 percent and 1 percent.[459] Other studies have found that mass immigration of low-skilled workers reduces the number of hours native-born teenagers worked by 3 percent and the hours of low-skilled adults by 1 percent.[460] Economists insist that low-skilled Americans have advantages with union memberships, a better understanding of English and that younger low-skilled Americans develop advanced skills that protect their wages from being crippled by mass immigration.[461]

Yet a survey of over forty economists at major universities from MIT, Harvard, Yale, Berkeley, Princeton, the University of Chicago, Stanford, Colombia, and Northwestern in 2013 found a majority agreed to the question that many low-skilled American workers would be substantially worse off if a larger number of low-skilled foreign workers were legally allowed to enter the US each year.[462]

"There can be winners and losers. Similarly, skilled workers will face greater competition for jobs and their wages may fall," said Harvard Professor Oliver Hart, who participated in the survey.

More important than what economists' working papers said was how Americans, especially those in low-skilled sectors of

---

459 The National Academies of Science, Engineering, Medicine, "The Economic and Fiscal Consequences of Immigration." *The National Academic Press,* (Washington DC, 2017). p, 242.

460 Christopher L. Smith, "The Impact of Low-Skilled Immigration on the Youth Labor Market." *The University of Chicago Press Journals,* January 2012.

461 (The National Acadmies of Science, Engineering, Medicine, 2017, p. 121).

462 "Low-Skilled Immigrants," *Chicago Booth,* December 10, 2013, http://www. igmchicago.org/surveys/low-skilled-immigrants

the economy, felt. In 2018, a Gallup poll showed 12 percent of Americans worried they would lose their jobs to immigrants, which doesn't seem like much on face value but in real terms, it represents over 15 million people.

Although this includes low-skilled workers who have seen wages in certain fields like meat processing not only stagnate but decline over several decades as employers flooded the industry with non-union foreign labor,[463] it also includes college-educated workers who had to compete with foreign H1-b workers. This is what happened to 250 high-skilled Disney World employees who worked managing the company's data system and were not only fired in the summer of 2015, but were also forced to train their foreign replacements, and to the 350 tech workers who were laid off from their jobs at Northeast Utilities in 2013 and were also forced to train their foreign replacements.[464]

Foreign-educated immigrants pose a unique threat to middle-class workers, especially those who are older and would have a difficult time finding employment in the same field and learning new skills. American companies are more than willing to hire college-educated foreign labor despite the fact that they're less skilled than college-educated Americans[465] because their visa status is tied to their employment. Meaning if they leave their job, they'd have to leave the country. The narrative employers give to the public about why they constantly need foreign tech

---

463   Dean Baker, "Meatpacking Didn't Always Have Bad Pay." *Center for Economic and Policy Research,* July 12, 2012, http://cepr.net/blogs/beat-the-press/meatpacking-didnt-always-have-bad-pay

464   Julia Preston, "Pink Slips at Disney. But First, Training Foreign Replacements." *The New York Times,* June 3, 2015, https://www.nytimes.com/2015/06/04/us/last-task-after-layoff-at-disney-train-foreign-replacements.html

465   Jason Richwine, "Foreign-Educated Immigrants Are Less Skilled Than U.S. Degree Holders." *Center for Immigration Studies,* https://cis.org/Report/ForeignEducated-Immigrants-Are-Less-Skilled-US-Degree-Holders

workers is much different; they insist that there is a shortage of Americans in the STEM (Science, Technology, Engineering, and Math) field. This is a fallacy; barely half of Americans with a STEM-degrees are currently employed in the field.[466]

The anxiety felt by over 15 million Americans is not understood in Washington. Even the Trump administration, who campaigned on the issue, has broken promises to voters and regularly increased visas for both low- and high-skilled workers.[467, 468] Trump's promise of ending chain migration, which would have reduced the number of immigrants without a high school degree by 71 percent and the number of immigrants without a college degree by 41 percent,[469] never came close to becoming law. And so, his working-class base has to wait longer for any reforms on legal immigration.

Nonetheless, a majority of Americans as of 2018 still prefer Trump's plan to move immigration to a merit-based system. The survey by Public Religion Research Institute found that 63 percent of Americans wanted to implement a merit-based

---

466   "52% of STEM-Trained College Graduates Are Employed in STEM
        Workforce." *Pew Research Center's Social & Demographic Trends Project,*
        January 8, 2018, https://www.pewsocialtrends.org/2018/01/09/
        women-and-men-in-stem-often-at-odds-over-workplace-equity/
        ps_2018-01-09_stem_1-15/
467   Steve Holland, "Trump Immigration Plan May Increase Visas for Highly
        Skilled Workers: Sources." Reuters, April 25, 2019, https://www.reuters.
        com/article/us-usa-trump-immigration/new-trump-immigration-plan-may-
        increase-visas-for-highly-skilled-workers-idUSKCN1S02WD
468   Heather Long, "Trump Administration Nearly Doubles H-2B Guest Visa
        Program, Which Brings Many Mexican Workers." *The Washington Post,*
        April 8, 2019, https://www.washingtonpost.com/business/2019/04/06/
        trump-administration-nearly-doubles-h-b-guest-visa-program-which-brings-
        many-mexican-workers/
469   Michael Clemens and Jimmy Graham, "How the Trump Administration Plan
        Would Shape the Composition of Immigration: First Numerical Estimates."
        Center for Global Development, January 30, 2018, https://www.cgdev.org/blog/
        how-trump-administrations-plan-would-shape-composition-immigration-first-
        numerical-estimates

immigration system that favored immigrants based on their skills, education, and ability to speak English including a majority of whites (66 percent), blacks (59 percent), and Hispanics (54 percent).[470]

Aside from taking jobs from native-born workers, Americans are opposed to immigrants using welfare programs and being a net drain on society. This is another area of concern when it comes to immigration that elites brush aside as xenophobic fears with no basis in reality.

The fact is that America's archaic immigration system does not prioritize immigrants by their potential to contribute economically or otherwise to the US. A majority of immigrants earn their privilege of coming into the US based on familial relations which means sometimes the US imports the very rich, but most of the time, the very poor.

As of 2010, 20 percent of all immigrants living in the US were in poverty and about 57 percent were living in or near poverty according to a study by the National Academies of Sciences, Engineering, and Medicine. The poverty rate among immigrants is significantly higher than native-born Americans, which stood at 13.5 percent with 31 percent living in or near poverty in 2010. For absolutely no rhyme or reason, the US immigration policy is importing poverty, adding to the population of people dependent on government assistance and increasing the economic inequality within the country.[471]

As mentioned previously, immigrants perform differently depending on their native country's SAT score, their personal level of education, and a few other variables. Overall, the divide based upon regions of the world shows that immigrants from Europe, East Asia, and South Asia are less likely than Americans to be in poverty while immigrants from the Middle East, Central

---

470   "PRRI 2018 American Values Survey" *PRRI*, October 1, 2018, https://www. prri.org/wp-content/uploads/2018/10/AVS-2018-Topline-COMBINED.pdf

471   (The National Acadmies of Science, Engineering, Medicine, 2017, p. 121).

America, Mexico, Sub-Saharan Africa, and the Caribbean are more likely to be in poverty.

We can break this down even further because not all immigrants from the same region have an equal level of economic potential. For example, immigrants from the Dominican Republic have one of the highest levels of poverty among any immigrant group in the US, with nearly half living in or near poverty. That doesn't mean all immigrants from the Caribbean have equal rates of poverty; immigrants from Jamaica have a poverty rate that's lower than native-born Americans. By nationality, immigrants from countries like the Philippines, India, Germany, the UK, and Poland have half the poverty rate of native-born Americans. Immigrants from countries like Japan, Canada, South Korea, Pakistan, Russia, and as mentioned previously Jamaica also all have poverty rates below Americans.

While immigrants from those countries are less likely to be in poverty and need government assistance, migrants from Mexico, Honduras, and Guatemala all have a poverty rate that is more than twice as high as the average American. Over 25 percent of immigrants from said countries are in poverty and more than 60 percent are in or near poverty.[472] Other immigrant populations from countries like Haiti, Cuba, Ecuador, El Salvador, Vietnam, and Iran also have poverty rates higher than native-born Americans.

This increased flow of low-skilled immigration puts a strain especially on state and local governments who were forced by law to feed, hospitalize, educate, and in some cases imprison them.

Immigrant households with children are more likely to be enrolled in a welfare program than native-born households with children in nearly every state, with the only exceptions being Mississippi, Montana, North Dakota, and West Virginia.

---

472   The National Academies of Science, Engineering, Medicine, 2017, p. 120.

In some states like Colorado, Nebraska, and Wisconsin, immigrant households were twice as likely to be enrolled in a welfare program as native-born households.[473] This is unsurprising given that immigrant children are about twice as likely to be in poverty as American-born children.

A study by the Center for Immigration Studies found that 63 percent of noncitizen households in 2014 accessed at least one welfare program, compared with just 35 percent of native households. Some of the program's noncitizens used at a higher frequency than native households included food programs, Medicaid, and cash payments from Earned Income Tax Credits.[474]

Supporters of open borders and mass immigration are quick to point out that while immigrants, both legal and illegal, use welfare, they also pay taxes.

According to the Institute on Taxation and Economic Policy, illegal aliens paid about $11.7 billion in state and local taxes in 2014.[475] That seems like a lot, but it's s nothing compared with illegal immigrants' financial costs, which are imposed mostly on state and local governments. A study by The Heritage Foundation estimated costs of illegal immigrants' public education, welfare, and other benefits amounts to be a net fiscal burden of $54.5 billion annually.[476]

Legal immigrants fare better, which should be expected given that they have more access to the job market and are

---

473   Ibid. p. 99
474   Steven A. Camarota and Karen Zeigler, "63% of Non-Citizen Household Access Welfare Programs." *Center for Immigration Studies,* November 20, 2018, https://cis.org/Report/63-NonCitizen-Households-Access-Welfare-Programs
475   Matthew Gardner, et al., "Undocumented Immigrants' State & Local Tax Contributions." *Institute on Taxation,* last updated March 2017, https://itep.org/wp-content/uploads/immigration2017.pdf
476   Jason Richwine and Robert Rector, "The Fiscal Cost of Unlawful Immigrants and Amnesty to the U.S. Taxpayers." *The Heritage Foundation,* May 6, 2013, https://www.heritage.org/immigration/report/the-fiscal-cost-unlawful-immigrants-and-amnesty-the-us-taxpayer

better educated in general. According to a study by the New American Economy, the US's foreign-born population earned $1.3 trillion in 2014, contributed $328.2 billion in taxes, and had $927 billion in disposable income.

Like American citizens, legal immigrants' welfare burden depends on their level of education, with those with a college education having a tax surplus and those without having a fiscal deficit. As of 2010, legal immigrants with a college degree give $24,529 more in taxes than they absorb in welfare, whereas those without a high school degree receive $36,993 more in welfare than they pay in taxes. Overall, legal immigrants have a net fiscal deficit of $4,344 per household, meaning they take more in welfare than they give in taxes.

Part of this tax deficit could be closed by taxing remittances, which is the money both legal and illegal immigrants send back to their nation of origin. According to the World Bank Group, remittances from the US added up to $123 billion[477] in 2014, and that number ballooned to nearly $150 billion in 2017.[478] That is to say that the US's foreign-born population sends between 13 to 16 percent of their disposable income outside of the US.

Individual states have tried several times to stop illegal immigrants from receiving welfare. In 1975, Texas adopted a law that restricted universal junior high and high school to just American citizens and legal immigrants. This bill was struck down by the Supreme Court as unconstitutional in the 1982 case *Plyler v. Doe.* In 1994, California voters overwhelmingly passed Proposition 187, which would have prohibited illegal aliens from receiving nonemergency services like healthcare

---

477   Andy Kiersz, "Here's Where Migrant Workers In America Send Their Money." *Business Insider,* April 7, 2014, https://www.businessinsider.com/world-bank-us-remittance-map-2014-4

478   "Remittance Flows Worldwide in 2017." *Pew Research Center's Global Attitudes Project,* April 3, 2019, https://www.pewresearch.org/global/interactives/remittance-flows-by-country/

and public education. It passed by a margin of 59 to 41 percent and won the support of a majority of whites, blacks, and Asians as well as nearly one-third of all Hispanics.[479] The law was immediately challenged and then appealed, but in 1999 the Democrats took over the state and they withdrew the appeal, essentially killing the law.[480]

So, with inaction at best and amnesty at worst coming from most politicians, it is not hard to see how voters seeking to stop foreigners from taking their tax dollars would flock to Trump. During the 2016 presidential campaign, Trump lumped in illegal immigrants that abuse welfare with criminal aliens and visa overstayers, and it was music to the ears of voters who felt that Americans were being taken advantage of by people who broke the law to get into the US.

"Our enforcement priorities will include removing criminals, gang members, security threats, visa overstays, public charges—that is, those relying on public welfare or straining the safety net, along with millions of recent illegal arrivals and overstays who've come here under the current Administration," Trump said in the speech. "Immigration law doesn't exist just for the purpose of keeping out criminals. It exists to protect all aspects of American life—the worksite, the welfare office, the education system and much else. That is why immigration limits are established in the first place."[481]

For nearly fifty years before the 1965 Immigration Act, the idea of a majority of immigrants being fiscal deficits would have been unthinkable. Immigration between 1924 to 1965 was

---

479   Tim Golden, "Prop. 187 Approved in California." *Migration News*, December 1994, https://migration.ucdavis.edu/mn/more.php?id=492

480   Patrick J. McDonnell, "Davis Won't Appeal Prop. 187 Ruling, Ending Court Battles." *Los Angeles Times*, July 29, 1999, https://www.latimes.com/archives/la-xpm-1999-jul-29-mn-60700-story.html

481   Nolan D. Mccaskill, "Full Text: Donald Trump Immigration Speech in Arizona." *Politico*, September 1, 2016, https://www.politico.com/story/2016/08/donald-trump-immigration-address-transcript-227614

based on a national origins quota system, meaning that visas were distributed to countries based upon the number of people of each nationality in the US at the time of the 1890 Census. The law completely excluded Asian immigrants, though that was revised in 1952.[482]

One benefit of that policy, however, was that most immigrants entering the US had comparable educations to American citizens and were actually earning more than native-born Americans. In 1970, native-born men earned about $62,398 annually and foreign-born men earned $62,443 in 2012 dollars.

After the 1965 Immigration Act, that all changed as most immigrants came from less developed countries with fewer freedoms and lower SAT scores than America. By 2012, the average native-born man earned far more than immigrants, with natives taking in $65,674 and foreign-born men earning $55,824. Foreign-born men's wages were weighted down by immigrants from places like Vietnam, the Philippines, Latin America, and Mexico.[483]

Congress's decision to change immigration was followed by a drastic widening of economic inequality, especially between Americans of different races. The racial gap between black and white Americans narrowed from 1970 to 2016.[484] This is due to two factors: black Americans who were the descendants of slaves no longer receive the level of discrimination as they once did, which has allowed them to advance economically, although the advancement has been very slow. Secondly, many groups of

---

482   United States State Department, "The Immigration and Nationality Act of 1952 (The McCarran-Walter Act)." *Office of the Historian,* date accessed December 19, 2019, https://history.state.gov/milestones/1945-1952/immigration-act

483   (The National Acadmies of Science, Engineering, Medicine, 2017, p. 106).

484   Rakesh Kochar and Anthony Cillufo, "Racial and Ethnic Income Inequality in America: 5 Key Findings." *Pew Research,* July 12, 2018, https://www.pewresearch.org/fact-tank/2018/07/12/key-findings-on-the-rise-in-income-inequality-within-americas-racial-and-ethnic-groups/

black immigrants have higher rates of income than native black Americans, especially those from countries like South Africa, Ghana, Nigeria, West Indian, and Jamaica.[485] The only group with substantially lower income than native blacks are Somalian immigrants.

Yet the inverse is happening among Hispanics and Asians as the US continues to bring in immigrants who are less likely to do as well as native-born Americans—including native-born Hispanics and Asians.

Hispanics earned about 65 percent as much as whites in 2016, which is down substantially since 1970 when Hispanics earned 74 percent as much as whites. Asian immigration is much more complex given that for centuries, many Asian countries have had a caste system where citizens are either very wealthy and highly educated or have very little.[486] Although this situation is changing in Asia, the US has continued to absorb many impoverished Asian immigrants like Burmese and Bhutanese people, who have respective poverty rates of 35 and 33 percent. The gap in income distribution between the top 10 percent of Asians and the bottom 10 percent is growing at a faster rate than any other racial group in America.

To a rational thinker, that's to be expected because all Asians, like all immigrants, are not the same. Congress crafted an immigration policy that doesn't prioritize immigrants based upon merit, so we're getting the best with the worst. We're basically throwing everything the world has to offer at our country and seeing what sticks, which sometimes produces fabulous results—but a lot of times, it doesn't.

---

485   United States Department of Commerce, "Selected Population Profile in the United States, 2016 American Community Survey 1-Year Estimates." *The Census*, 2016, https://factfinder.census.gov/faces/tableservices/jsf/pages/productview.xhtml?src=bkmk

486   John West, *Asian Century…on a Knife's Edge*, Palgrave Macmillan, (London: January 25, 2018). p.57-87.

As America continues to grow more racially and ethnically diverse, people become more individualistic and less inclined to support the public good both personally and financially. Those feelings are only compounded when native-born workers feel that their tax dollars are being used to subsidize recent immigrants and their children, driving them further and further into the arms of national populists.

THE UNITED KINGDOM

Immigration was a key motivating factor for Brits leading up to the vote on whether to remain in or leave the EU. For many working-class voters, their reason for supporting Nigel Farage's campaign to Brexit from the rest of Europe was the fear that the EU's free movement of people, known as the Schengen Agreement, would hurt them economically.

National populist economics was something that Farage, a former commodities trader and like Trump, not a member of the working class, had been campaigning on for years before Brexit. During the EU parliamentary election in 2014, Farage said the UK should change anti-discrimination laws to allow businesses to hire only British citizens[487] and warned about the free movement of people from Eastern Europe coming into the UK to work.

"We must be completely mad, as a country, to be giving people from Eastern Europe in-work benefits…. Even if I thought, which I don't, there was an economic benefit to mass immigration some things are more important than money, namely the shape of our society and giving our own youngsters a chance to work," Farage said in January 2014.

---

487   Owen Bennett, "Put UK Workers FIRST: Nigel Farage Says
       British Businesses Should Be Able to Discriminate." *Express.co.uk*,
       April 24, 2015, https://www.express.co.uk/news/uk/513546/
       Nigel-Farage-British-businesses-put-UK-workers-first

In that election, Farage's UKIP party won the largest share of the vote with 26.6 percent because it addressed the concerns that Labour and the Tories simply wouldn't touch, including how the free movement of people could hurt the working class. By that point, the UK had seen a wave of migration from Eastern Europe, especially since Poland entered the EU in 2004. In the preceding decade, more than eight hundred thousand Poles moved to the UK for employment opportunities; the influx of Polish immigrants was so large that they replaced Indians as the most common non-UK country of birth among the nation's residents.[488]

Adding to the anxiety among workers was the fact that Bulgaria and Romania nationals had gained the right to work in the UK at the beginning of that 2004 as well.[489]

Farage used the Schengen Agreement to campaign against the EU, warning Brits that hundreds of millions of people living in economically unstable countries like Greece and Italy or low-income former communist nations like Romania and Bulgaria could flood into the UK.

"I think you know the difference. We want an immigration policy that is not just based on controlling not just quantity but quality," Farage said during a radio interview in May 2014. "I am making one very simple point in this election. We cannot have any form of managed migration into Britain and remain a member of the European Union because we have an open door to nearly half a billion people…We would be far better off if the policy that did not discriminate against doctors from

---

488   Rohit Sudarshan, "Understanding the Brexit Vote: The Impact of Polish Immigrants on Euroscepticism." *Humanity in Action,* May 2017, https://www. humanityinaction.org/knowledge_detail/understanding-the-brexit-vote-the-impact-of-polish-immigrants-on-euroscepticism/

489   Mark Lowen, "Bulgarians and Romanians Free to Work in UK as Controls End." *BBC News,* January 1, 2014, https://www.bbc.com/news/uk-politics-25549715

New Zealand or engineers from India in favor of anybody regardless of background and skills coming from southern and eastern Europe and that is the great debate."

Farage focused on immigration from within the EU and the cost to the nation-state economically rather than changes that were happening culturally because of high levels of immigration from Muslim countries. It was something that many working-class Brits were concerned with, given the fact that the UK had not enacted any major labor laws to protect working-poor Brits from the onslaught of Eastern Europeans. By the time Brexit rolled around two years later, voters were citing their opposition to mass immigration from Eastern Europe as part of their decision to leave.[490]

It's not like their concerns were unwarranted. The number of immigrants from EU countries living in the UK tripled from 1995 to 2015[491] with the biggest group being Eastern Europeans; it was having a direct effect on the wages of the poorest members of British society. A report by the Migration Advisory Committee found that EU immigration was having a negative effect on the wages of the bottom 25 percent of UK-born workers from 1992 to 2017. Their wages decline by about 5 percent, while the earnings of the top 10 percent increased by 3.5 percent during that same period.[492]

There were also concerns with non-EU migrants who had lower employment rates than Brits, carried a fiscal deficit

490   Siraj Datoo, "Brexit Supporter Uses The Slur 'Paki' While Talking To BBC Reporter But Says He's Not Racist." *Buzzfeed,* June 28, 2016, https://www. buzzfeed.com/sirajdatoo/brexit-supporter-uses-the-slur-paki-while-talking-to-bbc-rep?utm_term=.yjWql9QJL#.rozWdz4Gx

491   Jonathan Wadsworth, et al., *Brexit and the Impact of Immigration on the UK*, The London School of Economics, (London: May 2016). p. 2.

492   Chris Giles, "The Effects of EU Migration on Britain in 5 Charts." *The Financial Times,* September 18, 2018, https://www.ft.com/ content/797f7b42-bb44-11e8-94b2-17176fbf93f5

in terms of the amount welfare they used, and contributed £840 less in taxes than citizens of the UK.[493]

Yet the main focus on the Brexit campaign, especially where Farage was concerned, was centered around avoiding mass uncontrollable immigration from within the EU.

EUROPE

Europe's welfare state is the most generous in the world and allows its citizens to have more favorable living conditions than most other countries. This is especially true in Scandinavia, where the welfare state is a cherished public commodity that every political party supports.

Yet waves of mass immigration, especially from Muslim-majority countries, started invoking fear in some Scandinavian people that the millions of new, mostly poor immigrants, were absorbing the welfare state without properly contributing. This led to the rise of national populist parties in some of the most tolerant societies on the planet, especially in Sweden, which experienced a rapid ethnic change due to mass immigration and a rapid increase in the number of asylum seekers from 2005 to 2018.

Before the 1970s, almost all of Sweden's immigration came from its neighboring Nordic countries like Finland and Denmark. During the '80s, Sweden began importing refugees from nations like Iraq and Iran. The number of refugees they accepted was considered large for the time but pales in comparison to the numbers taken in during the refugee crisis. Luckily for the Swedes, many of these refugees were part of

---

493   Mark Lowen, "Bulgarians and Romanians Free to Work in UK as Controls End." *BBC News,* January 1, 2014, https://www.mirror.co.uk/news/politics/5-brexit-immigration-myths-experts-13266987

their country's educated upper-middle-class[494] and the Swedish government worked very hard and successfully on assimilating both groups.[495]

The '90s marked the beginning of a radical transformation as the number of refugees and immigrants from majority-Muslim countries and former states within the Soviet Union began flocking to Sweden in unprecedented numbers. The population of some migrant groups grew by more than 1,000 percent in a span of a quarter of a century from 1980 to 2004: the Turkish population grew from 14,357 to 34,965; Somalians went from 146 to 15,294; Iraqis from 631 to 70,117; Iranians from 3,348 to 53,982; Ethiopians from 1,797 to 11,213; and former Yugoslavians from 37,982 to 134,940.[496]

Overall, the foreign-born population swelled by nearly 60 percent from 1990 to 2010 when it hit 1.33 million.[497] Aside from the sheer population increase, the demographics were radically altered and the population of non-EU immigrants in Sweden hit over 9 percent for the first time ever.

The situation became increasingly unmanageable as refugees became a burden on Swedish society. Refugees had higher levels of unemployment, greater dependency on the welfare

---

494   Peter S. Goodman, "The Nordic Model May Be The Cushion Against
       Capitalism. Can It Survive Immigration?" *The New York Times,* July 11,
       2019, https://www.nytimes.com/2019/07/11/business/sweden-economy-
       immigration.html

495   Lee Roden, "What Lessons Can Sweden Learn from Its Yugoslavian
       Refugees?" *The Local,* September 18, 2017, https://www.thelocal.
       se/20170918/what-lessons-can-sweden-learn-from-its-yugoslavian-refugees

496   Charles Westin, "Sweden: Restrictive Immigration
       Policy and Multiculturalism." *Migration Policy,* March
       2, 2017, https://www.migrationpolicy.org/article/
       sweden-restrictive-immigration-policy-and-multiculturalism/

497   Katya Vasileva, "6.5% of the EU population are foreigners and 9.4% are
       born abroad." *Eurostat,* July 14, 2011, https://ec.europa.eu/eurostat/web/
       products-statistics-in-focus/-/KS-SF-11-034

state, higher crime rates and school dropout rates, and lower participation in civic society.[498] A government study on crime from 1997 to 2001 showed how immense the problem had gotten. The study found that immigrants including refugees were three times more likely to be investigated for assault and five times more likely to be investigated for a sex crime.[499]

It became an untenable situation that increasingly worried and annoyed Swedes and opened the door for the Swedish Democrats (SD) under the leadership of Jimmie Åkesson.

The SD had been around for decades on the fringe of the political right, a bastion of white supremacists and neo-Nazis until Åkesson and three fellow Gen-Xers, Björn Söder, Mattias Karlsson, and Richard Jomshof cleansed the party of its extremists in 2005. Together, they purged the party of its more sinister members and attempted to make it mainstream.

During the 2010 election, the SD made the issue of protecting Sweden's welfare from mass immigration the main part of their party's platform. The party released a controversial ad featuring an old woman hobbling to collect her pension when she is surrounded and bypassed by women wearing burqas and pushing strollers. The voiceover said, "All politics are about priorities; now you have a choice. The ad was incredibly controversial, Swedish TV refused to broadcast it, but it went viral on the internet and help the SD breakthrough."[500]

On September 19, 2010, the SD won nearly 6 percent of the national vote which awarded them twenty seats in the Riksdag, the first time the party had held legislative seats.

---

498   Charles Westin, THE EFFECTIVENESS OF SETTLEMENT AND INTEGRATION POLICIES TOWARDS IMMIGRANTS AND THEIR DESCENDANTS IN SWEDEN, *International Labour Office Geneva*, 2000.

499   "Immigrants behind 25% of Swedish Crime." *The Local,* December 14, 2005, https://www.thelocal.se/20051214/2683

500   "TV4 Refuses to Air Sweden Democrat Ads." *The Local,* August 27, 2010, https://www.thelocal.se/20100827/28622

It was a model that Åkesson copied again and again and was rewarded by voters over the course of the last decade. During the 2014 election, even before the refugee crisis, Åkesson told Swedes that they must make a choice between Sweden's welfare state or mass immigration.

"The Prime Minister has confirmed it—the election is a choice between mass immigration and welfare. You choose on Sept. 14," Åkesson said in the run-up to the 2014 election.[501] In that election, the SD won nearly 13 percent of the votes and gained twenty-nine more seats in the Riksdag, which put them as the third-largest party in Sweden.

Åkesson's ascension in Swedish politics all came before the 2015 refugee crisis, which brought more than one hundred fifty thousand immigrants and refugees to Sweden in a single year, causing crime, political unrest, and social decay.

CRIME

The subject of immigration and crime is a murky one, especially because of hesitance on the part of both victims and authorities to report a criminal's nation of origin. Some countries, provinces, states, and municipalities do not demand to know where a criminal was born and report if they are a citizen or a noncitizen.

A study conducted by the University of Illinois at Chicago found that in the US, 70 percent of illegal aliens, 49 percent of legal immigrants, and even 28 percent of American-born Hispanics are not likely to call to police even if they were a victim of a crime because they fear being asked about their

---

501   Johan Ahlander, "Asylum Seekers or Welfare? Swedish Election Breaks Immigration Taboo." Reuters, September 1, 2014, https://www.reuters.com/article/us-sweden-election-immigration-idUSKBN0GW29X20140901

immigration status.[502] This number was lower in sanctuary cities than non-sanctuary cities, but the number was still substantial, with 39 percent of Hispanics in Cook County, Illinois and 40 percent in Los Angeles County, California saying they wouldn't report crimes committed against them.

In 2018, noncitizens made up 64 percent of all federal arrests, but that was mostly due to immigration offenses. Among nonimmigrant crimes, noncitizens (13.7 percent of the US population as of 2018)[503] are overrepresented in some crimes, but not all of them. Among violent crimes prosecuted at a federal level, noncitizens were just 6.4 percent, and among weapons charges, they were only 4 percent. The crimes where noncitizens were overrepresented include property crimes (they make up 19 percent), fraud (22 percent), drugs (20 percent), and regulatory crimes (42 percent).[504]

Those statistics don't include foreign-born criminals, who were naturalized and became American citizens.

The US isn't the best country when it comes to reports of immigration and crime; other nations like Denmark, for example, give exceptional details on not only the immigration status of criminals but also how many generations they've been in the country.

A 2016 Danish report found that immigrants from some countries like the US, Sweden, Germany, China, and Thailand

---

502   Nik Theodore, "Insecure Communities: Latino Perceptions of Police Involvement in Immigration Enforcement." *Department of Urban Planning and Policy*, University of Illinois at Chicago, May 2013, https://greatcities.uic.edu/wp-content/uploads/2014/05/Insecure_Communities_Report_FINAL.pdf

503   Jason Lange, "U.S. Foreign-Born Population Swells to Highest in over a Century." Reuters, September 13, 2018, https://www.reuters.com/article/us-usa-immigration-data/u-s-foreign-born-population-swells-to-highest-in-over-a-century-idUSKCN1LT2HZ

504   United States Department of Justice, Mark Motivans. "Immigration, Citizenship, and the Federal Justice System, 1998-2018." *Bureau of Justice Statistics*, August 2019, https://www.bjs.gov/content/pub/pdf/icfjs9818.pdf

were less likely to commit crimes, while immigrants from Lebanon (who are mostly Palestinian), Somalia, Turkey, Iraq, and Pakistan have the highest crime indexes of any foreign-born groups. The report also found that the children of immigrants were much more likely to commit crimes than their immigrant parents in nearly every case. The children of Syrians, Lebanese, Moroccans, and Indians have especially higher crime indexes.[505]

Young men who come from a non-Western background had an especially high number of criminal convictions. A study in 2018 found that in the course of a year, 13 percent of all non-Western men ages 17–24 are convicted of a criminal code violation. This is three times higher than Danish men of the same age.[506]

The refugee crisis of 2015 brought hundreds of thousands of those young, non-Western men to Europe, especially to Sweden and Germany.

There have been multiple studies in both countries and results have been conflicting, but there's certainly data that finds many of these refugees would go on to commit crimes throughout both countries. Soon after Germany began admitting more refugees than any other nation in Europe, news broke that over twelve hundred German girls were sexually assaulted, raped, and robbed in cities all over the country on New Year's Eve.[507]

---

505   Denmark, Statistics Denmark, "Indvandrere i Danmark." *Udgivet af Danmarks Statistik*, November 2016,
http://www.dst.dk/Site/Dst/Udgivelser/GetPubFile.aspx?id=20704&sid=indv2016

506   Anders Topp Thomsen, "GRAFIK Indvandrede og efterkommere halter efter etniske danskere." *Kontakt DR*, March 1, 2018, https://www.dr.dk/ligetil/grafik-indvandrede-og-efterkommere-halter-efter-etniske-danskere

507   Rick Noack, "Leaked Document Says 2,000 Men Allegedly Assaulted 1,200 German Women on New Year's Eve." *The Washington Post*, April 19, 2019, https://www.washingtonpost.com/news/worldviews/wp/2016/07/10/leaked-document-says-2000-men-allegedly-assaulted-1200-german-women-on-new-years-eve/

Leaked documents showed that more than two thousand men, mostly of North African descent, were responsible.[508,509] The story went viral almost instantly and created more concerns of Western degeneration awareness.

Studies on how much the refugees contributed to crime in Germany are conflicting, with some insisting the effects were negligible,[510] and others claiming that they were pretty significant. A 2018 report by the Interior Minister found that asylum seekers, which make up just 2 percent of the German population, were responsible for 8.5 percent of all crimes other than immigration violations.[511] The report found that refugees from countries like Syria committed fewer crimes while those from North Africa, Afghanistan, and Pakistan committed more crimes.

Another study by *The Wall Street Journal* found that all foreign nationals were vastly overrepresented in crime statistics. While foreigners only made up 12.8 percent of the population, they accounted for 34.7 percent of crime suspects. The study found that foreign nationals were especially overrepresented in several types of crimes, making up the suspects in about 70 percent of organized crimes, 75 percent of pickpocketing, 55 percent of forged official documents, 41 percent of burglaries, 37 percent of rapes and sexual assaults, 34 percent of social

508   "String of New Year's Eve Sexual Assaults Outrage Cologne."
       Duetsche Welle, April 1, 2016, https://www.dw.com/en/
       string-of-new-years-eve-sexual-assaults-outrages-cologne/a-18958334
509   Von Eva Quadbeck, "Silvester-Täter kamen mit Flüchtlingswelle ins Land."
       RP Online, June 9, 2016, https://rp-online.de/politik/deutschland/berlin/
       silvester-nacht-von-koeln-taeter-kamen-mit-fluechtlingswelle-ins-land_
       aid-9233833
510   "Report: Refugee-Related Crimes in Germany Increases Less than Influx of
       Asylum Seekers." *Deutsche Welle*, February 17, 2016, https://www.dw.com/en/
       report-refugee-related-crimes-in-germany-increase-less-than-influx-of-asylum-
       seekers/a-19053227
511   Von Martin Lutz, et al., "Kriminalstatistik: Bayern Ist Das Sicherste
       Bundesland." *DIE WELT,* April 27, 2018, https://www.welt.de/politik/
       deutschland/article175907770/Kriminalstatistik-Bayern-ist-das-sicherste-
       Bundesland.html?wtrid=onsite.onsitesearch

benefit fraud, and 29 percent of murders and manslaughters.[512] Another report from 2019 found that Germans were significantly more likely to be the victims of a crime committed by an immigrant rather than visa-versa.[513]

Sweden, like Germany, also took in a massive number of refugees—the most refugees per capita of any other nation on the globe.[514] The political class celebrated their arrival as a success story[515] celebrating Swedish tolerance, but some studies doubt the level of success.

Like many other countries, Sweden does not keep official crime data on immigration and crime. The last time they held an official government-sponsored report was in 2005, and it showed that those born abroad were 2.5 times as likely to be registered as a suspect in a crime as native Swedes.[516, 517] Immigrants from different areas produce different levels of crime; those from North Africa and the Middle East are more

512   Bojan Pancevski, "An Ice-Cream Truck Slaying, Party Drugs and Real-Estate Kings: Ethnic Clans Clash in Berlin's Underworld." *The Wall Street Journal*, October 17, 2018, https://www.wsj.com/articles/ethnic-crime-families-provoke-german-crackdown-1539604801

513   Marcel Leubecher, "Gewalt von Zuwanderern gegen Deutsche nimmt zu." *DIE WELT*, September 4, 2019, https://www.welt.de/politik/deutschland/article191584235/BKA-Lagebild-Gewalt-von-Zuwanderern-gegen-Deutsche-nimmt-zu.html

514   Admir Skodo, "Sweden: By Turns Welcoming and Restrictive in Its Immigration Policy." *Migrationpolicy.org*, May 27, 2019, https://www.migrationpolicy.org/article/sweden-turns-welcoming-and-restrictive-its-immigration-policy

515   Carl Bidt, "The Truth About Refugees in Sweden." *The Washington Post*, April 1, 2019, https://www.washingtonpost.com/news/global-opinions/wp/2017/02/24/the-truth-about-refugees-in-sweden/?utm_term=.548e1b21de99

516   Lee Roden, "Why Sweden Doesn't Keep Stats on Ethnicity and Crime." *The Local*, May 8, 2018, https://www.thelocal.se/20180508/why-sweden-doesnt-keep-stats-on-ethnic-background-and-crime

517   Peter Martens and Stina Holmberg, "Crime among persons born in Sweden and other crime." *National Council for Crime Prevention*, 2005, https://www.bra.se/download/18.cba82f7130f475a2f1800025850/1371914734437/2005_crime_among_persons_born_in_sweden_and_other_countries.pdf

likely to commit crimes than those from places like Finland. The government has yet to commission another official report on the subject.

One area in Sweden where migrants are far overrepresented is in gang-related crimes. A study done in 2012 by Amir Rostami, a researcher from the University of Stockholm, found that 76 percent of gang members in Sweden were either immigrants or the children of immigrants.[518] The 2015 refugee crisis made the situation worse as gangs recruited new members from the hundreds of thousands of migrants coming from the Middle East and North Africa.[519]

Gangs in Sweden contribute heavily to gun violence in the country. A report by the newspaper *Dagens Nyheter* in 2017 found that about 90 percent of all murders or attempted murders in the country were carried out by immigrants or the children of immigrants.[520] Gun murders increased from an average of four per year in the early '90s to seventeen in 2011, to forty-three in 2017.[521,522]

Gang-related violence has caused a dramatic uptick in the number of shootings, arson attacks, and bombings;[523] yes,

---

518 "Sweden Has a Problem with Hand Grenades." *Euronews,* April 11, 2018, https://www.euronews.com/2018/04/10/ sweden-has-a-problem-with-hand-grenades-and-here-s-why

519 "Police: Gangs Recruiting Afghan Asylum Seekers into Drug Trade." *Radio Sweden,* December 4, 2018, https://sverigesradio.se/sida/artikel. aspx?programid=2054&artikel=7104779

520 Lasse Wierup, "Vanligt Med Utländsk Bakgrund Bland Unga Män Som Skjuter." *Dagens Nyheter,* 20 May 2017, https://www.dn.se/nyheter/sverige/ vanligt-med-utlandsk-bakgrund-bland-unga-man-som-skjuter/

521 Paulina Neuding, "Sweden's Violent Reality Is Undoing a Peaceful Self-Image." *POLITICO,* April 17, 2018, https://www.politico.eu/article/ sweden-bombings-grenade-attacks-violent-reality-undoing-peaceful-self-image-law-and-order/

522 "Why Are Young Men in Sweden Shooting Each Other?" *The Economist,* March 8, 2018, https://www.economist.com/europe/2018/03/08/ why-are-young-men-in-sweden-shooting-each-other

523 Richard Milne, "Sweden Bomb Attacks Reignite Debate over Gang Violence." *The Financial Times,* June 12, 2019, https://www.ft.com/ content/0af96328-8d07-11e9-a1c1-51bf8f989972

Sweden now has a problem with bombings. In 2017, there were 211 reported incidents of explosions throughout Sweden. That number dropped to a still outrageously high 162 bombings in 2018. It spiked again during the first six months of 2019 when Sweden endured 120 bombings, an increase of 45 percent from the same time the prior year. Most of these were centered in Stockholm or the city of Malmö, which has a very heavy foreign-born population.[524, 525, 526, 527, 528]

Some of the suburbs of Malmö and Stockholm and have become so gang-riddled that it has created a hazardous situation for policing and emergency services, creating dozens of vulnerable areas or as they're popularly referred to, no go zones. As of 2019, the Swedish police have identified sixty areas as vulnerable, with twenty-two being especially vulnerable.[529] This is not unique to Sweden: the UK, Germany, France, Brazil, and South Africa all have high-crime areas where gangs, whether they are made up of foreign-born residents or not, make it extremely difficult to police.

In both Germany and Sweden, national populist parties like the Alternative for Deutschland (AfD) and SD were able to use these crime statistics to their benefits and attract new voters

524 "NFC Utreder Sprängdåd Allt Mer - Nyheter (Ekot)." *Swedish Radio*, May 4, 2018, https://sverigesradio.se/sida/artikel.aspx?programid=83&artikel=6945601

525 "Antalet Sprängdåd i Sverige Har Ökat." *SVT Nyheter*, April 15, 2019, https://www.svt.se/nyheter/snabbkollen/antalet-sprangdad-i-sverige-har-okat

526 Lisa Röstlund, "Antalet Sprängdåd i Sverige Ökar." *Dagens Nyheter*, August 20, 2019, https://www.dn.se/nyheter/sverige/antalet-sprangdad-i-sverige-okar/

527 "Olagliga Sprängningar På Rekordnivå - P4 Stockholm." *Swedish Radio*, June 16, 2019, https://sverigesradio.se/sida/artikel.aspx?programid=103&artikel=7243467

528 Jon Hall, "Bombings and Explosions Up 45% in Sweden This Year." *Scriberr News*, September 2, 2019, https://www.scriberrnews.com/2019/09/02/in-2019-bombings-and-explosions-up-45-in-sweden/

529 "Here's the New Police List of Trouble Suburbs in Sweden." *The Local*, June 3, 2019, https://www.thelocal.se/20190603/sweden-vulnerable-areas-decrease-positive-trends-police

who were not just members of the working poor, but also white-collar workers who feared for their safety.

Unlike in the 2010 and 2014 Swedish elections where the SD focused on protecting the welfare state, the 2018 election message was that crime has become out of control. The SD campaigned on a tough-on-crime platform and promised to stop the flow of mass immigration into Sweden that was bringing these foreign criminals. The SD's messaging worked; on September 9, they won 17.5 percent of the national vote, nearly a 4.7 percent increase from four years prior. They were especially victorious in the southern part of the country that was heavily populated with foreign-born residents and won their first mayorship and twenty-one out of thirty-three municipalities in Skåne.[530, 531, 532] They were so successful that they, along with the center-right Moderate Party, defeated the center-left SD from power in the suburbs of Malmö for the first time since 1911.[533]

A study in 2019 found that the concerns over immigration including the criminality of immigrants was the number one issue that drove voters to the SD and the ruling elite chose to ignore these concerns at their own peril.[534]

530 Richard Orange, "Sweden Democrats Biggest in Two-Thirds of Skåne Districts." *The Local,* September 11, 2018, https://www.thelocal.se/20180911/sweden-democrats-biggest-in-two-thirds-of-skne-districts

531 Simon Johnson, "Sweden's Far-Right Eyes Election Gains as Gang Violence Rises." Reuters, 26 June 2018, https://www.reuters.com/article/us-sweden-election-crime-insight/swedens-far-right-eyes-election-gains-as-gang-violence-rises-idUSKBN1JM0QQ

532 Steven Erlanger, "As Sweden Votes, the Far Right Gains Even in an Immigrant Bastion." *The New York Times,* September 7, 2018, https://www.nytimes.com/2018/09/07/world/europe/sweden-election-far-right.html

533 Richard Orange, "Moderates Take Power across Skåne with Help of Sweden Democrats." *The Local,* November 27, 2018, https://www.thelocal.se/20181127/how-the-moderates-have-taken-power-all-over-skne-with-sd-help

CHAPTER 6

TERRORISM

THE ISLAMIC TERRORIST attacks on September 11, 2001, was arguably the first singular event of the 21st century that reshaped global politics. The reaction to the attacks by citizens around the world and the response by Western government changed the fabric of society, launching decades-long wars and caused a cultural backlash against Islam.

In an effort to save neoliberalism, many Western governments like the US adopted a neoconservative worldview that justified nation-building and increasing their military presence around the world. At the same time, absorbing millions of people from the Islamic majority countries, some of whom had negative opinions of Western societies and had no intentions of assimilating and others who outright wanted to destroy them. "We fight them over there, so we don't need to fight them over here" became a rallying cry for Americans justifying former President George W. Bush's wars.

As the US and its allies sought to remake the world, Bush told Americans that their patriotic duty was to go shopping and visit Disney World, proving that we were resilient consumers and that the terrorists really hadn't won.[535] At the same time, the neoliberal agenda marched on. Mass immigration continued a near-record pace, the opioid epidemic that would claim half a million American lives grew, and globalization rapidly displaced manufacturing workers across the Rust Belt. All the conditions that led to the rise of Donald Trump blossomed in the aftermath of the 9/11 attacks.

Western governments' answer to the growing threat of Islamic terrorism was to continue on their neoliberal project toward more open borders, mass consumerism, and military adventurism without questioning the foundation of their philosophy and its long-term ramifications.

This is not to say that terrorism in itself pushes a majority of voters toward national populist parties; a study by the European Journal of Political Research found the inverse was true and that the citizens of Germany became more favorable toward the EU after experiencing an Islamic terrorist attack.[536] Yet, it is the overall reaction by governments and their refusal to implement longstanding reforms in the wake of terrorism that creates a condition that drives people toward national populism.

A perfect example can be found in the difference between the US' reaction to the 9/11 attacks and Denmark's.

POST-9/11

The September 11 attacks were a rallying moment for the US, then-President George W. Bush's approval ratings shot up to 90

---

535   Robert Reich, "How Did Spending Become Our Patriotic Duty?" *The American Prospect*, December 19, 2001, https://prospect.org/article/how-did-spending-become-our-patriotic-duty

536   Erik Gahner Larsen, et al, "Do Terrorist Attacks Feed Populist Eurosceptics? Evidence from Two Comparative Quasi-Experiments." European Journal of Political Research, May 21, 2019, https://ejpr.onlinelibrary.wiley.com/doi/abs/10.1111/1475-6765.12342

percent.[537] There was almost nothing he couldn't have received bipartisan support on in an effort to combat terrorism and keep the homeland safe. The 9/11 Commission Report made several important recommendations on how to accomplish that goal including a biometric exit-entry system, a US border screening system, a secure identification system, a layered security system, an interagency center to target illegal aliens and human traffickers, tighter controls on student visas, more immigration agents for the FBI Joint Terrorism Task Force, increased global standards for travel documents, 24/7 staffing on the border, a physical barrier at the border, and addressing the problem of migrants who destroy their travel documents (immigration fraud).[538] Under Bush's watch, most of those recommendations were delayed, only partially enacted, or completely ignored. Others were temporary fixes: under Bush, the number of visas offered to certain troubled regions of the world like Pakistan was cut significantly only to see huge increases during the Obama administration. [539, 540, 541, 542, 543]

537   "Presidential Approval Ratings – George W. Bush." *Gallup,* November 26, 2019, https://news.gallup.com/poll/116500/presidential-approval-ratings-george-bush.aspx

538   National Commission on Terrorist Attacks, *THE 9/11 COMMISSION REPORT,* W. W. Norton & Company, (Washington DC: 2004). pp. 186-187, 385-394.

539   United States Senate, "Vital 9/11 Commission Recommendations Remain Incomplete, Unaddressed." *Democratic Policy Committee,* February 8, 2007, https://www.dpc.senate.gov/dpcdoc.cfm?doc_name=fs-110-1-26

540   "DHS Intends to Ignore 9/11 Commission Recommendations." *Federation of American Immigration Reform,* March 4, 2011, https://www.fairus.org/press-releases/dhs-intends-ignore-911-commission-recommendations

541   Alane Kochems, "The September 11 Commission Report Card: The Good, the Bad, and the Ugly." *The Heritage Foundation,* December 13, 2005, https://www.heritage.org/homeland-security/report/the-september-11-commission-report-card-the-good-the-bad-and-the-ugly

542   Kelly Moore, "9/11 Border Lessons Still Ignored in US, Belgium: Column." *USA Today,* July 10, 2018, https://www.usatoday.com/story/opinion/2016/03/25/brussels-terror-securing-border-911-commission-column/82218750/

543   Sara McElmurry, et al., "Balancing Priorities: Immigration, National Security, and Public Safety." *Chicago Council on Global Affairs,* November 1, 2016, https://www.thechicagocouncil.org/publication/balancing-priorities-immigration-national-security-and-public-safety

The US continued its neoliberal agenda and Americans rallied around Bush's war efforts as his administration missed a golden opportunity to secure America's borders, fully reorganize many areas of the US legal immigration system, and crack down significantly on illegal immigration.

Bush was careful to thread the needle that the US was not at war with Islam, and he did not make any effort to reduce immigration from Muslim-majority countries.[544] Quite the opposite, Bush tripled the number of Muslim refugees entering the US every month from 2001 to 2005.[545] From 2001 to 2018, the US imported over 2 million people from Muslim-majority nations, including many from troubled regions of the world.[546] This angered a portion of American voters, especially those within the Republican Party, and gave an opening for a candidate like Trump, who campaigned against political correctness and mass immigration, which led to rising poll numbers when he called for a temporary ban on all Muslim immigration in December 2015. Ultimately, when he became president that was narrowed down to a travel ban on eight countries identified as terror-prone; several polls showed that a plurality or majority supported this policy.[547,548]

---

544   United States White House, "Backgrounder: The President's Quotes on Islam." *The White House,* accessed December 19, 2019, https://georgewbush-whitehouse.archives.gov/infocus/ramadan/islam.html

545   David Bier, "Trump Has Cut Christian Refugees 64%, Muslim Refugees 93%." *Cato Institute,* October 3, 2018, https://www.cato.org/blog/trump-has-cut-christian-refugees-64-muslim-refugees-93

546   Daniel Horowitz, "Have We Learned Anything about Our Immigration System 18 Years after 9/11?" *Conservative Review,* September 11, 2019, https://www.conservativereview.com/news/learned-anything-immigration-system-18-years-9-11/

547   "American Voters Want Second Opinion On Obamacare, Quinnipiac University National Poll Finds; Voters Support Immigrants, But Also Back Muslim List." *Quinnipiac University Poll,* January 12, 2017, https://poll.qu.edu/national/release-detail?ReleaseID=2416

548   Dana Blanton, "Fox News Poll: Views on (Trump's) Proposed Ban on Non-U.S. Muslims." *Fox News,* July 10, 2017, https://www.foxnews.com/politics/fox-news-poll-views-on-trumps-proposed-ban-on-non-u-s-muslims

While America's focus moved toward nation-building abroad, Denmark began looking inward in the face of a rising threat from Islamic fundamentalism.

The citizens of Denmark had one of the earliest signs of Western degeneration awareness, understanding that an attack on the US would ultimately lead to attacks on European countries. Denmark held its national election exactly ten weeks after the terrorist attacks, and 9/11 was very much in the minds of Danish voters. Pia Kjærsgaard's Danish People's Party (DPP) held their national convention only days after 9/11 and made the opposition to Islam the main center of their party's message in the upcoming election, with one candidate declaring, "[Muslims] are only waiting until they are enough to kill us."[549] At the convention, Kjærsgaard used explicit references to 9/11 and Danish culture.

"It has been mentioned that 9/11 became the cause for a 'clash of civilizations.' I don't agree. Because a clash of civilizations would require that there were two civilizations, and that is not the case. There is only one civilization, and that is ours," Kjærsgaard said.

On November 20, the DPP received 12 percent of the vote, winning twenty-two seats and becoming the third-largest party in Denmark. The party provided parliamentary support for Denmark's first majority government composed entirely of conservative parties since 1901. In exchange for the DPP's support in the coalition government, the right-wing governing parties of Denmark implemented some of the policy positions on immigration to reduce the number of new entrants from non-Western countries.[550] Including a sweeping measure

---

549   Susi Meret, "The Danish People's Party, the Italian Northern League and the Austrian Freedom Party in a Comparative Perspective: Party Ideology and Electoral Support." (PhD diss., Aalborg University, 2010) p.127.

550   Manuel Alvarez-Rivera, "General Aspects of the Electoral System." *Electionresources.org*, last updated June 5, 2019, http://electionresources.org/dk/

in 2002 restricting family reunification, *The Washington Post* characterized this law as one of the first Muslim bans in the West.[551]

The DPP and other right-wing governments held together a governing coalition from 2001 till 2011 and then again from 2015 to 2019. Over the fourteen years they governed Denmark, the DPP successfully pushed eighty different immigration restrictions into law[552] including a drastic cut to the number of foreigners who became naturalized citizens from 16,662 in 2002 to just 2,836 in 2018, with the largest cuts coming from immigrants from Turkey, Somalia, and Pakistan according to government data.[553]

Aside from cuts to legal immigration, the DPP pushed forward new regulations on refugee resettlement and assimilation.

In 2005, the government required all potential UN resettlement refugees be assessed for their integration potential to ensure that all refugees would assimilate into Danish society. They began to see a shift in the demographics of refugees; for example, most Iranian refugees accepted to Denmark in the coming years were Christian and not Muslim. During the refugee crisis of 2015, Denmark was the only Nordic country to reject a majority of asylum claims, accepting just 29 percent of Iraqis and 35 percent of Afghans who applied.

During the height of the refugee crisis, the Danish Parliament reduced benefits for new immigrants—including refugees—

---

551   Samantha Ruth Brown, "Analysis | Denmark Already Had a Muslim Ban. It Was Just Called Something Else." *The Washington Post*, April 18, 2019, https://www.washingtonpost.com/news/monkey-cage/wp/2017/03/23/denmark-already-has-a-muslim-ban-its-just-called-something-else/?utm_term=.8fdb13b76728

552   Anders Widfeldt, *The Growth of the Radical Right in Nordic Countries: Observations from the past 20 years*, The Migration Policy Institute, (Washington DC: 2018) p.19.

553   Statistics Denmark, "Population and Elections." *StatBank Denmark*, accessed December 18, 2019, https://www.statbank.dk/10025

and adopted a law seizing asylum seekers' valuables to pay for their resettlement.[554, 555]

One of the most conversational laws pushed by the DPP, especially in the eyes of the media, is a policy enacted in 2018 that mandated all children over the age of one who lived in heavily populated Muslim ghettos be placed in Danish cultural classes for twenty-five hours a week. The policy has the intended goal of abolishing the ghettos and fully assimilating all the nation's Muslims by 2030.[556]

The DPP's focus on terrorism continued throughout the last two decades as Europe gripped with dozens of either attempted or successful terrorist attacks from Islamic extremists; Denmark remained relatively peaceful. In 2015, Denmark experienced its only successful terrorist attack by an Islamic extremist when the son of Jordanian immigrants killed two civilians and wounded five police officers in an attempt to murder cartoonist Lars Vilks over his illustration of Muhammad.[557]

In the aftermath of the terror attack, the DPP campaigned even harder over the subject of immigration and Islam, promising to prosecute imams who influenced their adherents to fight for ISIS.[558] In their Danish election just four months later, the DPP won their largest share of the vote in their party's

---

554   Arwa Damon and Tim Hume, "Denmark Adopts Law Approving Seizure of Migrant Assets." *CNN*, January 26, 2016, https://www.cnn.com/2016/01/26/europe/denmark-vote-jewelry-bill-migrants/index.html

555   "Denmark Enacts Cuts to Refugee Benefits." *The Local*, August 26, 2015, https://www.thelocal.dk/20150826/denmark-passes-controversial-refugee-benefit-cuts

556   Ellen Barry and Martin Selsoe Sorensen, "In Denmark, Harsh New Laws for Immigrant 'Ghettos'." *The New York Times*, July 2, 2018, https://www.nytimes.com/2018/07/01/world/europe/denmark-immigrant-ghettos.html

557   Griff Witte and Karla Adam, "Danish Attacks Echo France." *The Washington Post*, February 16, 2015, https://www.washingtonpost.com/world/danish-police-kill-copenhagen-shooting-suspect/2015/02/15/8bed7a70-b50a-11e4-9423-f3d0a1ec335c_story.html

558   Malcom Brabant, "Denmark's Radical Parties Vie for Power As Terror Casts a Shadow over Poll." *The Guardian*, May 30, 2015, https://www.theguardian.com/world/2015/may/30/denmark-radical-parties-power-terror-shadow-poll.

history—21 percent of the vote—making them the nation's second-largest party.

Although their immigration policies have been panned by media outlets and neoliberal politicians, the DPP's restrictive stance on immigration became so popular with voters that both conservative and liberal parties adopted many of their plans. In the 2019 election, the center-left Social Democrats won the election campaigning on capping the number of immigrants from non-Western countries, expelling certain refugees, and mandating work requirements in exchange for public benefits.[559]

The Social Democrats' leader and current Prime Minister of Denmark, Mette Frederiksen, dismissed the open-border ideology that has engulfed most left-wing parties around the world, saying during one of the debates, "You are not a bad person just because you are worried about immigration."[560]

It's plausible that had center-left parties moved toward the DPP's position before 9/11, the national populist party would have never risen to power in the first place.

TERRORISM IN THE TROPICS

Islamic terrorism isn't the only type of violent extremism that spurred a populist response by voters. In South America, citizens endured a brutal military campaign by Marxist revolutionaries; it was especially bad in Colombia where citizens suffered through a series of assassinations, kidnappings, drug dealing, illegal mining, extortion, murder, and bombings that

---

559   Richard Orange, "Mette Frederiksen: the Anti-immigration Left Leader Set to Win Power in Denmark." *The Guardian*, May 14, 2019, https://www.theguardian.com/world/2019/may/11/denmark-election-matte-frederiksen-leftwing-immigration.

560   Jon Henley, "Denmark's Centre-left Set to Win Election with Anti-immigration Shift." *The Guardian*, June 4, 2019, https://www.theguardian.com/world/2019/jun/04/denmark-centre-left-predicted-win-election-social-democrats-anti-immigration-policies.

ultimately led to the election of the national populist Centro Democrático (Democratic Centre) in 2018.

Colombia, like many other South American governments, had been battling the revolutionary socialist guerilla organization the Revolutionary Armed Forces of Colombia (FARC) since 1964. The situation became much worse, however, once their neighbor Venezuela democratically elected Hugo Chávez in 1998 and slowly turned his country into a state sponsor of leftist guerilla movements throughout Latin America.

The Venezuelan government before Chávez was hostile toward Venezuelan guerilla groups like FARC and the National Liberation Army (ELN), though they regularly allowed them to evade Colombian troops by hiding in their country.[561] After Chávez was elected, however, the country took a turn to openly supporting FARC.

The Colombian government attempted to end the violent conflict through peace negotiations from 1999 through 2002 during the same time Chávez met with Raúl Reyes, a FARC commander, and offered protection to the group. When the peace process failed on February 20, 2002, the Colombian government under President Álvaro Uribe seized back the safe zone and began an assault on FARC.[562]

Seven weeks later, in neighboring Venezuela, a coup against Chávez unfolded and the nation's military detained the president and transported him off the mainland. The United States and several European nations quickly recognized a new interim government.

Chávez immediately reached out to FARC, ELN, and Fidel Castro and his loyalist in the Venezuelan presidential guard,

561   "How Venezuela Complicates Peace Talks in Colombia." *The Economist*, last modified October 22, 2018, https://www.economist.com/the-economist-explains/2018/10/22/how-venezuela-complicates-peace-talks-in-colombia.

562   Amanda Taub, "Colombia's War with FARC and Why It Might Finally End, Explained." *Vox*, December 18, 2014, https://www.vox.com/2014/12/18/7412615/farc-colombia-ceasefire.

the latter of whom returned Chávez to power when they reoccupied the presidential palace at Miraflores.[563]

After that, Chávez dramatically changed his approach to FARC and other socialist guerillas. Believing that another coupe was around the corner and the military wasn't loyal to him, Chávez began training FARC's terrorists in guerrilla and urban warfare in case there was a full-on invasion of Venezuela and they would need to defend him.

In late 2002, Chávez developed a Contingency Plan that authorized terrorists trained by Chávez's government to attack, neutralize, or liquidate opposition supporters, political leaders, and resources through sabotage and targeted assassination.[564]

FARC set up drug trafficking operations in Venezuela that helped to fund them after Uribe's aggressive tactics to dismantle the organization destroyed many of their cocaine trafficking routes. The terrorist organization also funneled US$400,000 to Chávez's ally Ecuadorian President Rafael Correa's campaign, helping secure his victory.

With the help of Chávez, FARC set up narco-states in Venezuela, Colombia, and Bolivia. As Colombia moved closer to the United States, Chávez created an alliance with Marxist governments in Cuba, Bolivia, Ecuador, and Nicaragua as part of his Bolivian revolution to fight against American imperialism.

Chávez created the Bolivarian Continental Movement (MCB), which integrated various revolutionary groups as a way to fight against imperial powers—namely, the United States. FARC was named as one of the earliest members of this new umbrella organization. Upon its founding, MCB decided to establish cells in every Latin American country.

---

563   Miguel Goncalves, "Conditional Convenience: Venezuelan Support for FARC Since Hugo Chávez." *The Yale Review of International Studies,* January 2014, http://yris.yira.org/essays/1251.

564   Luis Fleischman, *Latin America in the Post-Chávez Era: The Security Threat to the United States,* Potomac Books, (Dulles, Virginia).

FARC became a political, military, and social tool for Chávez to expand his Bolivian revolution throughout South and Central America, especially against America's ally Colombia.

Between 2002 through 2008, Chávez and FARC continued significant cooperation and Chávez even stated that FARC was the real army that occupies territory in Colombia rather than a terrorist group. Chávez went so far as to provide FARC a safe haven in Venezuela as the terrorist organization was being beaten down by the Colombian military. A 2008 raid of a FARC camp in Ecuador revealed that Chávez even subsidized a FARC office in Caracas.[565]

FARC and Chávez's relationship declined significantly though in the latter half of 2008 as FARC became unable to accomplish Chávez's goals, and there was mounting international pressure on Chávez to distance himself from the terrorist organization.

Colombian politics also helped move Chávez away from FARC. In 2010, Colombia elected President Juan Manuel Santos, who vowed to pursue a less aggressive stance against Chávez and FARC. Chávez began working closely with Santos and the two countries even conducted intelligence operations against FARC together. Chávez passed an anti-terrorism funding law as FARC's leadership suffered a series of deaths and imprisonments. Their membership sunk from twenty thousand members in 2002 to just nine thousand in 2011.

With its back against the wall, FARC lashed out in a wave of attacks—notably, mortar bombings in the town of San Miguel, Putumayo and at the Colombian military base in La Macarena.[566] Under Santos's leadership, the number of terrorists killed or captured declined while the number of attacks rose.

---

565   José R. Cárdenas, "The FARC's Enablers." *Foreign Policy*, May 16, 2011, https://foreignpolicy.com/2011/05/16/the-farcs-enablers/.

566   Office for the Coordinator for Counterterrorism, "Chapter 2. Country Reports: Western Hemisphere Overview." *U.S. Department of State*, July 31, 2012, https://2009-2017.state.gov/j/ct/rls/crt/2011/195546.htm.

Uribe was furious at the rise of terrorism in Colombia and his successor's soft approach on FARC; he created a new political party, the Democratic Center, in 2014. The party ran former Treasury minister Óscar Iván Zuluaga for president in that year's election on a platform of ending negotiations with FARC.[567]

In their first time at the ballot box, the Democratic Center won nineteen seats in the House and Senate and made it to the second round of the presidential election, narrowly losing to Santos by only six points.[568] Four years later, the Democratic Center nominated Urbine's protégé, forty-one-year-old Iván Duque Márquez, who won the presidency against a former guerrilla.[569] The party also won a majority of seats in the Colombian Congress.

---

567 John Otis, "Colombia's Election Hinges On How To End War." *Time*, June 13, 2014, https://time.com/2853801/colombia-election-president/.

568 "Santos Re-elected in Colombian Poll." *BBC News*, June 16, 2014, https://www.bbc.co.uk/news/world-latin-america-27862555.

569 Nicholas Casey and Susan Abad, "Colombia Elects Iván Duque, a Young Populist, As President." *The New York Times*, June 17, 2018, https://www.nytimes.com/2018/06/17/world/americas/colombia-election-ivan-duque.html.

CHAPTER 7

SOVEREIGNTY

THE BELIEF IN national sovereignty is a clear dividing line in Western nations. The term globalist has become both a slur and a badge of honor depending on who you ask.

At the very heart of the issue is a question of values: do you value international cooperation and the dream of a more unified future, or do you value regionalism, self-determination, and democracy. Both worldviews have their own advantages as well as drawbacks. Globalists can spur international agreements promising mutual protection and cooperation, while nationalists can offer their citizens democratic representation. Those likely to benefit from globalization, like the highly educated, connected, and wealthy, are genuinely more in favor of a system where they're not in full control because it doesn't matter given that they're not likely to lose their economic or social standing.

They don't have the fear of seeing their coal mine closing or their factory job laying off workers because their government has complied with international environmental benchmarks set in the Paris Agreement or Kyoto Protocol. Mutual protection compacts between countries are also less likely to affect wealthy families given that their children are less likely to serve in the military.[570] They'll never know the fear of having a relative dying in defense of another nation's borders. So, while they won't have to bear the burdens of globalism, they have all the social benefits of knowing their tax dollars are being used to promote beliefs they agree with like a more environmentally friendly future and spurring female entrepreneurship in third world countries. They can feel like they are contributing to a progressive global community that makes the world a better place without having to actually sacrifice very much to make that happen.

Those who don't find themselves with the same level of privilege tend to oppose globalism because it takes decision-making out of the hands of local and national governments that protect their economic and cultural interests. The loss of their nation's sovereignty may lead to many more repercussions in their day-to-day lives that could rob them of the financial stability, cultural or regional hegemony, and basic dignity.

One group of people view nationalism as a set of values that belong in the dust bin of history, while the other looks at it as their only hope to protect their way of life. This conflict is what has changed the political dynamics of nearly every Western country. Before the rise of national populism, the range of acceptable political discourse (known as the Overton window) was confined to right-wing or left-wing neoliberalism. Bush, Obama, Clinton, McCain, Romney…all different variations of the same political discussion.

That changed with the rise of national populism challenged the notion that voters were powerless to stop nation-states'

---

570   Kathy Roth-Douquet and Frank Shaeffer, "Why Aren't the Rich and the Famous in Uniform?" *Today*, May 26, 2006, https://www.today.com/popculture/why-aren-t-rich-famous-uniform-wbna12990432#.Vw0NtPwo6Ul.

subjugation to international organizations. National populists told those on the losing end of globalism that they didn't have to surrender their heritage, culture, democracy, and the remaining institutions that protect their interests. The ruling elite's willingness to surrender their nation's sovereignty has caused a widespread voter backlash among voters who began to support national populists.

This fight to protect the nation-state sprawls across the globe, from the US exiting the Paris Climate Agreement to Brazil leaving the UN Compact on Migration to Salvini warring with the EU over international agreements involving refugees. Yet there is no better example in recent history of the issue of sovereignty moving voters away from the ruling elite than the British vote to exit the EU.

BREXIT

When the UK joined the European Economic Community (EEC) in 1973[571] the decision to join was overwhelmingly supported by the British people. When the UK held a national referendum on the decision to join the EEC in 1975, 67 percent of Brits voted in favor of their country's membership. Still, the Brits decided to opt-out of the European Monetary System, which led to the creation of the Euro; Margaret Thatcher, who would become prime minister in 1979, had deep reservations about further tying the UK to the EU.

On September 8, 1988, Thatcher delivered a speech known as the Bruges Speech at the College of Europe where she warned about the growing dominance of the EU outside of what was originally intended.

---

571   "ON THIS DAY 1973: Britain Joins the EEC." BBC, December 15, 2019, http://news.bbc.co.uk/onthisday/hi/dates/stories/january/1/ newsid_2459000/2459167.stm.

"I want to see us work more closely on the things we can do better together than alone. Europe is stronger when we do so, whether it be in trade, in defense or in our relations with the rest of the world," Thatcher said in her speech. "But working more closely together does not require power to be centralized in Brussels or decisions to be taken by an appointed bureaucracy. Indeed, it is ironic that just when those countries such as the Soviet Union, which have tried to run everything from the center, are learning that success depends on dispersing power and decisions away from the center, there are some in the Community who seem to want to move in the opposite direction."

"We have not successfully rolled back the frontiers of the state in Britain, only to see them re-imposed at a European level with a European super-state exercising a new dominance from Brussels," Thatcher continued. "Certainly, we want to see Europe more united and with a greater sense of common purpose. But it must be in a way which preserves the different traditions, parliamentary powers and sense of national pride in one's own country; for these have been the source of Europe's vitality through the centuries."[572]

Thatcher foresaw that the EU, which was created to establish an area of free trade and a common customs union between member states was turning into a European project. Politicians in Brussels hoped to transform the EU into something at resembled the United States, where a central state with a large bureaucracy would govern across all formally independent nations.

In 1992, Prime Minister John Major signed the Maastricht Treaty, which turned the EEC into the EU and forfeited even more of the UK's sovereignty over the issues of inflation, public

---

572   Margaret Thatcher, "Speech to the College of Europe ("The Bruges Speech")." *Margaret Thatcher Foundation*, September 20, 1988, https://www.margaretthatcher.org/document/107332.

debt, and deficit. Opinion polls at the time found that only 31 percent of the British public approved of the Treaty,[573] but there was no national referendum on the issue despite the concerns of many politicians and the public at large. The UK would go on to introduce over 52,000 laws from 1990 through 2017 as a result of EU legislation. These laws especially affected the UK on issues as varied as trade, agriculture, financial services, employment, and the environment.[574] In addition to the series of laws, the EU issued hundreds of thousands of directives and regulations dealing with everything from labor relations to home appliances like vacuum cleaners and electric ovens.[575, 576]

Less than a decade later, in 1997, the British lost control of their immigration system when they signed the Treaty of Amsterdam which included the Schengen Agreement, allowing the free movement of people throughout the EU member states.

At the time of the agreement, most members of the EU were Western countries including France, Germany, Sweden, the Netherlands, Austria, Italy, Spain, and Greece with fairly equivalent levels of income, education, and welfare. Joining the Schengen Agreement was not going to cause a massive increase in the number of low-skilled immigrants.

Like most of the principles that originally guided the EU, that all changed as poorer Eastern European nations like

---

573   Vernon Bogdanor, "Futility of a House with No Windows." *The Independent*, July 26, 1993, https://www.independent.co.uk/voices/futility-of-a-house-with-no-windows-1487252.html.

574   Thomson Reuters, "EU Laws Introduced in the UK over Last 25 Years Highlights Scale of Challenge Facing Lawmakers Following Brexit." Reuters, March 27, 2017, https://www.thomsonreuters.com/en/press-releases/2017/march/eu-laws-introduced-in-the-uk-highlights-scale-of-challenge-facing-lawmakers-following-brexit.html.

575   Matthew Holehouse, "EU to Launch Kettle and Toaster Crackdown After Brexit Vote." *The Telegraph*, May 11, 2016, http://www.telegraph.co.uk/news/2016/05/10/eu-to-launch-kettle-and-toaster-crackdown-after-brexit-vote2/.

576   Marian L. Tupy, "The European Union: A Critical Assessment," *Cato Institute*, June 22, 2016, https://www.cato.org/publications/economic-development-bulletin/european-union-critical-assessment#cite-9

Poland, Hungary, Romania, and Bulgaria joined the EU and the UK was swamped with more than a million low-skilled workers and had no say in the matter.

In 2002, Thatcher started the genesis that led to Brexit. In her book *Statecraft: Strategies for a Changing World*, Thatcher said the EU was fundamentally unreformable and the UK should consider leaving, becoming the first former prime minister to raise the possibility.[577]

"We trade globally," she wrote, "and we must think globally—not confined within the bounds of a narrow Europe…That such an unnecessary and irrational project as building a European superstate was ever embarked upon will seem in future years to be perhaps the greatest folly of the modern era…And that Britain, with her traditional strengths and global destiny, should ever have been part of it will appear a political error of historic magnitude."[578]

Thatcher voiced her concerns about the growth of the EU throughout her retirement, believing that the EU was moving from its intended purpose as an economic agreement into a political project that the British people had not endorsed. [579] During one speech, she warned that the idea of a European superstate to rival the US would never work because the continent had no common language or culture.[580]

---

577   Andy McSmith, "Tories Maintain Silence over Thatcher's Europe Outburst." *The Telegraph*, March 19, 2002, https://www.telegraph.co.uk/news/uknews/1388179/Tories-maintain-silence-over-Thatchers-Europe-outburst.html.

578   Jordan Weissmann, "Watch Margaret Thatcher Explain Why the Euro Is a Terrible Idea in 1990." *The Atlantic*, April 8, 2013, https://www.theatlantic.com/business/archive/2013/04/watch-margaret-thatcher-explain-why-the-euro-is-a-terrible-idea-in-1990/274768/.

579   Ethan Thoburn, "How Maggie Was Right About The EU Decades Ago." *The Bruges Group*, June 21, 2019, https://www.brugesgroup.com/blog/how-maggie-was-right-on-europe-decades-ago.

580   Nile Gardiner, "What Margaret Thatcher Really Thought About Brexit." *CapX*, March 20, 2015, https://capx.co/what-margaret-thatcher-really-thought-about-brexit/.

Most Conservative Party politicians stayed silent on Thatcher's warning while Prime Minister Tony Blair used it to attack Tories as being prone to isolationism. How can anyone seriously argue for withdrawal from Europe? Blair said. The policy to talk about withdrawal, to end up ruling out a single currency forever, whatever the economic circumstances, is not an act of patriotism. It is an act of folly. The vice president of the European Commission at the time, Neil Kinnock, went a step further and referred to Thatcher's words as pub bore politics.[581]

Thatcher's words weren't lost on everyone, however; an emerging politician named Nigel Farage became the leader of the small, Eurosceptic, UKIP promising to make the former prime minister's proposal a reality.

From the beginning, Farage laid out a vision that the UK needed to leave the EU. At one event in 1997, he told a room of UKIP voters, What started as a murmur in the pubs and clubs and wherever people congregate in this country is now beginning to reach a crescendo raw and what people are saying is 'Get Britain Out.'[582] Farage had been elected as chairman of the UKIP in 1998 and was one of their first three members elected to the European Parliament the following year.

UKIP with its Eurosceptic vision was considered a fringe party extremely far out of the mainstream. David Cameron famously referred to them in 2006 as fruitcakes, loonies, and closet racists.[583] Farage took over the party in 2006 hoping to transform it but stepped down from leadership in 2009 to run for Parliament only to retake control the following year.

---

581   Andy McSmith,"Tories Maintain Silence over Thatcher's Europe Outburst." *Telegraph.co.uk.*, last modified March 19, 2002, https://www.telegraph.co.uk/news/uknews/1388179/Tories-maintain-silence-over-Thatchers-Europe-outburst.html.

582   Alex Hunt, "How UKIP Became a Political Force." *BBC News*, November 21, 2014, https://www.bbc.com/news/uk-politics-21614073.

583   Ros Taylor, "Cameron Refuses to Apologise to Ukip." *The Guardian*, April 4, 2006, https://www.theguardian.com/politics/2006/apr/04/conservatives.uk.

After his return to leadership in 2010, Farage began using his platform as an MEP to increase his visibility as well as UKIP's. During one session of the EU Parliament, Farage berated President of the European Council Herman Van Rompuy as having the charisma of a damp rag, and the appearance of a low-grade bank clerk and accused him of being the quiet assassin of European democracy.[584] The video went viral around the UK and Europe and UKIP began growing in membership with every new social media post of Farage attacking leaders within the EU. From 2010 to 2013, UKIP's membership more than doubled from 15,535 to 32,447.

As Europe suffered through Greece's debt crisis and the UK underwent austerity measures to curb spending, Farage's public image and support among British citizens grew exponentially.

He appealed to working-class Labour voters over the drastic cuts in education, welfare, and healthcare[585] as well as to Tory voters over issues like sovereignty and immigration. The idea that the political elite both in London and Brussels were out of touch with mainstream British society took hold.

In the run-up to the 2014 EU parliamentary election, Farage attacked the political class for lying to the British public about the EU's control of British sovereignty and mass immigration from Eastern European countries like Poland, which he claimed hurt working-class Brits. The Liberal Democrat leader Nick Clegg accused Farage of not being a serious politician and being a dangerous con, which only emboldened his supporters.

Farage campaigned across the UK as an everyman, telling fellow patriots that they were made powerless due to the elite

---

584 Associated Press, "Ukip's Nigel Farage Tells Van Rompuy: You Have the Charisma of a Damp Rag." *The Guardian,* February 25, 2010, https://www.theguardian.com/world/2010/feb/25/ nigel-farage-herman-van-rompuy-damp-rag.

585 Thiemo Fetzer, "Did Austerity in the UK Lead to the Brexit Crisis?" *Harvard Business Review,* August 23, 2019, https://hbr.org/2019/08/ did-austerity-in-the-uk-lead-to-the-brexit-crisis.

who sold out their country to global forces like the EU that threatened the very basis of British democracy. The UKIP campaign poster featured the British flag being burned from its center with the EU Flag underneath featuring the slogan Who really runs this country? 75 percent of our laws are now made in Brussels.[586]

In several speeches, Farage compared the EU to the dystopian book *1984* as well as the authoritarian regime in North Korea that had reduced (the British Parliament) to the level of a large council.[587]

The electorate was offered a clear and opposing dichotomy: they could either vote for UKIP and fight to regain the sovereignty that was their birthright or vote for the status quo. On May 22, 2014, UKIP won 27 percent of the vote, becoming the largest party from the UK in the EU Parliament.[588] Experts derided UKIP's victory as nothing more than a protest vote that would ultimately end up as meaningless;[589] they couldn't understand that a massive uprising was occurring across the country against the EU.

One person who did notice Farage's rise was Prime Minister David Cameron—even before UKIP's election victory in 2014. Under pressure from members of the Conservative Party, Cameron announced on January 23, 2013, that if the British voters chose to re-elect the Conservative Party in the 2015

---

586   Hatty Collier and Patrick Wintour, "Nigel Farage Launches Ukip Campaign Amid Criticism of 'racist' Rhetoric." *The Guardian*, April 22, 2014, https://www.theguardian.com/politics/2014/apr/22/ nigel-farage-ukip-european-elections-campaign.

587   Catherine MacMillian, "The European Union as a Totalitarian Nightmare: Dystopian Visions in the Discourse of the UK Independence Party (UKIP)," *Romanian Journal of English Studies*, Istanbul 2019. p. 161.

588   "Vote 2014 Election Results for the EU Parliament UK Regions News." *BBC News*, 2014, https://www.bbc.com/news/events/vote2014/eu-uk-results.

589   Douglas J. Elliott, "What Do the European Union Election Results Mean?" *Brookings*, May 26, 2016, https://www.brookings.edu/blog/ up-front/2014/05/26/what-do-the-european-union-election-results-mean/.

election, the party would put a referendum on EU membership on the ballot before the end of 2017.[590] The campaign tactic worked, the Tories won a majority in the 2015 election and even forced Farage to resign from UKIP after he lost the election for Parliament.[591]

Cameron's Foreign Secretary Philip Hammond made good on Cameron's promise and introduced the European Union Referendum Act of 2015, allowing the Secretary of State to appoint the date for the referendum on membership in the EU, which took place on June 23, 2016.[592]

The referendum thrust Farage back into the spotlight; he along with a few high-profile British politicians like former London Mayor Boris Johnson and Chair of the Parliamentary Labour Party John Cryer backed the Leave campaign. Opposition to the referendum included the government of the United Kingdom, Scotland, and Wales; the Labour, Liberal Democrat, and Scottish National Parties; and Prime Minister David Cameron and most of his cabinet members, including future Prime Minister Theresa May.

Although there were many different factions of the Leave Campaign, they focused on two main issues: sovereignty and immigration. Johnson's effective slogan Take Back Control[593] emphasized that Britain's membership in the EU had forced

---

590   "David Cameron promises in/out referendum on EU." *BBC News,* January 23, 2013, https://www.bbc.com/news/uk-politics-21148282.

591   Andy McSmith, "Ukip Leader Nigel Farage Resigns After Losing South Thanet Seat?" *The Independent,* May 8, 2015, https://www.independent.co.uk/news/uk/politics/generalelection/ukip-leader-nigel-farage-loses-in-south-thanet-10235307.html.

592   "European Union Referendum Act 2015 (c. 36)." *British and Irish Legal Information Institute,* December 17, 2015, http://www.bailii.org/uk/legis/num_act/2015/ukpga_201536_en_1.html.

593   Dr. Tim Haughton, "It's the slogan, stupid: The Brexit Referendum." *University of Birmingham,* https://www.birmingham.ac.uk/research/perspective/eu-ref-haughton.aspx

them to send £350 million per week to Brussels that could otherwise have gone to funding the UK's healthcare system.[594] Justice Minister Michael Gove, who co-convened Vote Leave, also argued that EU regulations cost the British economy £600 million every week.[595] Our membership of the EU stops us being able to choose who makes critical decisions which affect all our lives, Gove said about the referendum.[596]

Johnson also emphasized that the UK has lost control of its borders; one month before the election, the Office of National Statistics published information stating that net migration to the UK had increased by 81 percent since 2012 and an astonishing 333,000 people immigrated to the country in 2015 alone.[597]

"(There is) no public consent for the scale of immigration we are seeing," Johnson said to the BBC. "(immigration has become) completely out of control...I think that they (the figures) show the scandal of the promise made by politicians repeatedly that they could cut immigration to the tens of thousands and then to throw their hands up in the air and say there's nothing we can do because Brussels has taken away our control of immigration."[598]

---

594   Kate McCann and Tom Morgan, "Nigel Farage: £350 Million Pledge to Fund the NHS Was 'a Mistake'." *The Telegraph,* June 24, 2016, https://www.telegraph.co.uk/news/2016/06/24/ nigel-farage-350-million-pledge-to-fund-the-nhs-was-a-mistake/.

595   Michael Gove, "Michael Gove Makes Case for EU Exit: 'It's Time to Take Back Control'." *The Guardian,* April 19, 2016, https://www.theguardian. com/politics/2016/apr/19/michael-gove-makes-case-eu-exit-bbc-today.

596   "Dreaming of Sovereignty." *The Economist,* March 19, 2016, https://www. economist.com/britain/2016/03/19/dreaming-of-sovereignty.

597   Alan Travis, "Net Immigration to UK Nears Peak As Fewer Britons Emigrate.I *The Guardian,* May 26, 2016, https://www.theguardian.com/uk-news/2016/ may/26/net-migration-to-uk-nears-peak-fewer-britons-emigrate.

598   Jon Stone, "Boris Johnson Attacks His Own 'cynical' Tory Manifesto Promise on Immigration." *The Independent,* May 26, 2016, https://www.independent. co.uk/news/uk/politics/boris-johnson-attacks-cynical-tory-manifesto-promise-on-immigration-a7050246.html.

Leavers also insisted that if nations like Turkey, Montenegro, Serbia, and Albania joined the EU, more than 5 million more mostly Muslim immigrants would be added to this number.[599]

Farage, who campaigned with a separate organization to Johnson, also focused on the same points. In one of his most controversial campaign events, Farage unveiled a poster featuring thousands of migrants crossing into Europe with the words Breaking Point The EU has failed us all splashed against the image.

"Frankly, as you can see from this picture, most of the people coming are young males and, yes, they may be coming from countries that are not in a very happy state, they may be coming from places that are poorer than us, but the EU has made a fundamental error that risks the security of everybody."[600]

Although many accused Leavers of being racist or anti-immigrant, it was the question of sovereignty that was at the heart of their campaign, as well as the question of who gets to decide the laws that govern the people of Britain, including their economy and immigration system.

Remainers like Cameron promised to make reforms within the EU system, including allowing the UK to opt-out of further political integration, housing and welfare requirements for migrants, prevent the UK from contributing to further euro-zone bailouts and lower administrative burdens.[601] They also insisted that leaving the EU would bring the UK to the brink

---

599   Chris Morris, "Reality Check: Did Johnson Talk Turkey During Brexit Campaign?" *BBC News*, last modified January 18, 2019, https://www.bbc.com/news/uk-politics-46926119.

600   Jon Stone, "Nigel Farage's Anti-immigrant Poster Reported to Police over Claims It Incites Racial Hatred." *The Independent*, June 17, 2016, https://www.independent.co.uk/news/uk/politics/nigel-farages-anti-immigrant-poster-reported-to-police-over-claims-it-incites-racial-hatred-a7087801.html.

601   "EU reform deal: What Cameron wanted and what he got." *BBC News*, February 20, 2016, https://www.bbc.com/news/uk-politics-eu-referendum-35622105.

of an economic collapse, inflict an immediate recession, and cause the loss of 820,000 jobs.[602]

Johnson told voters in a BBC interview that every concession that Cameron had received and would receive from the EU was not enough to protect British sovereignty. "We were told were going to get wholesale changes. Anybody looking at the agreement that we have before us now would be in no doubt that this is not fundamental reform," Johnson said in the interview. "The government lawyers just blew up. They said this basically voids our obligations under the 1972 European Communities Act. It doesn't work. You cannot express the sovereignty of Parliament and accept the 1972 European Communities Act."[603]

What Remainers didn't understand was that the Leave Vote, being executed by Johnson, Farage, and Gove, was delving into the zeitgeist of millions of Brits. An Ipsos poll taken right before the vote found that the most important issues facing the British people were immigration, healthcare, and the EU[604] all the major points the Brexiteers campaigned on.

On election day, 17.41 million Brits voted to Brexit from the EU, the largest democratic mandate in British political history. The Leave campaign succeeded by a margin of 52 to 48 percent.

After seeing the results, Farage exclaimed that it was a victory for the sovereignty of the UK and the end of the EU, "The EU is failing, the EU is dying. I hope we've knocked the first brick out of the wall. I hope this is the first step toward a Europe of sovereign nation states."[605]

---

602   Rebecca Perring, "Brexit BULL! Remain 'experts' RUBBISH Britain but Our Stats Show They Keep Being WRONG." *Express. co.uk.*, July 18, 2019, https://www.express.co.uk/news/uk/1155003/ Brexit-latest-news-project-fear-OBR-brexit-report-no-deal-brexit.

603   BBC, "EU reform on UK sovereignty not achievable, says Johnson." *BBC News,*

604   "Concern About Immigration Rises As EU Vote Approaches." Ipsos MORI, June 23, 2016, https://www.ipsos.com/ipsos-mori/en-uk/ concern-about-immigration-rises-eu-vote-approaches.

605   Estelle Shirbon, "Triumph for 'Brexiteer' Nigel Farage, British Scourge of the EU." Reuters, June 24, 2016, https://www.reuters.com/article/ us-britain-eu-farage-triumph-idUSKCN0ZA2JT.

Brexiteers' strategy of focusing on the issues of sovereignty and immigration worked. A survey by Lord Ashcroft found that British voters were motivated to leave the EU because they wanted to reclaim their democracy and regain control of their borders. The issue of sovereignty and living under laws created by politicians they voted for was cited as the most important reason voters chose to leave the EU, followed in second place by their desire to have complete control of their immigration system.[606]

The entire British political system was turned on its head; Cameron resigned and Theresa May, who also supported the UK remaining in the EU, became the second female prime minister after Thatcher. In her first speech as prime minister, May declared, "As we leave the European Union, we will forge a new, bold, positive role for ourselves in the world, and we will make Britain a country that works, not for the privileged few, but for every one of us."[607]

When laying out the terms of Brexit, May laid out a twelve-point plan to negotiate the terms of leaving the EU, including the UK's ability to control their own laws including immigration, set up new trade agreements, and forge an agreement for British nationals who lived in Europe. She emphasized that her Brexit agreement would not (be a) partial membership of the European Union, associate membership of the European Union, or anything that leaves us half-in, half-out.

May promised to deliver on what the majority of Brits voted for: a clean break from the EU. Unfortunately, that's not what she delivered.

On July 12, 2018, May's government released The Future Relationship between the UK and the EU, otherwise known as

---

606   Lord Ashcroft, "How the United Kingdom voted on Thursday…and why." *Lord Ashcroft Polls*, June 24, 2016, https://lordashcroftpolls.com/2016/06/how-the-united-kingdom-voted-and-why/.

607   "EU reform on UK sovereignty not achievable, says Johnson," *BBC News*, March 6, 2016, bbc.com/news/uk-politics-35739518/.

the Chequers agreement. Unlike her proposal for a true Brexit, the Chequers agreement allowed the UK to have access to the European Single Market preventing the UK from subsidizing any of their nation's industries and keeping beholden to EU regulations on the environment, climate change, and consumer protection. It also forced the UK to continue to make appropriate (financial) contributions.[608]

In addition to being under Brussels' control economically, May's deal forced UK courts to adhere to rulings made by European judges in cases related to EU-set rules. This makes the EU courts supreme to the UK's. Not exactly the idea of an independent nation.[609]

Lastly, on the issue of immigration, while May promised to end the free movement of people in the plan, she did not create a border between the Republic of Ireland and Northern Ireland, meaning that someone from the EU could simply go to Ireland and then walk over to Northern Ireland and enter the UK.[610]

To say the plan was not received well by Brexiteers would be an extreme understatement; one British MEP said to these authors that it was a deal you'd only sign on to if you lost a war.

Within days of the release of the Chequers agreement, May's Brexit Secretary David Davis and Foreign Secretary Boris Johnson resigned in opposition.[611, 612]

---

608   Simon Rushton, "Chequers Deal: Theresa May's Divisive Brexit Plan Explained." *Inews.co.uk.*, November 12, 2018, https://inews.co.uk/news/politics/brexit/chequers-deal-brexit-plan-agreement-what-explained-theresa-may-219525.

609   Alex Barker, "The Soft-Brexit Chequers Deal: What It Means." *Financial Times,* July 9, 2018, https://www.ft.com/content/aeb53c82-82ac-11e8-96dd-fa565ec55929.

610   "Chequers Plan 'will Avoid Hard Border'." *BBC News,* September 16, 2018, https://www.bbc.com/news/uk-northern-ireland-45539190.

611   Heather Stewart, "Brexit Secretary David Davis Resigns Plunging Government into Crisis." *The Guardian,* July 9, 2018. https://www.theguardian.com/politics/2018/jul/08/david-davis-resigns-as-brexit-secretary-reports-say.

612   "Johnson: It is Not Too Late to Save Brexit." *BBC News,* last modified July 18, 2018, https://www.bbc.com/news/uk-politics-44871629.

In his resignation speech, Johnson hit on all of the major points where May had failed the UK in Brexit negotiations, "We burned through negotiating capital. We agreed to hand over a £40 billion exit fee, with no discussion of our future economic relationship. We accepted the jurisdiction of the European Court over key aspects of the withdrawal agreement. And, worst of all, we allowed the question of the Northern Irish border, which had hitherto been assumed on all sides to be readily soluble, to become so politically charged as to dominate the debate…it is not too late to save Brexit. We have time in these negotiations. We have changed tack once and we can change again."[613]

Parliament would reject every proposal that May offered. She inevitably was forced to resign from office for her inability to secure a proper Brexit that gave the British people what they wanted: a return to national sovereignty.

On July 24, 2019, May stepped down as Prime Minister and was replaced with Johnson.[614] After several failed attempts to move the ball on Brexit, Johnson purged Conservative Party members opposing his deal. [615] With Brexit stalled, new elections were called in October and held in December.[616]

---

613   "Full Text of Boris Johnson's Resignation Speech in the House of Commons." *Brexit Central,* July 24, 2018, https://brexitcentral.com/full-text-boris-johnsons-resignation-speech-house-commons/.

614   William Booth, Karla Adam, "Theresa May Resigns, Boris Johnson Becomes U.K. Prime Minister, in Elaborate Transition of Power." *The Washington Post,* July 25, 2019. https://www.washingtonpost.com/world/europe/boris-johnson-uk-prime-minister/2019/07/24/42bcel26-ac93-11e9-9411-a608f9d0c2dc_story.html.

615   Yaron Steinbuch, "Boris Johnson kicks out 21 Conservative MPs who opposed him." *The New York Post,* September 4, 2019, https://www.nypost.com/2019/09/04/boris-johnson-kicks-out-21-conservative-mps-who-opposed-him/.

616   Stephen Castle and Mark Landler, "Boris Johnson Calls for December Election in Push to Break Brexit Deadlock." *The New York Times,* October 24, 2019, www.nytimes.com/2019/10/24/world/europe/boris-johnson-election-brexit.html.

The election held on December 12th, 2019, was one of the most consequential in British history. The Tories under Johnson campaigned on a united pledge to get Brexit done while both Labour and the Liberal Democrats promised to hold a second referendum. It was a clear and concise difference between what a right-wing government would offer voters as opposed to a left-wing.

Johnson's party won nearly 44 percent of the vote, the highest percentage of any party since 1979 and the Tories netted a total of 365 seats, the largest Conservative-led government since 1987. The Liberal Democrat leader Jo Swinson was defeated in her district and it was the worst results for the Labour Party since 1935.[617]

The Tories election victory came even as Johnson had a disapproval rating 20 points higher than their approval.[618] Voters were willing to turn a blind eye to their distaste for Johnson to achieve Brexit, even in areas that had historically voted Labour.

Just eight days after the election, the new Parliament passed Johnson's Withdrawal Agreement, and Queen Elizabeth ratified the bill on January 23, 2020, allowing the UK to officially split with the EU on January 31st.[619,620]

618   "Conservatives hold 12-point lead over Labour heading into final week of the election campaign." *Ipsos*, December 5, 2019, https://www.ipsos.com/ipsos-mori/en-uk/conservatives-hold-12-point-lead-over-labour-heading-final-week-election-campaign.

619   Mark Landler and Stephen Castle, "U.K. Parliament Advances Brexit Bill in Lopsided Vote, All but Assuring January Exit." *The New York Times*, December 20, 2019, www.nytimes.com/2019/12/20/world/europe/brexit-parliament.html.

620   Macer Hall, "Boris Johnson Secures Brexit! EU Set to Rubber-Stamp Deal as Queen Signs It into UK Law." *Express.co.uk*, January 23, 2020, www.express.co.uk/news/politics/1232079/brexit-news-boris-johnson-eu-deal-the-queen-royal-assent-law.

CHAPTER 8

ECONOMIC INEQUALITY AND ANXIETY

ISSUES LIKE IMMIGRATION, sovereignty, and corruption are the largest motivating factors for national populists, but economic anxiety and fears of globalism also play a critical factor in explaining the rise and ideology of national populism.

Free trade, globalism, and laissez-faire economics have become orthodoxy to most center parties on both the left and right. Although this has been fairly standard for most right-wing parties over the last half century, the evolution among liberals has created an opportunity for national populists to broaden their appeal to voters who typically vote for left-wing parties.

In the later part of the 20th century and the first two decades of the current century, leaders of left-wing parties like Clinton, Obama, Blair, and Hollande oversaw their parties' transformation. Those left-wing parties abandoned the key constituency of working-class voters in favor of a cosmopolitan, multicultural, educated, and woke future.

Left-wing parties who had been advocates for laborers, union workers, and low-skilled natives for over a century now began viewing them as backwards culturally and worthy of being left behind by globalism. Working-class people found it increasingly difficult to find work, start a family, and create a life that provided them with a level of dignity they expected from living in a Western society. Many became victims of despair, depression, and drug overdoses.

Workers found themselves on the losing end of globalism, abandoned by traditional center-left parties, but were still unwilling to trust traditional right-wing parties that had a long history of opposing labor unions and protections for workers. Left with few other options, a portion of former left-wing voters found themselves voting for national populists like Le Pen, Trump, and the Law and Justice Party (PiS) in Poland.

Unlike most traditional right-wing parties, national populists are centrists on economic issues; they're supportive of protecting industries like manufacturing, mining, and logging, support a welfare state that helps young families and seniors and are skeptical of free trade and globalism. [621,622]

Trump won the Rust Belt, which including the states of Ohio, Pennsylvania, Wisconsin, and Michigan, by appealing to voters who had been on the losing end of globalism for decades. The billionaire reality TV star campaigned on rene-gotiating NAFTA, attacking free trade agreements, and ending global trade deals. It paid off substantially; in 2012, union voters supported former president Obama by eighteen points

---

621   Ronald F. Inglehart and Pippa Norris, *Trump, Brexit, and the Rise of Populism: Economic Have-Nots and Cultural Backlash,* John F. Kennedy School of Government or of Harvard University. (Cambridge: 2016). p. 36.

622   Felix Kersting, "The Economics of Populism in the Present." Exploring Economics, May 15, 2019, https://www.exploring-economics.org/en/discover/economics-populism-present/.

over pro-free trade Republican Mitt Romney; in 2016 they supported Clinton over Trump by only eight points.[623,624]

Likewise, Le Pen, who was trounced in the second round of the 2017 French presidential election, winning only 34 percent of the general election vote, received the majority of the vote of blue-collar workers.[625] In the legislative elections later on that year, Le Pen's party won a third of the legislative seats in the department of Pas-de-Calais, a working-class area.[626]

The PiS took control of the Polish government in 2015 and implemented a series of socially conservative but fiscally centrist economic proposals to support families. Some of the policies they put forth included a $125 monthly stipend for every child in a family, increased pension payments, and the elimination of income taxes for everyone under the age of twenty-six.[627] Despite all these new tax cuts and social programs, the Polish government still managed to cut deficit spending.[628]

Defending his economic populism, the PiS leader Jaroslaw Kaczynski declared at one rally, "A person whose pockets are empty is not really free…(this is the end of the) post-colonial concept of Poland as a source of cheap labor."

---

623   Felix Kersting, "The Economics of Populism in the Present." Exploring Economics, last modified May 15, 2019, https://www.exploring-economics. org/en/discover/economics-populism-present/.

624   "How Groups Voted in 2016." *Roper Center for Public Opinion Research*, last modified 2016, https://ropercenter.cornell.edu/how-groups-voted-2016.

625   "How Groups Voted in 2012." *Roper Center for Public Opinion Research*, 2013, https://ropercenter.cornell.edu/how-groups-voted-2012.

626   "Résultats Des élections Législatives 2017." Ministere De L'Interieur, June 2017, https://www.interieur.gouv.fr/Elections/Les-resultats/Legislatives/ elecresultlegislatives-2017/(path)/legislatives-2017//062/index.html.

627   Marc Santora, "In Poland, Nationalism With a Progressive Touch Wins Voters." *The New York Times*, October 10, 2019, https://www.nytimes. com/2019/10/10/world/europe/poland-election-law-and-justice-party.html.

628   Marcin Goclowski and Joanna Plucinska, "Polish Government Touts Deficit Cut Ahead of Election." Reuters, August 27, 2019, https://www.reuters.com/article/us-poland-budget/ polish-government-touts-deficit-cut-ahead-of-election-idUSKCN1VH1DC.

In another interview with a Catholic radio host, Kacynski insisted these policies weren't socialist. "I've been even called upon to confess, so to speak, that I am a Socialist. Well, I'm not a Socialist, I'm a supporter of social solidarity…(the PiS) want to support the development of small, medium and smallest entrepreneurship. The economy should benefit the whole society, instead of just one group and leaving the rest of the society in God's good grace." [629]

PiS managed all of these economic moderate positions while remaining fervently against mass immigration and refugee resettlement and supportive of Poland's ties to the Catholic Church. On October 13, 2019, Polish voters rewarded the PiS with the highest share of the vote that any party had received since Poland returned to democracy after the fall of the Soviet Union.[630] Exit polls showed that a majority or plurality of voters of every age voted for the PiS.[631]

Economic populism appeals to both left and right-wing voters, there's an overlap in the issues that appeal to Trump supporters and Bernie voters, between the Leave campaign and Brits who want Jeremy Corbyn to be the next prime minister. Yet the reason they support populist economics comes from different ideological sources. Those that find themselves supporting left-wing candidates seek an egalitarian society based on social justice, while those voting for national populists seek a fair economic model that prioritizes communities, workers, and families. It's not that national populists don't believe that business owners have the right to be successful;

---

629   Marc Santora, "In Poland, Nationalism With a Progressive Touch Wins Voters." *The New York Times*, October 10, 2019, https://www.nytimes.com/2019/10/10/world/europe/poland-election-law-and-justice-party.html.

630   Mary Sibierski, "Populists set to win Poland vote, raising fears of new EU tensions." AFP, October 14, 12, https://www.afp.com/en/news/15/populists-win-poland-vote-raising-fears-new-eu-tensions-doc-1lb8mn13.

631   "Poland, Ipsos exit poll." Twitter, last modified October 13, 2019, https://twitter.com/EuropeElects/status/1183487545826521089.

they do, it's just they owe some loyalty to the communities, civic institutions, and people that create the stable and successful environment that allows those companies to thrive.

Libertarians incorporated their economic policies into several generations of right-wing parties. Center-right parties told those on the losing end of globalism to embrace the chaos of market forces because ultimately, it would allow them to purchase cheap goods and download new apps, even as it robbed them the dignity of a well-paying job and poisoned the health of communities and families across the working-class areas of the country. The concerns for how these policies were detrimental to workers and what would happen to them if they were forced to compete with the cheapest labor on Earth were seemingly unheard. This purely globalist approach to the economy became a secular religion to the political class, especially in the US.

The push for globalism went without the consent of the American people. Since 1988, a consistent majority of Americans have told pollsters at *The New York Times* they prefer restrictions over unbridled free trade.[632] But as has been the case on other issues like sovereignty and immigration, the public's opinion mattered very little.

Over the past few decades, there have been two defining moments that led millions of people to skepticism toward globalism and the current economic system: the Great Recession, which led to the billion-dollar bailouts of companies and countries that were too big, to fail, and the hollowing out of Middle America after NAFTA and the normalization of trade deals with China.

Those events culminated in the rise of national populism in Europe, the UK, and America.

---

632   "Poll." *The New York Times*, March 2016, https://assets.documentcloud.org/documents/2773278/Poll.pdf

THE GREAT RECESSION

The Great Recession occurred throughout most of Europe and North America in late 2007 when the financial crisis and subprime mortgage crisis devastated the American economy and rippled throughout most of the West, destroying millions of jobs and trillions of dollars in wealth.

It came at a particularly difficult time, especially in an America that was suffering through two Middle Eastern wars, the hollowing out of manufacturing jobs in Middle America, and a looming opioid crisis that was beginning to kill more than fifteen thousand people per year.[633] According to the Bureau of Labor Statistics, the recession occurred in the US from late 2007 until June 2009, though its effects, including higher unemployment rates, continued to linger for years afterward. In January 2010, unemployment hit double digits in eighteen states.[634]

Presidents Bush and Obama turned to Keynesian economics, pouring nearly $500 billion in bailout and stimulus plans into the economy during the recovery.[635, 636] The recovery took more than half a decade to reach every geographical corner of the US, but even then, however, it wasn't equal among race, geography, or education.

---

633   Jon Collins, "Prince's Death Another Loss in a Decades-long Opioid Overdose Epidemic." *MPR News*, June 3, 2016, https://www.mprnews.org/story/2016/06/03/prince-overdose-opioid-epidemic.

634   "State Unemployment Rates, January 2007 to January 2017 : The Economics Daily: U.S. Bureau of Labor Statistics." *U.S. Bureau of Labor Statistics*, March 17, 2017, https://www.bls.gov/opub/ted/2017/state-unemployment-rates-january-2007-to-january-2017.htm.

635   Tam Harbert, "Here's how much the 2008 bailouts really cost." *MIT Sloan*, February 21, 2019, https://mitsloan.mit.edu/ideas-made-to-matter/heres-how-much-2008-bailouts-really-cos.

636   Renae Merle, "A guide to the financial crisis — 10 years later." *The Washington Post,* September 10, 2018, https://www.washingtonpost.com/business/economy/a-guide-to-the-financial-crisis–10-years-later/2018/09/10/114b76ba-af10-11e8-a20b-5f4f84429666_story.html.

Only one Wall Street banker, Kareem Serageldin, went to jail for handing out risky loans and crashing the world economy.[637] Most big financial institutions were saved, but business on Main Street stagnated and Americans across the political spectrum from the Tea Party and Occupy Wall Street protested the elite. Even when Washington spent billions to save America's car manufacturers, they continued to move production and investment overseas, showing no loyalty to the American taxpayer and worker.[638]

By 2016, upper-income Americans had completely recovered from the recession, with their net worth increasing to $810,800 from $740,100 in 2007. They were the only ones to see a return to pre-recession prosperity, while middle- and lower-income Americans' net worth in 2016 was still 30 to 40 percent lower on average than it had been in 2007. For low-income white Americans, net worth declined from $42,700 in 2007 to just $22,900 in 2016.[639]

Millions of Americans who had been on the losing end of globalism for decades found themselves on the losing end of the recovery. Voters who felt the system was designed to work against them moved from Occupy Wall Street to the Bernie Sanders campaign and from the Tea Party to Donald Trump. Rural counties, especially in the South, Appalachia, and the West, had much slower recoveries, with twenty-two counties'

637 Jesse Eisinger, "Why Only One Top Banker Went to Jail for the Financial Crisis." *The New York Times Magazine,* April 30, 2014, https://www.nytimes.com/2014/05/04/magazine/only-one-top-banker-jail-financial-crisis.html.

638 Edward Niedermeyer, "Even After Bailout, GM and Chrysler Invest Billions Abroad." *Washington Examiner,* November 5, 2012, https://www.washingtonexaminer.com/weekly-standard/even-after-bailout-gm-and-chrysler-invest-billions-abroad.

639 Rakesh Kochhar and Anthony Cilluffo, "How U.S. Wealth Inequality Has Changed Since Great Recession." *Pew Research Center,* November 1, 2017, https://www.pewresearch.org/fact-tank/2017/11/01/how-wealth-inequality-has-changed-in-the-u-s-since-the-great-recession-by-race-ethnicity-and-income/.

economies not recovering at all since the recession. A majority of midsize counties in Midwestern states like Iowa, Illinois, Michigan, Minnesota, and Wisconsin that swung heavily for Trump in 2016 had reached their pre-recession job peaks by 2016.[640]

The recession was arguably even more painful and politically divisive in Europe, where the recession hit in 2007 and 2011. Aside from the recession, Europe was engulfed in a series of crises including over debt, bailouts, and austerity. Unemployment rates, especially for Europeans under twenty-four, climbed to over 20 percent in Belgium, Finland, France, Hungary, Poland, Sweden, the UK, over 40 percent in Italy, and 50 percent in Greece and Spain.[641]

Greece's economy was devastated by the financial crisis, which was followed by a sovereign debt crisis where Greece was incapable of paying back its debt. Other countries like Portugal, Spain, Cyprus, and Ireland also found themselves in a similar financial state and required bailouts from the EU, the International Monetary Fund, and the European Central Banks.[642]

Not only did these bailouts and austerity measures not sit well with citizens of their respected countries, but they also did not fare well with voters from more fiscally responsible countries and pushed them toward national populist parties. One of the clearest examples of that was in Finland.

Finnish voters were enraged over the EU's response to the debt-ridden countries and their government's participation in the bailouts. A Think If Laboratories poll conducted

---

640   Dr. Emilia Istrate, *County Economies 2016: Widespread Recovery, Slower Growth*, NACO, February 8, 2017, https://www.naco.org/resources/county-economies-2016-widespread-recovery-slower-growth.

641   Antonio Flores and Jens Manuel Krogstad, "EU Unemployment Nears Pre-recession Low."*Pew Research Center*, July 18, 2018, https://www.pewresearch.org/fact-tank/2018/07/18/eu-unemployment-rate-nears-pre-recession-low/.

642   Library, CNN, "European Debt Crisis Fast Facts." CNN, January 28, 2019, https://www.cnn.com/2013/07/27/world/europe/european-debt-crisis-fast-facts/index.html.

in April 2011 found that nearly 60 percent of Finns opposed the bailout.[643]

It couldn't have come a worse time for Finland's governing class, which supported the bailout. Portugal's application for an EU bailout occurred on the first day of early voting in the Finnish election, and the national populist True Finn party and their leader Timo Soini used it to their benefit,[644] promising that they would block the bailout to Portugal if elected.[645]

Soini reminded voters that when Finland was going through an economic crisis in the 1990s, no European country rushed to their aid. The True Finns spoke to both populist conservatives who said bailouts were not responsible as well as progressives who felt banks needed to be held accountable. We are against any new contributions to bailouts. This is not the way to do it, Soini told The Associated Press. Banks have to be made responsible for lending money too freely, and countries in trouble should sell their assets.[646]

Although the European bailout of Portugal and Greece was the main driver of the True Finns' message, Soini also emphasized positions that were popular to both progressives and conservatives, from raising capital gains to hardline stances on immigration, including cutting social welfare for foreigners and lowering refugee quotas.[647]

---

643   "MTV3 poll harsh condemnation of crisis countries." *Yle Uutiset,* April 8, 2011, https://yle.fi/uutiset/3-5339621.

644   Jouni Turenen, "Portugal escalated the electoral battle." *Yle Uutiset,* April 8, 2011, https://yle.fi/uutiset/3-5339295.

645   Ian Traynor, "Eurosceptic True Finns Party Surprise Contender in Finnish Election." *The Guardian,* April 15, 2011, https://www.theguardian.com/world/2011/apr/15/eurosceptic-true-finns-contender-finnish-election.

646   Matti Huuhtanen, "Finnish Nationalists Challenge EU Bailouts in Election That Has Europe on Edge." The Associated Press, April 15, 2011, https://web.archive.org/web/20110721204006/www.1310news.com/news/world/article/212885–finnish-nationalists-challenge-eu-bailouts-in-election-that-has-europe-on-edge.

647   "True Finns Publish Election Manifesto." *Yle,* June 6, 2011, http://yle.fi/uutiset/news/2011/02/true_finns_publish_election_manifesto_2391059.html?origin=rss.

On election night, April 17, 2011, forty-seven incumbents lost their re-election in a Parliament of only two hundred members. The True Finns were the big winners, coming in third and nearly tying the leading center-right and center-left parties. They more than quadrupled their support from the previous election, receiving 560,075 votes or 19.1 percent, just 39,000 votes short of coming in first place.[648]

In the face of the protest vote against Brussels, an unnamed representative of the EU told *The Wall Street Journal* that the result would not affect the bailout for Portugal regardless of what the voters wanted.[649] During the negotiation over the new government, the leading Social Democrats and National Coalition Party agreed to continue to fund the bailout of Portugal. The True Finns stuck to their guns and withdrew from government formation talks, accusing Social Democrats who campaigned against the bailout of selling out their voters.[650]

While Italy, Spain, Greece, and Ireland all looked to outside help to get their financial houses in order after the fiscal crisis, the UK looked inwards, which ultimately resulted in a vote to leave the EU.

The UK's Tory and Liberal Democrat coalition government's response to an age of irresponsibility was to institute austerity measures to cap spending and reduce the deficit. Tory leadership insisted that it would help fend off a future economic crisis.[651]

---

648   "True Finns the biggest winner in the elections. Coalition Party the largest party in the Parliamentary elections 2011." *Statistics Finland,* April 29, 2011, https://www.stat.fi/til/evaa/2011/evaa_2011_2011-04-29_tie_001_en.html.

649   "EU: Finnish Election Won't Affect Portugal Bailout Package." *The Wall Street Journal,* April 5, 2011, https://web.archive.org/web/20110421045228/online.wsj.com/article/BT-CO-20110418-703792.html.

650   Terri Kinnunen and Jussi Rosendahl, "UPDATE 4-Finland Delays Vote on EU Bailout for Portugal." Reuters, May 10, 2011, https://www.reuters.com/article/finland-bailout-idUSLDE74910V20110510.

651   Thomas Goulding and Ben Chu, "This is the Truth About Whether or Not Austerity is Really over." *The Independent,* July 6, 2017, https://www.independent.co.uk/news/uk/austerity-end-over-tories-pay-cap-what-is-it-over-public-spending-explained-a7825726.html.

Cameron delivered a speech on April 26, 2009, where he proposed a new age of austerity in which the UK government would become more transparent and would slash government spending.[652]

Real spending per capita decreased in education, housing subsidies, and other welfare benefits, and between 2010 and 2019, the UK curbed spending by more than £30 billion.[653] Cameron was successful in his efforts as the deficit shrank from £153 billion to just £24.7 billion in 2019.[654] Aside from cutting spending, the austerity measures had an unintended consequence of pushing voters to support Farage and the Leave campaign during Brexit.

During the 2014 EU elections, when Farage's party won the plurality of votes, over one in four UKIP voters said they supported the nationalist party as a protest vote against the establishment parties.[655] A study conducted by economics professor Thiemo Fetzer also found that voters most affected by austerity measures, especially the 2012 Welfare Reform Act, increasingly shifted to UKIP by a margin of 3.5 to 11.9 percent in various districts during the 2014 election as well as the Leave campaign in 2016.[656] Fetzer insisted that the referendum would have resulted in a Remain victory had it not been for austerity measures.[657]

---

652   Deborah Summers, "David Cameron Warns of 'new age of Auterity'." *The Guardian,* April 26, 2009, https://www.theguardian.com/politics/2009/apr/26/david-cameron-conservative-economic-policy1.

653   Benjamin Mueller, "What Is Austerity and How Has It Affected British Society?" *The New York Times,* February 24, 2019, https://www.nytimes.com/2019/02/24/world/europe/britain-austerity-may-budget.html.

654   "UK Debt Balloons to £1.8b, Deficit Shrinks." *The Standard,* April 24, 2019, http://www.thestandard.com.hk/breaking-news.php?id=126673&sid=2

655   *The Sun Survey Results,* YouGov, 2014, https://d25d2506sfb94s.cloudfront.net/cumulus_uploads/document/v1aduveoca/YG-Archive-Pol-Sun-results-300414-EU-Why-Vote-UKIP.pdf.

656   Thiemo Fetzer, "Did Austerity in the UK Lead to the Brexit Crisis?" *Harvard Business Review,* August 23, 2019, https://hbr.org/2019/08/did-austerity-in-the-uk-lead-to-the-brexit-crisis.

657   Thiemo Fetzer, "Austerity Caused Brexit." *VOX,* April 8, 2019, https://voxeu.org/article/austerity-caused-brexit.

Additional studies found that austerity measures coupled with the globalist policies pushed voters that had been on the losing end of neoliberal economic policies for decades. Those in areas that lost manufacturing areas and lost jobs due to trade and automation were also more likely to vote to leave the EU, despite the fact that many of them had previously voted for the Labour Party.[658] What those voters wanted and still want to this day is not the neoliberal promise of creating a Singapore on the Thames, with low taxes and workers with little protection. They want an economy that looks out for the interests of the workers.

THE DESPAIR OF MIDDLE AMERICA

A positive side effect of Trump's election victory was that for the first time, elites took notice that millions of people throughout Middle America had been on the losing side of globalism and were pissed about it. For decades, those people were nearly invisible to coastal elites, who had long ignored the growing depression among working-class people in former industrial hubs across the US.

Elites living in high-income zip codes couldn't relate to Trump's message of Making America Great Again, because the last three decades had been marked by new technological innovations, high incomes, and longer lives. The neoliberal promise of untold riches would come from globalization and for millions of educated, high-skilled, white-collar workers, they weren't wrong. As mentioned in chapter one, over the course of time, those more likely to get a college education and a six-figure job slowly moved away from working-class people. They both literally and figuratively gated themselves off from

658 Italo Colantone and Piero Stanig, "Global Competition and Brexit." *American Political Science Review* 112, no. 2 (May 2018), 201–218.

the suffering of their countrymen, who were living in cities that were shells of their former selves and dying of despair, depression, and drugs.

Throughout the 1970s and '80s, manufacturing began to decline for a number of reasons, including several recessions, inflation, lack of innovation in the Rust Belt, and especially the new rise of foreign competition.[659] When Congress voted for free trade deals in the '90s and normalized trade relations with China in 2000, that number began to plummet.[660] From 2000 to 2016, America lost more than 5 million manufacturing jobs and the percentage of workers in manufacturing dipped from 13 percent to just 8 percent.[661]

Manufacturing employment remained fairly steady; between August 1984 and August 2000 the number of manufacturing jobs fluctuated from 18 million to a low of 16.7 million before rising again to 17.3 million.[662]

The culprit for most of those job losses was growing trade deficits, especially those under President George W. Bush, which cost manufacturing workers more than 3.6 million jobs and an additional 1.4 million were lost during the Great Recession. This devastation was followed by the slowest recovery in domestic manufacturing output in over sixty years.

---

659 Salman Ahmed, et al., "How Trade Did and Did Not Account for Manufacturing Job Losses," *Carnegie Endowment For International Peace*, December 10, 2018, https://carnegieendowment.org/2018/12/10/how-trade-did-and-did-not-account-for-manufacturing-job-losses-pub-77794

660 Drew DeSilver, "U.S. Manufacturing Producing More with Fewer Workers." *Pew Research Center*, last modified July 25, 2017, https://www.pewresearch.org/fact-tank/2017/07/25/most-americans-unaware-that-as-u-s-manufacturing-jobs-have-disappeared-output-has-grown/.

661 Heather Long, "The U.S. Has Lost 5 Million Manufacturing Jobs Since 2000." *CNN Money*, March 29, 2016, https://money.cnn.com/2016/03/29/news/economy/us-manufacturing-jobs/.

662 Robert E. Scott, *Manufacturing Job Loss: Trade, Not Productivity, Is the Culprit*, Economic Policy Institute, n.d., August 11, 2015, https://www.epi.org/publication/manufacturing-job-loss-trade-not-productivity-is-the-culprit/.

During the '90s, when economists, business leaders, and politicians were pushing Presidents George H. W. Bush and Bill Clinton to embrace free trade, the manufacturing deficit remained fairly stable, reaching about $110 billion in 1996. That number exploded to over $300 billion by 2000 and $558.5 billion in 2006.[663]

Nobel Prizewinning economist Paul Krugman admitted in a 2019 article that he and his fellow economists who championed free trade during that time period miscalculated how it would impact manufacturing jobs. In his op-ed, Krugman wrote that the surge in the trade deficit caused a fall in employment. A reasonable estimate is that the deficit surge reduced the share of manufacturing in GDP by around 1.5 percentage points, or more than 10 percent, according to Krugman. Which means that it explains more than half the roughly 20 percent decline in manufacturing employment between 1997 and 2005.[664]

Trade deals like NAFTA and normalizing trade deals with China cost the US economy millions of jobs across the country, but especially in the Rust Belt, Appalachia, and other parts of rural America.

The think tank Public Citizen, founded by Ralph Nader, estimated that one million jobs were lost because of NAFTA.[665] The free trade deal between the US and its neighbors Mexico and Canada had a detrimental effect on certain industries, and

---

663   Robert E. Scott, *Manufacturing Job Loss: Trade, Not Productivity, Is the Culprit.* Economic Policy Institute, n.d., August 11, 2015, https://www.epi.org/ publication/manufacturing-job-loss-trade-not-productivity-is-the-culprit/.

664   Paul Krugman, "What Economists (Including Me) Got Wrong About Globalization." *Bloomberg*, October 10, 2019, https://www.bloomberg.com/opinion/articles/2019-10-10/ inequality-globalization-and-the-missteps-of-1990s-economics.

665   Joseph Williams and Lori Wallach, *NAFTA at 20: One Million Lost U.S. Jobs, Higher Income Inequality, Doubled Agriculture Trade Deficit With Mexico and Canada, Displacement and Instability in Mexico, and Corporate Attacks on Environmental Laws.* citizen.org, December 28, 2013, http://www.citizen.org/ wp-content/uploads/press-release-nafta-at-20.pdf.

normalizing trade relations worsened the pain being felt by workers across the country.

A 2013 paper by economists David Autor, David Dorn, and Gordon Hanson found that exposure to Chinese imports experienced trade shocks in multiple industries, including manufacturing. Local labor markets in the US saw a reduction in employment, labor force participation, and wages. They also saw an increased need for state and federal welfare assistance, including unemployment, disability, retirement, and Medicaid.[666]

Experts sold NAFTA and normalizing trade with China on the promise that it would lead to a growth in the Mexican economy that would reduce the number of migrants coming to the US[667] and would push the communist country to embrace economic liberalism.[668] Those promises never came to fruition.

American men were especially hurt by the manufacturing jobs being shipped overseas and plants across the country closing. Without the opportunity to earn a living wage, those that chose to look for work were forced into low-skilled jobs and lost out on the opportunity to buy a house, get married, or have children. A study by economists from MIT, UC San Diego, and the University of Zürich found that the decline in fertility, marriage, and stable homes throughout this region of the country was all related to the loss of economic stability that came after the free trade deals wiped out millions of manufacturing jobs.[669]

---

666   David H. Autor, David Dorn, and Gordon H. Hanson, *The China Syndrome: Local Labor Market Effects of Import Competition in the United States.*, *The American Economic Review,* (Nashville: 2013)

667   Mónica Verea, "Immigration Trends After 20 Years of Nafta." *ScienceDirect. com.,* July 2014, https://www.sciencedirect.com/science/article/pii/ S1870355016300052.

668   Reihan Salam, "Normalizing Trade Relations With China Was a Mistake." *The Atlantic,* June 8, 2018, https://www.theatlantic.com/ideas/archive/2018/06/ normalizing-trade-relations-with-china-was-a-mistake/562403/.

669   David Autor, David Dorn, and Gordon Hanson, "When Work Disappears: Manufacturing Decline and the Falling Marriage-Market Value of Young Men." *The National Bureau of Economic Research,* February 16, 2017, https:// www.nber.org/papers/w23173.

White men without a college education were left to compete in industries that were radically being altered by automation and mass immigration. Low-skilled Americans who could find decent-paying jobs in industries like drywalling or meatpacking plants were forced to compete with non-unionized foreign labor, and wages collapsed as a result.[670]

Of course, many didn't look for new jobs. Around the same time Middle America was suffering through massive demographic changes that eroded social capital and job-killing trade deals, they were dealt with another blow: the opioid epidemic.

The opioid epidemic started with pill mills began in the former industrial town of Portsmouth, Ohio, where a doctor named David Procter created a cash-only business that peddled highly addictive drugs for the depressed region of Southern Ohio and Northern Kentucky.[671] Procter built up his pill mill business by building additional clinics throughout the country, preying on low-skilled workers who suffered from chronic pain that eventually turned them into addicts. He was also known to extort sex from women who found themselves addicted to opioids.[672]

In 1996, Purdue Pharma released a new drug OxyContin, which they claimed had low risks of being addictive.[673] *Los Angeles Times* reporter Sam Quinones reported that Oxy

---

670   David Barboza, "Meatpackers' Profits Hinge On Pool of Immigrant Labor." *The New York Times,* December 21, 2001, https://www.nytimes.com/2001/12/21/us/meatpackers-profits-hinge-on-pool-of-immigrant-labor.html.

671   Philip Eil, "The Pill Mill That Ravaged Portsmouth." *Cincinnati Magazine,* July 5, 2017, https://www.cincinnatimagazine.com/features/pill-mill-portsmouth/.

672   Shannon Firth, "'Dreamland' Author Takes an Opioid Epidemic Trip." *Medical News and Free Online CME* | MedPage Today, November 26, 2016, https://www.medpagetoday.com/psychiatry/addictions/61691.

673   Art Van Zee, "The Promotion and Marketing of OxyContin: Commercial Triumph, Public Health Tragedy." *PubMed Central (PMC),* February 2009, https://www.ncbi.nlm.nih.gov/pmc/articles/PMC2622774/.

prescriptions for chronic pain increased from 670,000 in 1997 to 6.2 million in 2002.[674]

Procter's model was recreated in town after town across the country. Once the availability of prescription drugs became harder to come by, Mexican drug cartels flooded cities throughout the country with black tar heroin and eventually, Chinese-produced fentanyl and other synthetic drugs.

From 1999 to 2017, the opioid epidemic killed more than two hundred thousand Americans across the country, but the crisis was concentrated in states that voted for Bush in 2004 like Ohio, Kentucky, West Virginia, and New Mexico. Bush was more focused on remaking the world in the neoconservative image than he was at protecting his fellow Americans that had just voted to re-elect him.

Aside from not cracking down on Mexican drug cartels that were killing Americans, the Bush administration also let Purdue Pharma get away with a sweetheart deal. After it was exposed that Purdue executives knowingly lied to the public about the risks of addiction with the drug, prosecutors recommended that top Purdue Pharma executives be indicted on felony charges and face potential jail time. Officials at Bush's Justice Department chose to ignore the recommendation and instead settled for a $634 million fine.[675] Terrance Woodworth, a former Drug Enforcement administration official who was involved with the investigation into Purdue Pharma, said it was a missed opportunity to slow the trajectory of the opioid crisis. It would have been a turning point, Woodworth said to *The New York Times* and it would have sent a message to the entire drug industry.

---

674   Nancy Rommelmann, "The Great Opiate Boom." *The Wall Street Journal*, June 5, 2015, https://www.wsj.com/articles/the-great-opiate-boom-1433531938.

675   Barry Meier, "Origins of an Epidemic: Purdue Pharma Knew Its Opioids Were Widely Abused." *The New York Times*, May 29, 2018, https://www.nytimes.com/2018/05/29/health/purdue-opioids-oxycontin.html.

From 2006 to 2012, three of America's largest drug companies manufactured over 65 billion oxycodone and hydrocodone pain pills.[676]

Starting in the year 2000, middle-aged mortality rates for non-Hispanic white men began rising. America became the only developed nation in the world to have this distinction.[677]

This situation only continued to worsen, nearly unnoticed by politicians in Washington, D.C. for another decade and a half.[678] For the first time since the World Wars and the 1918 influenza pandemic, life expectancy in the US declined from 78.9 years to 78.6 from 2014 to 2017.[679] Preventable deaths were especially high for people aged twenty-five to forty-four, who were increasingly dying from diseases related to poor lifestyle habits, drug overdoses, and suicide. In 2016, about 20 percent of all deaths among Americans aged twenty-four to thirty-five were due to opioids.[680]

Even before life expectancy began to fall on a national level, the difference in life expectancy between areas of the country varied by as much as twenty years. Americans living in

---

676   Scott Higham, Sari Horwitz, and Steven Rich, "76 billion opioid pills: Newly released federal data unmasks the epidemic." *The Washington Post,* July 16, 2019, https://www.washingtonpost.com/ investigations/76-billion-opioid-pills-newly-released-federal-data-unmasks-the-epidemic/2019/07/16/5f29fd62-a73e-11e9-86dd-d7f0e60391e9_story.html.

677   Anne Case and Angus Deaton, "Rising Morbidity and Mortality in Midlife Among White Non-Hispanic Americans in the 21st Century." *PNAS,* December 8, 2015, https://www.pnas.org/content/112/49/15078.

678   Olga Khazan, "Americans Are Dying Even Younger." *The Atlantic,* November 29, 2018, https://www.theatlantic.com/health/archive/2018/11/ us-life-expectancy-keeps-falling/576664/.

679   Lenny Berstein, "U.S. life expectancy declines again, a dismal trend not seen since World War I." *The Washington Post,* last modified November 29, 2018, https://www.washingtonpost.com/national/health-science/ us-life-expectancy-declines-again-a-dismal-trend-not-seen-since-world-war-i/2018/11/28/ae58bc8c-f28c-11e8-bc79-68604ed88993_story.html.

680   Olga Khazan, "Another Shocking Opioid Statistic." *The Atlantic,* June 1, 2018, https://www.theatlantic.com/health/archive/2018/06/ another-shocking-opioid-statistic/561671

the elite suburbs outside Denver, Colorado had a life expectancy of nearly eighty-seven years old in 2014, while those living in the Mississippi Delta, Native American reservations of South Dakota, and in parts of Appalachia were dying in their mid-sixties[681] Deaths by despair hit states in the Midwest and Rust Belt especially hard; Missourians born in 2012 had a life expectancy about a year shorter than those born in 2018.[682] After decades of globalism, black men in Harlem, who in 1980 had a lower life expectancy than citizens of Bangladesh, were living longer lives than white men in Appalachia.[683]

What was the response from Washington to this growing crisis in America's rural communities? Elitist conservatives writing in *National Review* said those communities deserved to die,[684, 685] while liberals like President Obama said voters in those areas were bitter, they cling to guns or religion or antipathy to people who aren't like them or anti-immigrant sentiment or anti-trade sentiment as a way to explain their frustrations.[686]

681   Susan Scutti, "Life Expectancy Differs by 20 Years Between Some US
      Counties." CNN, May 9, 2017, https://www.cnn.com/2017/05/08/health/
      life-expectancy-by-county-study/index.html.
682   Charles F. Lehman, "Missouri Sees Sharp Drop in Life Expectancy."
      Washington Free Beacon, September 29, 2019, https://freebeacon.com/issues/
      missouri-sees-sharp-drop-in-life-expectancy/.
683   "Black Men in America Are Living Almost As Long
      As White Men." *The Economist,* June 15, 2019, https://
      www.economist.com/united-states/2019/06/15/
      black-men-in-america-are-living-almost-as-long-as-white-men.
684   David French, "Working-Class Whites Have Moral Responsibilities
      — In Defense of Kevin Williamson." *National Review,*
      March 14, 2016, https://www.nationalreview.com/corner/
      working-class-whites-have-moral-responsibilities-defense-kevin-williamson/.
685   Kevin D Williamson, "Chaos in the Family, Chaos in the State: The White
      Working Class's Dysfunction." *National Review,* March 18, 2016, https://www.
      nationalreview.com/2016/03/donald-trump-white-working-class-dysfunction-
      real-opportunity-needed-not-trump/.
686   Ed Pilkington, "Obama angers midwest voters with guns and religion
      remark." *The Guardian,* April 14, 2008, https://www.theguardian.com/
      world/2008/apr/14/barackobama.uselections2008.

Despair and desperation had been killing their communities and their loved ones for decades, and the best elitists could do was say move on. It wasn't an answer that voters were willing to accept. So, when a candidate emerged in 2016 and offered to stand up for those beaten down by globalism, challenge the orthodoxy of neoliberalism, and blow up the system that robbed so many people of their dignity, just enough forgotten working- and middle-class voters elected him president.

CHAPTER 9

THE NATIONAL POPULIST FUTURE

AS WE HAVE covered in this book, the world is witnessing an unprecedented backlash against the political establishment. Voters have turned to national populism as a rebellion against the elites who have been completely unresponsive to their cultural, political and economic concerns. In this chapter, we will explore the longevity of national populism, what national populists must do to achieve their goals, what elites must do to relieve the growing populist tensions across the globe, and what happens if they don't.

NATIONAL POPULISTS MUST LEARN TO GOVERN.

Although national populists are winning elections and finally getting a seat at the table, most have not proven that they can bring about the change they promise voters. It's clear that these fledgling movements are not equipped with the institutional structures required to govern effectively.

As with any fledgling political movement, this will change over time. Think tanks, media outlets, and political organizations will adapt or be born out of these movements and help to galvanize the principles of the movement in each country. This type of organization doesn't happen overnight and may not occur in time to address the grievances of national populists. This is especially true in places like the US and the UK, where center-right parties like the Tories and the Republicans still insist on pushing forward on a neoliberal agenda.

In lieu of starting a new nationalist party, the best bet for national populists in countries like that is to try and reform these parties from within, the way Åkesson did with the Swedish Democrats. It's something that national populists in the US should have been doing since Trump was first elected president: running candidates for both state and legislative office who have a national populist worldview.

Once national populists gain a foothold in office, they must begin the process of delivering for the people even if it means working with the political establishment. Working with the political establishment is important; it could show that the point of national populists isn't to act merely as disruptors but as reformers. It also may be the only way national populists deliver on any of their promises unless they're in full control of the government, as is the case in Hungary, Poland, and India.

National populists need to move forward on their own agenda based on the premise of raising the living standards of the working and middle class, promoting a pro-family agenda, protecting sovereignty, combating terrorism, reducing immigration levels, and promoting social cohesion. There isn't an easy one size fits all remedy to these problems. Every country, state, and region undergoing a national populist revolution requires different answers to these very complex issues.

PAST POLITICS

Although the neoliberal agenda has created the national populist revolution with their policies, the answer to combating the series of crises they created isn't only political. It would help if governments around the globe elected leaders that better reflected the interests of their citizens, who have been on the losing end of globalism and mass immigration, but it doesn't mean winning a few elections will reverse every issue.

Poland and Hungary, for example, have both elected national populist parties to run their countries; despite instituting legislation to promote natality, their birthrates remain under replacement levels. Every future generation of Poles and Hungarians will be smaller than the generation before them.

Likewise, local states and municipalities across the US have spent billions of dollars combating the opioid epidemic, and yet it continues to ravage communities across the country.

Yes, there's more that governments can do to help the people, but there's also a lot national populists can do to help themselves.

If national populists really believe that nations are families rather than the neoliberal premise that they're marketplaces, then they're going to have to start acting like it. Communicating on the internet is not going to produce the goals they want. They're going to have to create physical communities centered around local institutions, faith-based organizations, and small businesses. Entrepreneurs are going to have to create businesses that value workers; boomers will need to help millennials and generation Z as they attempt to build a family and reinvest in their nation's culture.

It's not going to be easy and could seem overly idealistic, but it is the model that many small religious communities in the US have used to create stability and organize for both political and economic influence, even if it's just locally.

THE ELITES MUST LEARN TO LISTEN

The rise of national populism is the most significant political development of the last hundred years, and yet most liberals still don't understand it. Since World War II, the differences between the center-right and center-left have merged into a de facto super party with very little daylight between both sides. In the process, a very large portion of the electorate has had no voice.

In the aftermath of Brexit and President Donald Trump's election, one would have reasonably expected an amount of circumspection. But the national populist revolution has been challenging for the political establishment to come to grips with.

To their core, the elites believe the national populist revolution is the product of a fleeting tantrum of old, white, racist males. Every voter concerned by massive unchecked immigration of low-skilled workers is met with a charge of being a racist. Every voter concerned by the gutting of heartland manufacturing jobs to the East is met with the suggestion to learn to code.

The disdain elites have for working-class people is nothing new and it is palpable. In 2011, former National Security Advisor Zbigniew Brzezinski said, "We have a large public that is very ignorant about public affairs and very susceptible to simplistic slogans by candidates who appear out of nowhere, have no track record, but mouth appealing slogans."[687]

It's all so absurd. Liberals must embrace the legitimate concerns voters raise about globalization, trade, and mass migration, especially if they don't want to continue to fan the flames national populists.

---

687   Mark Finkelstein, "Zbig Brzezinski: 'Ignorant' Americans Susceptible to 'Simplistic Slogans.'" July 13, 2011, https://www.newsbusters.org/blogs/nb/mark-finkelstein/2011/07/13/zbig-brzezinski-ignorant-americans-susceptible-simplistic.

The essence of this movement is a belief that media doesn't reflect us, democracy doesn't represent us, and the economy isn't working for us. The erosion of faith in the system is undermining the very legitimacy of our democratic institutions. And like the hydra from ancient Greek mythology, every time the establishment tries to cut down both left- and right-wing populists, they grow an additional—oftentimes more extreme—head. They mocked and ignored the concerns of Pat Buchanan's voters in 1996 only to have Donald Trump win the presidency; they cheated Bernie Sanders voters out of gaining a voice in the 2016 election only to have AOC rise from the ashes in 2018.

Millions of people across the globe have turned to national populists to fill the void left after elites have them feeling neglected, loathed, and derided. And as the elites continue to bury their heads in the sand, dismissing the concerns of working- and middle-class voters, and rejecting the popular will of the people, it is the elites who are undermining democracy.

Illiberal globalists who have worked tirelessly over the last few years to thwart the gains made by national populists have stopped democracy from self-regulating, releasing tension under pressure of the electorate. And there are three different ways this could play out in the future.

WHAT HAPPENS IF THEY DON'T LISTEN?

The first is that liberals start listening and give national populists a seat at the table, their ideas are given legitimacy and are debated and discussed without being marginalized, and their politicians and political parties are members of coalition governments over time.

This is what has happened in places like Australia, Austria, Denmark, New Zealand, and Switzerland. National populist parties and politicians have places inside the government and in larger center-right and even some center-left coalitions. None of those states have fallen into dictatorships or have rolled back democracy. Concerns over immigration and globalism are fairly debated and concessions are made on both sides.

If national populists don't rise through normal democratic means, then they will gravitate to strong men who promise to completely dismantle the current economic and political system. Potentially, this leads to an erosion of freedoms and an authoritarian form of populism.

Ian Bremmer wrote, "Perhaps the most worrying element of the strongman's rise is the message it sends. The systems that powered the Cold War's winners now look much less appealing than they did a generation ago. Why emulate the US or European political systems, with all the checks and balances that prevent even the most determined leaders from taking on chronic problems, when one determined leader can offer a credible shortcut to greater security and national pride? As long as that rings true, the greatest threat may be the strongmen yet to come."[688]

This is a symptom of failing democratic institutions often seen in developing countries in Latin America and the Middle East. The president of Egypt, strongman Abdel Fattah al-Sisi, is a classic example: he strips the rights of opposition parties, imprisons opponents, and erodes the freedom of the press.

If elites still choose to ignore the will of the people, and if government bureaucracies thwart democratically elected leaders, then the future will become much more dystopian.

A certain portion of the population will fall into the belief that their voices are actively being suppressed and that there is

---

688   Ian Bremmer, "The 'Strongmen Era' is here. Here's what it means for you." last modified May 3, 2018, http://time.com/5264170/the-strongmen-era-is-here-heres-what-it-means-for-you/.

no legitimate to address discontent aside from using violence. Those actions are rightfully condemned by all people wanting to live a civilized society.

Unfortunately, it happens on both sides of the political aisle, from Robert Bowers, who murdered eleven Jewish worshippers at the Tree of Life synagogue in Pittsburg, Pennsylvania—alleging Jewish support for mass migration—to James Hodgkinson, a radicalized Bernie Sanders volunteer who took to the practice baseball fields of Republican congressmen. Hodgkinson shot and nearly killing numerous members of Congress in the attack. Online, Hodgkinson expressed fury that President Trump had been elected, called for taxing the rich and other far-left rhetoric.

Domestic terrorism is the latest outlet of people who cannot use democratic means and legitimate forms of protest to resolve their political grievances. Counterterrorism consultant Dr. Marc Sageman said that most people get involved with terrorism because they are disillusioned and have lost the belief in self-efficacy. Sageman also said that one of the best ways to combat the rise in terrorism is by government leaders engaging challengers in the political arena.[689]

Of course, none of this has to happen. If the concerns of voters who have turned to national populists are heard, if bureaucrats allow for democratic changes to occur, if politicians start prioritizing their own citizens over that of special interest groups, international corporations, and political orthodoxies, and voters finally feel like their governments care about people like them, then the tides can turn to preserve liberalism.

If none of those things happen, then we may be witnessing the beginning of the end of liberal democracy as we know it.

---

689   Steve Hartsoe, "Why People Join Terrorist Groups." last modified January 23, https://today.duke.edu/2018/01/why-people-join-terrorist-groups.

RYAN GIRDUSKY'S ACKNOWLEDGMENTS

THE ENTIRE EXPERIENCE of writing and publishing this book was incredible and worthwhile. I owe three men, in particular, an immense amount of thanks for making this possible. First and foremost, my agent Thomas Flannery Jr., who believed in this project when I mentioned the idea in the spring of 2019. Secondly, my cowriter Harlan Hill who went through this journey with me from beginning to end. Lastly, to our publisher David Bernstein, who believed in Harlan's and my vision for this book when so many others didn't.

I also have to thank some of those closest to me who provided me with an amazing amount of support and understanding during the writing of this book. Especially my parents, John and Toniann, for everything, but most importantly for giving me the ability to dream as well as motivating me to have drive and ambition. I also have to thank my siblings, Dan and Ava, who keep me humble. To my close friends and family members, there are far too many of you to name, but thank you for your constant encouragement and allowing me to act like I was in witness protection during the writing of this book. To Claire Potter, the professor I wished I had, thank you for teaching me everything I know about book writing. John Binder, there are few words to describe how grateful I am for you and for your patience as I called you daily to read and then reread to you portions of this book. And a special thanks to those who pushed me when I needed it most, especially Andrew Koslosky, Gina Loudon, Ron Meyer Jr., and Amanda Prestigiacomo. Lastly to my sixth-grade history teacher, Mrs. Dandola, who I doubt will ever see this book. Nonetheless, I feel the need to publicly thank you for giving me my love of history, the news, and current events. Being in your classroom shaped my life for the better. Thank you.

HARLAN HILL'S
ACKNOWLEDGMENTS

IT IS IMPOSSIBLE to overstate the enormous sacrifices of my parents, Teresa Hill and Tommy Hill. Their selflessness and their strong parenting set the bar extremely high for when I—God willing—have children of my own.

To George Slotin, Raheem Kassam, and Phoebe Frank, thank you for being my best friends. Without your constant support and patience, I'm truly not sure where I would be today. My life is undoubtedly more full and happy because of you three.

To my coauthor, Ryan Girdusky, we became friends on the set of Newsmax TV, and in the years since, I've grown to think of you as a brother. Every week you push me to be a better friend, a more profound thinker, and a stronger leader. Your brutally candid advice on everything from girlfriends to politics is more important to me than you can imagine. I am so glad we undertook this project together.

ABOUT THE AUTHORS

Ryan James Girdusky is a political consultant and writer whose work has been featured in multiple publications including the *Washington Examiner, The American Conservative Magazine, The Week, Human Events,* The Daily Caller, and Townhall.com. From 2015 to 2017, Ryan was the senior writer for the conservative millennial website Red Alert Politics.

Harlan Hill is a Republican political consultant and commentator seen on Fox News, Fox Business, MSNBC, CNN, BBC, and Sky News. Hill is the managing partner of Logan Circle Group, a public relations and political consulting firm. He is an advisory board member of President Donald J. Trump's reelection campaign.